To Ken

Best Wishes to
an expert in
motivation!

J. Clark
10-7-08

Praise for *Talent*

"Leadership supply is a rate-limiting factor for advancing our global business strategy. We simply must continue to address the talent issue head-on. Ed's new book gives some clear how-to advice we can start using today!"

—**Sandy Ogg,** chief human resources officer, Unilever

"Business leaders glibly talk about people as the most important asset in their companies. Ed Lawler challenges these platitudes with a book that answers the question, 'Suppose we took people and human capital seriously—how would we design and lead our organizations?' Lawler has summarized his years of research and consulting in a hard-hitting and tremendously useful guide for the true people-centric organization."

—**David A. Nadler,** vice chairman, Marsh & McLennan Companies; author, *Building Better Boards*

"Human capital is the Holy Grail for creating sustainable competitive advantage, and *Talent* provides a step-by-step guide, chock full of the latest examples, to the strategies involved in achieving competitive advantage through people."

—**Peter Capelli,** professor of management; director, the Center for Human Resources, the Wharton School

TALENT

MAKING PEOPLE YOUR COMPETITIVE ADVANTAGE

EDWARD E. LAWLER III

Foreword by Dave Ulrich

JOSSEY-BASS
A Wiley Imprint
www.josseybass.com

Published by Jossey-Bass
A Wiley Imprint
989 Market Street, San Francisco, CA 94103-1741—www.josseybass.com

Jossey-Bass books and products are available through most bookstores. To contact Jossey-Bass directly call our Customer Care Department within the U.S. at 800-956-7739, outside the U.S. at 317-572-3986, or fax 317-572-4002.

Jossey-Bass also publishes its books in a variety of electronic formats. Some content that appears in print may not be available in electronic books.

Library of Congress Cataloging-in-Publication Data

Lawler, Edward E.
Talent : making people your competitive advantage / Edward E. Lawler III ; foreword by Dave Ulrich.
p. cm.
Includes bibliographical references and index.
ISBN 978-0-7879-9838-7 (cloth)
1. Personnel management. 2. Human capital—Management. I. Title.
HF5549.L2886 2008
658.3—dc22

2007050957

Printed in the United States of America

FIRST EDITION
HB Printing 10 9 8 7 6 5 4 3 2 1

CONTENTS

FOREWORD

As a discussion starter for doctoral students, I like to ask, "Who are the six most important and influential people in management thought in the last century?"[1] Their answers often include such scholars and authors as Peter Drucker, C. K. Prahalad, Michael Porter, and Tom Peters—and Ed Lawler!—and business leaders such as Jack Welch, Tom Watson, and Bill Gates. This question is like opening a debate in a sports bar about the best athlete in a given sport or position, so regardless of what names the students give, I like to prod them by suggesting another six people.

In the 1920s and 1930s, organizations were designed and run by efficiency experts who worked to scientifically prove the best ways to manage the physical settings of work. One groundbreaking experiment, conceived by Harvard researchers, was conducted at the Western Electric Company's Hawthorne plant. This experiment involved variations in the intensity of lighting and other factors such as pay rules, rest breaks, and work hours. In it, six workers were placed in a separate room doing assembly work similar to that of other employees, but under the watchful eye of management. While trying to find the ideal level of light and workforce practices needed to increase productivity, the researchers discovered that these six workers reacted more to their relationship to management than to their physical surroundings. That is, it didn't seem to matter what the experimenters changed in the environment—more light, less light, or whatever—performance always improved as long as the experimental group was the center of attention. In many ways, these six workers began the modern management era, where attention to the human element at work matters at least as much as workers' physical surroundings.[2]

In the ensuing decades, people and their work in organizations have received enormous attention as researchers and executives have tried to figure out how to create organizations that turn knowledge into productivity. We have seen insights on assumptions (Theory X and Theory Y), systems theory, sociotechnical processes, leadership, and organizations of all types (excellent, great, purposeful, and adaptive).

In recent years, attention to these more intangible aspects of organizations has increased, in response to the changing nature of business. Ed Lawler's new book is a marvelous synthesis of this work, addressing four basic questions:

- *Why* are the softer, more intangible issues (broadly defined as human capital) in business increasingly important today?
- *What* is meant by human capital?
- *How* should human capital be created, sustained, and managed?
- *Who* is responsible for the management of human capital?

Answers to these questions are the essence of this outstanding book. It offers a snapshot of how much the study of organizations and people has evolved since the original insights gleaned from the Hawthorne studies. Consistent with Lawler's earlier work, this book is a deft mixture of scholarship and practice. He synthesizes theory, reports research, but then advocates for practice based not only on the theory and research but on his unique insights from decades of observing and studying organizations.

WHY?

Recently my daughter and I were in Madrid. Before going, she checked out the travel guide and located a flamenco shop where she could get authentic clothing and music. We found the place, a very small storefront on a hidden side road. I marveled at how this small store could stay in business being away from the heavily trafficked shopping areas. Then, while my daughter shopped, I noticed that the two employees were very busy even when no one else was in the store. As I talked to them, they told me that the major part of their business was now done through the Internet. The store itself was a convenient warehouse for tapes, CDs, clothes, and other flamenco-related items. The local flamenco store in

Madrid competes worldwide in a modern business world shaped by a number of current business realities. The reasons?

- *Technology.* Automobiles and aircraft enabled people to be mobile and to remove space boundaries. Electricity removed boundaries of time (day and night). Today's technologies remove information and connection boundaries. MySpace, Facebook, and other Internet sites change how people connect. Google allows people anywhere in the world to have access to information. Almost anyone with a Web site and computer can access global connections, even a small flamenco store in Madrid.
- *Globalization.* Corner stores may be housed anywhere in the world. Flamenco stores in Madrid sell to customers anywhere in the world. The much-touted "global village" is upon us.
- *Knowledge.* My colleague Arthur Yeung makes a fascinating point about how businesses are organized in emerging markets. (See Figure 1.) Many countries are trying to succeed by using technology to do manufacturing, assembly, or service work (India, Pakistan, Philippines), but real value is created by the focusing less on assembly and more on R&D and engineering (going backward), and on marketing, branding, and distribution (looking forward). Ultimately, more value is created in a

FIGURE 1. NATURE OF WORK.

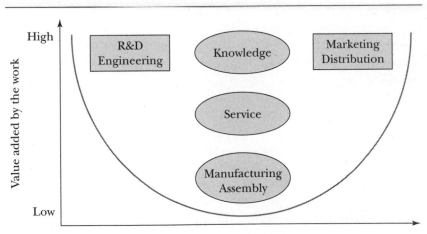

knowledge economy when countries or companies focus on high-value-added knowledge work.

- *Pace of change.* Few realize that Netscape, the firm that played a major role in forming the backbone of the Internet, is barely a decade old (incorporated in 1995). The Internet has become such a staple of society that we forget its novelty. Nokia has sold almost a billion phone devices, which now include not only voice but data, video, and access to the Internet. Companies that took fifty years to build can be lost in a couple of years in today's rapidly changing world. Netscape, purveyor of one of the first widely adopted Web browsers, still exists as a part of Time-Warner but is no longer a serious contender to the crown now held by Microsoft and its Internet Explorer.
- *Employees.* No one who interacts with those in their twenties or teens or preteens doubts that employees of this generation differ in significant ways from their elders. Sensitive to global issues, nimble with technology, and focused on short-term results, future employees will be the most talented and difficult to manage yet.
- *And so forth.* Customers, regulators, suppliers, investors, and others are going through dramatic change.

The world is changing. While companies used to be able to compete by accessing capital, creating products, and protecting their firm and product borders, the new source of competitiveness is shifting to the softer side of business—the people who create products, define borders, and raise capital, and the organizations in which they work. This book explains *why* human capital is so important and how it should be organized, managed, and developed.

WHAT

It is easy to fall into a trap of talking and thinking about human capital as "only" a talent issue. Organizations with talented employees are likely to outperform organizations with less talented employees, but not always. All-star pickup teams rarely beat an established and well-functioning team if the latter does not match up player by player on talent. While talent is necessary, it is not sufficient. Successful management in today's business world requires attention to both talent and teamwork, individual ability and organization capability.

Lawler captures both. He talks about talent and its importance, but then he defines the ultimate human capital (or organizational capability) not as an individual who has talent, but as the processes that create, manage, and organize talent (see Figure 2). Leadership as an organization capability matters more than gifted individual leaders.[3] Leadership focuses on the processes used to create future leaders. Sustainable, long-term success is not just a matter of having the leaders but of having the processes that reliably create them.

This book finds the balance between the challenge to source great talent and the challenge to meld individual talent into collective organization capability. In focusing on organizations as bundles of capabilities, it moves beyond defining organizations by their hierarchies. High-involvement organizations are characterized less by the number of levels of management and more by their use of some basic processes to ensure that knowledge turns into performance.

FIGURE 2.   MIX OF INDIVIDUAL ABILITY AND ORGANIZATION CAPABILITY.

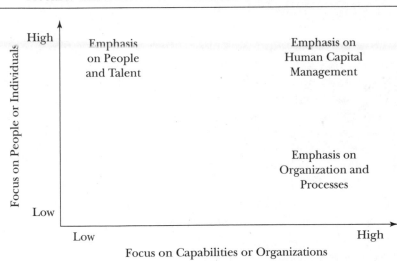

Leaders know that people and organizations matter. This book offers a language and approach to talking about people and organizations that is vivid and accessible.

HOW

Becoming a human-capital–centric (HC-centric) organization requires change, but where should those changes occur? This book offers an architecture that succinctly yet robustly defines how to go about organizing and leading an organization focused on human capital. Called the Star Model, it identifies the organization features about which choices need to be made to create the HC-centric organization.

- *Strategy.* Strategy defines the products, services, and markets an organization will focus on and how it will compete.
- *Competencies and capabilities.* Competencies are the knowledge, skill, and values possessed by individuals, while capabilities are the identity of an organization and what the organization is good at doing.
- *Structure.* Structure in an HC-centric organization focuses on turning individual competence into sustained organization capabilities. Authority is often shared throughout the organization.
- *Processes.* Information and decision processes in an HC-centric organization focus controls through values more than rules. Management by mindset replaces management by objectives.
- *Rewards.* HC-centric organizations allocate rewards less on tenure and hierarchy and more on performance. Individuals are rewarded for equity more than equality.
- *People.* People in an HC-centric organization are the centerpiece. Organizations that emphasize human capital are obsessed with finding people with outstanding talent, then working with them to make the whole work well together.
- *Identity.* An organization's identity is what it is known for by those who use its services. When this external identity, which can be called a firm brand, is aligned with internal organization and people practices, it becomes the culture of an organization.

For an organization to be more than the sum of the individuals working there, Lawler shows, the systems in the Star Model need to be aligned and integrated so they drive and implement strategy. A customer-share strategy will differ on all these dimensions from a product-innovation strategy. Being integrated means that any changes in one of the elements will require modifications in others. Sharing information with people should show up in how rewards are allocated.

To build organizations that combine talent and teamwork, Lawler then dives deep into three systems. For the people, or talent, element, he offers tips on sourcing, screening, securing, orienting, and motivating employees. For the performance management, or rewards, element, he draws on his vast and deep knowledge of incentive systems to offer guidance on how to define performance, manage motivation, conduct appraisals, set measures, and allocate financial and nonfinancial rewards systematically. For information and decision processes, he defines the core features of human capital analytics and proposes what human capital should look like.

WHO

So who is responsible for making this organization of the future operate successfully? It is not one person or role; in a true human-capital–centric organization, the responsibility must be shared. HR professionals must learn to deliver the administrative work but not be defined by it or bound up in it. They need to relate to the business, tie their processes to strategy, and build effective organizations. Line managers need to lead through sharing power, ownership, information, and incentives. Boards are stewards over fiscal and strategic firm investments, but they are also stewards over organization and people. Boards should make sure that organization and talent audits are done as rigorously and as frequently as financial, strategic, and product audits.

By sharing responsibility for the people and organization, boards, executives, and HR professionals each bring unique insights into the creation and maintenance of people and organizations.

SO WHAT?

To go forward, sometimes we need to capture what is. For the field of human capital (people and organizations), *Talent* offers a definition of what can be, a statement of the gap in getting there, and a blueprint for action.

As the internal elements of an HC-centric organization are defined, diagnosed, and developed, they will help employees become more competent and committed. Employee engagement inside an organization will show up in customer loyalty and investor confidence from the outside. As customer expectations turn into employee actions and organization capabilities, long-term success will follow.

When asked to pick thoughtful and relevant academics who have significantly shaped the field of management, particularly how managers shape organizations and people, Ed Lawler is high on my list (or anyone else's). This book shows why. By providing a rich combination of theory, research, stories, and personal insights, it synthesizes the state of human capital management, and makes operational what many still consider a soft and ambiguous area.

Alpine, Utah   DAVE ULRICH
February 2008

PREFACE

"I am fed up with being told it, and I am not going to listen anymore!" This outburst captures my reaction to hearing executives say how important their employees are. Time after time I have heard senior managers say, "People are my organization's most important asset" or "Employees are number one in my organization." Sounds good, but in many organizations, there's an enormous gap between the rhetoric and the reality. In too many organizations, people are *not* treated as important assets, and it seems particularly insincere and inappropriate when managers persist in saying they are.

Of course, it is one thing for me to say that organizations don't treat people as their most important asset—it is another to specify what an organization needs to do if it is going to act on this rather overused phrase. But that is why I've written this book. In these pages, drawing on research, consulting, observation, and experience, I've detailed what I believe organizations need to do in order to gain competitive advantage as a result of their ability to organize and manage talent. In other words, this book is about what an organization needs to do to act on the idea that people are its most important asset.

The starting point of any serious effort to treat people as a key source of competitive advantage is to determine whether in fact it makes sense to do it! Only under certain conditions is talent the logical go-to source of competitive advantage. Thus the first issue that I deal with in this book is whether the business conditions an organization faces are the ones that mean it should use an approach to management that actually puts talent front and center as a source of competitive advantage. If the answer to this question is that talent should be an important source of competitive advantage, it leads to the next choice an organization needs to make: which of two approaches to human-capital centric (HC-centric) management, high-involvement or global competitor, it needs to put in place.

Both these approaches put people first, but they use somewhat different management practices and produce different kinds of organizational performance. Choosing the right one is critical to making talent a source of competitive advantage. It has major implications for how an organization should be designed and managed and how it will perform.

Until recently it might have been possible to argue that a major barrier to managing organizations in a way that treats talent as the most important source of competitive advantage was a lack of knowledge about how to do it. I'm not sure this has been true for quite a while, but I am sure that it is no longer an obstacle.

Thousands of research studies on organizational effectiveness have provided an enormous amount of evidence on how to manage the human side of organizations effectively. The scientific literature not only provides useful theories; it contains a considerable amount of data on how effective a variety of practices are. If there is a knowledge problem at this time, it is the persistence of a knowing-doing gap. In other words, the knowledge exists, but it is not being used effectively.

Starting with the discussion of the star organization design model in Chapter Three and continuing through the next six chapters of the book, I point to how organizations that put talent first should be managed and contrast that with what the most common practices are in the United States and other developed nations.

For example, in the area of rewards, most organizations still have job descriptions and merit pay systems. They fail to use knowledge-based pay, profit sharing, and stock ownership plans that create a high level of involvement in the success of an organization.

With respect to their structure, they fail to use self-managing teams and flat structures that optimize member contact with the external world. As a result, they fail to create the right amount of organizational surface area so that the members of the organization are close to and in touch with key external individuals and issues.

In the discussion of talent management, I point out that many organizations lack the kind of employment deals and contracts that are appropriate for an HC-centric organization. Most organizations also fail to appropriately reward managers for developing individuals and individuals for developing themselves. The performance management systems of organizations all too often are seen as a bureaucratic pain in the posterior rather than as a key strategic tool in helping to develop and manage individual and organizational performance.

The information and decision processes in organizations often exclude many members of the organization from having input to key decisions. They also fail to deliver to them the kind of information they need in order to make good decisions and to be engaged in the business of the organization. The HR function in many organizations is poorly staffed and lacks the kind of decision-making sophistication that is required to adequately manage the organization's most important asset: its talent. Most corporate boards lack the information and expertise they need if they are to oversee an HC-centric organization. Last but certainly not least, most organizations fail to develop the kind of shared leadership approach that is needed in an HC-centric organization.

My hope is that by the time readers arrive at Chapter Ten they will have a comprehensive view of what an organization needs to look like if it is going to act on the idea that talent really is its most important asset. They then can proceed with the challenging task of creating an HC-centric organization. Chapter Ten provides some thoughts about how they should go about this.

The content of my book provides a benchmark against which executives can compare their organization's approach to management. I hope it will help them translate "people are our most important asset" into practice—or, if they are unwilling or unable to treat people as their most important asset, I hope it will persuade them to stop saying that they are!

ACKNOWLEDGMENTS

I owe thanks to many individuals and organizations for their contributions to this book. Although I'm the only author, I received help from many sources. Let me first thank the institutional sponsorship that my research has gotten for the last thirty years from the Marshall School of Business at the University of Southern

California. It has supported the creation and development of the Center for Effective Organizations, which has provided research support for my work. The Center has a terrific staff that provides me with both editorial and research support. In writing this book I received particularly strong support from Arienne McCracken, who did much of the manuscript preparation.

The Center for Effective Organizations is supported by more than fifty corporate sponsors, some of whom contributed to the data and ideas in this book; all of them contribute financial support to the Center. I owe them a large amount of gratitude.

Two members of the research staff at the Center for Effective Organizations deserve special thanks with respect to this book. Jim O'Toole, my coauthor on *The New American Workplace,* stimulated much of my thinking concerning the different approaches to managing organizations when human capital is critical. Chris Worley, the coauthor of my other recent book, *Built to Change,* provided a number of insights into change management, strategy, and organization design.

A special thanks to Dave Ulrich for contributing an insightful foreword. His contribution shows why and how he has had a major impact on how talent is managed in modern corporations.

Regina Maruca provided me with a great deal of editorial help. Not only did she improve my writing, she helped me clarify my thinking. Many thanks to Regina for being a great help and such a pleasure to work with.

Last but not least, my wife, Patty, provided support throughout the writing of this book. She read chapters, suggested titles, but more important, she provided love, support, and enthusiasm for the project.

Los Angeles, California   Ed Lawler
February 2008

TALENT

CHAPTER ONE

TALENT MATTERS

In the last several decades, an avalanche of business books, articles, speeches, and seminars have stressed the importance of human capital—people—in gaining competitive advantage. Executives seem to be paying attention. According to a recent survey of senior executives from all over the world, the two most important management challenges are

- Recruitment of high-quality people across multiple territories, particularly as competition for top talent grows more intense
- Improving the appeal of the company culture and work environment

Fifty-five percent of the respondents to that survey reported that they expect to spend more time on people management than on technology in the next three years. More than 85 percent of the respondents said that people are vital to all aspects of their company's performance particularly their top strategic challenges: increased competition, innovation, and technology.[1]

What's more, according to another recent survey of over a thousand global CEOs, 72 percent are more concerned about the availability of individuals with key skills than they are about energy and commodity prices and intellectual property rights.[2]

Apparently, people are front and center on managers' radar, as well they should be. Increasingly, companies in a wide variety of businesses are finding that people can be their number one source of competitive advantage. But it is not enough for leaders to say that people are important, or to put people issues high on their mental to-do list. What is needed are organizations that are designed and managed—from the boardroom to the front line—in ways that optimize talent attraction, retention, and performance. I call this type of organization human-capital–centric, or HC-centric.

Today, most organizations are still managed in a bureaucratic, structure-centric manner, and they have been managed that way for decades. In these companies, you'll often hear managers at all levels talking about the importance of people, but the walk really doesn't follow through on the talk. Their managers do make an effort to see that they attract and retain the people they need to make their bureaucratic structure operate efficiently, but they are not designed to make their human capital a competitive advantage.

In one of my favorite Dilbert cartoons, the boss says, "I've been saying for years that 'Employees are our most valuable asset.' It turns out that I was wrong. Money is our most valuable asset. Employees are ninth." When asked what came in eighth, he says: "Carbon paper." I realize that not everyone remembers carbon paper, but I hope those of you who don't still get the joke—and the real point: Lip service and window dressing are not enough.

To be clear, a bureaucratic, structure-centric approach to management can still work. A modest effort to attract, retain, and motivate talent is all that's needed in some organizations, because it achieves good enough performance from their human capital, and people are not their primary source of competitive advantage.

But for companies that are truly competing on the performance of their people—their human capital—it is not enough. They need to adopt an HC-centric approach to organizing. It is not just about controlling people costs because they are a major expense—it is about how well people perform, because their performance is the critical factor in determining whether the organization is effective.

COMPETITIVE REALITIES

So how do you tell whether an organization should be HC-centric or not? Multiple factors have contributed to the creation of the knowledge economy and the rise of talent as a potential source of competitive advantage. The extent to which an organization has been influenced by these factors is the major determinant of whether it needs to be HC-centric.

One of these factors is access to financial capital. Having access to financial capital used to be a major source of competitive advantage, but today financing is easily obtained and therefore is rarely a potential source of competitive advantage. In developed countries, financial capital moves quickly and efficiently and is easily accessed. Evidence of the ready availability of capital is prevalent. More and more corporations are buying back their stock because they have an abundance of cash, and private equity funds are buying major corporations with their large cash positions. Oh yes, new public offerings continue to be common, even though they are not as hot as they were in the dot-com era.

Another factor in the creation of a new competitive landscape—perhaps the most obvious change—is the information technology that has been created in the last decade. It has reshaped the global economy as well as the internal operations of corporations.

Information technology (IT) has contributed to the growing need for technical knowledge as well as to the development of new technical knowledge and businesses. Perhaps equally important is the impact of IT on the ability of organizations to move work across internal, external, and geographic boundaries. It is now possible to outsource manufacturing, software engineering, and many other activities to other companies and countries, and to coordinate the results on a global basis.

IT has made it possible for people to work more flexibly and to change what they work on with increased rapidity. It also can give people a better understanding of what they are doing and why they are doing it.

Time Magazine recognized the impact that IT has had when it made "you" the person of the year for 2006. According to *Time,* the World Wide Web is about people being able to do new and important things. It is about the "many" gaining power—and not just changing the world but changing how the world changes. In the case of organizations, it is changing what people do, how they do it, their importance to organizations, and how they are managed and organized most effectively.

Closely tied to the evolution of information technology is the increased amount of technical knowledge required for many of the products and services produced and offered in developed countries. This increase is fueling a parallel increasing need for knowledgeable, skilled, and motivated employees. It's also a major reason why the market values of S&P 500 companies are over three times their book values, and why the value of publicly traded companies' intangible assets has been growing for decades.[3] One estimate is that in 1982 intangible assets accounted for 38 percent of company assets, and that by 2000 they accounted for 85 percent.[4]

Another factor in the creation of a new competitive landscape is the result of the changes just described: The U.S. economy is increasingly service-driven. IBM, for example, once a computer and office equipment manufacturer (do you even remember IBM typewriters, or better yet, time clocks?), has evolved into a predominantly service-oriented organization. There also has been tremendous growth in food service organizations, such as McDonald's, and retailers, such as Wal-Mart (the largest U.S. employer). As a result, manufacturing employment now represents only 8 percent of the U.S. workforce, down from over 30 percent just a few decades ago.[5]

Why is the growth of service organizations important? The major reason is customer interface. One thing that distinguishes service organizations from manufacturing organizations is the importance of the relationship between the customer and the service provider. This often is distinctively personal and is critical to the success of the organization. It is noticeably dissimilar from the relationship between a manufacturing employee and the product. What works from a management point of view for producing a product often does not work when the issue is interfacing with customers.

Because of the amount of change that has taken place in the last several decades, it is increasingly clear that the source of competitive advantage in many industries has shifted from effective execution and reliable processes to the ability to innovate and change.[6] And it has changed from the ability to provide satisfactory customer service to the ability to excel in the area of customer relationships on a grand scale.

Simply stated, for companies that are truly competitors in the knowledge economy, what was good enough performance yesterday is rarely good enough today—and will almost never be good enough tomorrow. For most organizations, the best way to meet this challenge is to become HC-centric, to focus on making talent their most important source of competitive advantage.

The corporate landscape today is littered with once-successful large corporations that are failing, dying and going out of business because they have not changed. One only need look at the amount of change that has occurred in *Fortune Magazine*'s list of largest corporations to see just how unstable corporate performance has become. Between 1973 and 1983, 35 percent of the companies in the top twenty were new. The number of new companies increases to 45 percent when the comparison is between 1983 and 1993, and it increases even further, to 60 percent, when the comparison is between 1993 and 2003. The comparison between 2003 and 2007 shows a high level of change continuing (25 percent).

Some major corporations have disappeared entirely. Westinghouse used to be a peer of General Electric. Arthur Andersen used to be one of the world's largest public accounting firms before the Enron scandal. Polaroid used to be a cutting-edge technology imaging company. Digital Equipment Corporation was second only to IBM in the computer business.

I could go on and on, but it's hardly necessary. The simple fact is that fewer and fewer companies can be successful by practicing an old-school bureaucratic approach to management. Yes, it still works in transactional sales businesses (such as parking lot fee collection), in low-value-added manufacturing (garment sewing), and in food production (harvesting and packaging). But for companies that are competing on innovative products and services for which employee contact with customers is central, an HC-centric approach is essential.

TALENT AS A COMPETITIVE ADVANTAGE

What does it take to create an effective HC-centric organization? The first answer many give is "the right people." It is hard to argue with this, as talent is certainly critical to innovation, change, and high performance. Talent that brings needed expertise and ideas to corporations is fundamental to innovation, as is talent that accepts change and is capable of learning and executing new processes. The right talent is the fundamental building block when it comes to creating an organization capable of innovating and changing and using this as a source of competitive advantage.

What's more, acquiring the right talent is becoming an increasingly complex and challenging activity. The workforce itself has become more global, virtual, and diverse than it ever has been. Increasingly, a surplus of investment capital is chasing a scarcity of talented people.[7] The future is sure to hold more of the same; thus, organizations that excel at talent management will continue to enjoy a competitive advantage.

There is also a good reason to believe that, in the United States at least, the educational system is not keeping up with the expected need for talented, well-educated employees.[8] For example, the share of the U.S. workforce that has a post–high school education is not expected to rise significantly in the next twenty years, despite the fact that more and more of the work in the United States is expected to require at least a high school education.

Meanwhile, the supply of educated workers outside the United States is expected to continue to grow. Increasingly, customer service representatives, radiologists, engineers, software developers, and editors can be sourced many places in the world. The challenge for organizations, therefore, is to create an infrastructure that will allow them to find the talent they need, develop it, motivate it to perform, and retain it. The ability to do this and to do it well is a critical part of creating a competitive advantage that is difficult if not impossible to duplicate.

ORGANIZATION AS A COMPETITIVE ADVANTAGE

Finding, acquiring, and retaining the right talent is a necessary, but *not* a sufficient, step in creating an organization with a sustainable competitive advantage. To do this, an organization also has to have the right structures, systems, processes, and practices in place. All too often, organizations have great people, but do not manage or support them correctly. People are stifled by systems and processes that restrict experimentation, limit learning, hinder the transfer of knowledge, fail to motivate, and suppress innovation.[9] As a result, organizations fail to capitalize on the talent they have and in the long run perform poorly.

Why is this the case? Bureaucratic systems and processes are created in the name of execution, control, and the short-term optimization of performance. In a time of slow change or little change, innovation may not be an important source of competitive advantage, so a bureaucratic approach may be best.

But in periods of rapid change, emphasizing execution and historical best practices almost always causes an organization to lose its competitive advantage. It ends up using outdated practices because it lacks the ability to innovate and change. As a result, it cannot attract or properly manage the best talent, and its performance declines.

Even acquiring an existing organization that has the right mix of talent may not be enough to improve an organization's competitiveness. All too often, organizations that are mired in past practice mismanage the acquisition process, and as a result lose the very people and capabilities that were the justification for the deal.

One way to think about this is to distinguish between the need for organizations to "get better" and their need to "be different." For many businesses, most notably those based on knowledge and technology, "getting better" is simply not good enough. Focusing on improving processes (in the spirit of Six Sigma) or reducing costs is important, but if it is the predominant focus of the organization, it can lead to failure in the long term. What is needed is a strong emphasis on being different from what used to be good enough, and different from what competitors are offering, because that is how new competitive advantages are created.

Becoming different is possible only if an organization can be creative and innovative. This requires a strong emphasis on learning and gathering new knowledge from internal and external processes. It also requires an organization-wide understanding that any competitive advantage based on new products or tactics will probably be relatively short-lived. They can be copied, and the continuing growth of knowledge and innovation means that better products and services will appear quickly. The focus needs to be on creating an organization that can continuously innovate and change, not just come up with a new product or a new service offering.[10]

An organization that can develop the capability to innovate and manage change has a competitive advantage that can be a barrier to entry for other companies. Companies trying to compete quickly realize that success is not simply a matter of raising capital, buying new equipment, or recruiting top talent. Rather, it involves a much more complicated and difficult undertaking: developing internal systems that attract and retain the right talent and organize the talent in ways that lead to continuous innovation and change. In other words, it requires creating an organization that is HC-centric in its design, structures, policies, and practices.

PERFORMANCE AND CHANGE

Simply stated, the best way for organizations to gain a competitive advantage and to sustain it in today's business environment is to perform so well and change so fast that they string together a series of temporary competitive advantages. Needless to say, this is easy to say but extremely difficult to do. It requires a special combination of human capital and organizational policies, practices, and designs. It is precisely because it is difficult to create organizations that change quickly and easily that being able to do so is such a powerful and sustainable source of competitive advantage. If it were easy to do, it would not be a competitive advantage and a significant barrier to entry.

Why is it so difficult? In large part, the issue is the gap that exists between *knowing* and *doing*. Most managers know that talent is critical to innovation, change, and sustained organizational effectiveness. The surveys cited at the beginning of this chapter reflect this. So, too, does the increasing amount of lip service that is given to "people are our most important asset."

However, it is one thing to know talent is important and it is altogether another to make talent a source of competitive advantage. This requires both attracting and retaining the right talent and organizing and managing it effectively. Attracting and retaining the right talent is not easy, but most organizations can get it done if they devote enough resources to it. Actually developing and employing organizational structures and management practices that lead to talent being a source or the source of competitive advantage is another story, however. That requires a major change in managerial behavior as well as changes in most of the major features of an organization.

New companies, building from the ground up, can start with an HC-centric approach to management and create systems and practices that fit it. Older companies (and *old* here is a relative term) that have to transform themselves from being structure-centric organizations have a much harder time.

Hiring some highly talented individuals won't do it! Training programs won't do it, either! It requires much more than making some quick fixes to a structure-centric organization.

Structures need to change, and practices need to change, but even that is not enough. People inside and outside the organization need to change the way they think about the organization. The organization needs to become recognizable from all angles as HC-centric.

Becoming an effective HC-centric organization is difficult but well worth the effort required. For many organizations, it is the only sustainable competitive advantage that they can develop. In Chapter Ten I return to the topic of managing organizational change. Before examining it further, I need to provide an in-depth look at how an HC-centric organization should be organized and managed.

THE HC-CENTRIC ORGANIZATION

What does an HC-centric organization look like? To begin with, it's important to understand what its core is. Above all else, an HC-centric organization is one that aligns its features (reporting systems, compensation, division and department structure, information systems, and so on) toward the creation of working relationships that attract talented individuals and enable them to work together in an effective manner.

Staying at that high level of description for the moment, here are some of the major features of an HC-centric organization. (The rest of the book delves deeper into these features and provides much more detail.) In an HC-centric organization:

Business strategy is determined by talent considerations, and it in turn drives human capital management practices.

Talent considerations are central to both the development and to the implementation of business strategy. HC-centric organizations do not just take the business strategy and shape a human capital management plan to fit it; considerations of talent are upstream with respect to the business strategy. They are carefully considered when decisions are made about what business strategy to pursue and how to pursue it.

Once a business strategy is established, talent is front and center in terms of implementation. Careful attention is paid to making sure that employees understand the strategy and support it. In addition, the right mix of skills is developed in the organization so that it has the competencies and capabilities it needs to execute its strategy.

Every aspect of the organization is obsessed with talent and talent management.

HC-centric organizations do everything they can to attract, retain, and develop the right talent. They create a strong employer brand that is targeted to the talent they need. They carefully assess, develop, and recruit talent that fits the skill needs of the organization. To ensure that talent is managed correctly, HC-centric organizations have sophisticated measurement systems that assess the state of their talent and facilitate decision making about its development and allocation. Careful studies are done to ensure that the best training and development approaches are used and that these approaches are justified in terms of performance improvement and development. Key positions are identified based on their impact on the organization's performance, and special attention is paid to filling those positions with the right talent.

Performance management is one of the most important activities.

Performance management is a critical activity in HC-centric organizations. It is not enough to simply go through the business-as-usual and much-disliked annual exercise of assessing performance and driving rewards based on a performance assessment. Instead, a systemic process establishes strategy-driven goals, modifies goals as needed, assesses performance against goals, and provides feedback on performance. In addition, multiple meetings focus on skill development, knowledge development, and career opportunities for individuals. Performance management starts at the very top of the organization and is carried down, so it provides a sense of common direction, an understanding of the business strategy, and a guide for the behavior of all employees.

The information system gives the same amount of attention and rigor to measures of talent costs, performance, and condition as it does to measures of equipment, materials, buildings, supplies, and financial assets.

The information system looks at how the organization is performing in critical areas where talent is a key determinant of performance effectiveness, and it reports on the condition of the human capital. It does not just report the traditional financial numbers, because they are often misleading in organizations that are highly human-capital intensive.

Most traditional measures are designed for companies whose assets are made up of tangibles such as equipment, natural resources, and money. These measures typically give little indication as to how productive individuals are and what the competencies and capabilities of the organization are. They fail to inform both employees and investors about the performance and condition of the organization.

HC-centric organizations have measures that report on the productivity, condition, and value of their talent and how effectively it is being applied. These data are shared not just inside the organization but with key investors and legitimate stakeholders who need to know about the condition of the organization's talent and its performance effectiveness.

The HR department is the most important staff group.

HR has the best talent and the best IT resources, and executives throughout the firm use it as an expert resource when it comes to business strategy, organizational change, organization design, and talent management. It is staffed with the best possible individuals, and it is a critical career stopping point for anyone who aspires to senior management in the organization.

HR has the kind of analytic skills that allow it to assess the cost-effectiveness of HR programs and to determine the impact of job designs, structure changes, and other policies on organizational effectiveness and financial performance. It has valid benchmark analytics and metrics that allow it to compare how well the human capital of the organization is performing and also what its current level of skill, motivation, and commitment to the organization is.

The corporate board has both the expertise and the information it needs to understand and advise on talent issues.

Board members of HC-centric organizations have expertise in all aspects of human capital management; in particular, they have the ability to work with the analytics and metrics that assess the talent of the organization. The board receives regular information about the condition of the talent and the organization's utilization of it. Directors know what the commitment level of the talent is. They know a great deal about the availability and condition of talent, and they understand and monitor the ability of the organization to attract, retain, and develop new talent.

The board spends at least as much time on talent issues as it does on financial and physical asset allocation and management. It spends as much time reviewing talent metrics and analytics as it does reviewing the public reporting that the organization does on its financial performance.

Leadership is shared, and managers are highly skilled in talent management.

Managers in HC-centric organizations understand and use sound principles when making decisions about motivation, development, hiring, organization change, organization design, and performance management. They make talent decisions in a manner as rigorous and strategically relevant as the one they apply to decisions about other resources. They adopt a leadership style that enhances the brand of the organization as a desirable employer. They also are willing and able to share decision making and recognition with the individuals they work with. They are not obsessed with gaining power; if they are primarily driven to achieve upward mobility in their careers, they have no place in an HC-centric organization. HC-centric organizations have individuals at all levels who are able to respond to business developments and the need for change.

NEED FOR HC-CENTRIC ORGANIZATIONS

I believe that unless more and more organizations adopt the HC-centric approach, the already large gap between how much it is used and how much it should be used will increase. The reason for this is simple: the world is moving more and more toward one in which competitive advantage depends on organizations' performing in ways that require being HC-centric. There is no way to achieve the rate of change, the amount of innovation, and the focus on customers that is required in an increasing number of businesses without adopting the HC-centric approach to management.

How many HC-centric organizations are there? How many should there be? Before I can address either of these questions, I need to go into more detail about what HC organizations look like and what business conditions create the need for the HC-centric organization.

In Chapter Two, I consider in detail the situations where the HC-centric approach will produce the best results and also the situations where the structure-centric approach will produce the best results. Making the right choice is the first and most basic step in determining how effective an organization will be. It is not as simple as choosing one or the other; each has different versions that produce different results and fit different strategies.

CHAPTER TWO

MAKING THE RIGHT MANAGEMENT CHOICE

Which is the right management approach: structure-centric or HC-centric? The choice between the two is more complex than it might seem because each of these approaches offers two different ways to organize. In the case of a structure-centric approach, a company can organize either as a *hierarchical bureaucracy* or as a *low-cost operator.* An HC-centric organization can choose to be either a *high-involvement organization* or a *global competitor.* The choice of organizational approach is critical and warrants careful analysis. Fortunately, it is possible to identify some strong indicators of when each approach is likely to be most effective.

STRUCTURE-CENTRIC ORGANIZING

For decades, the most commonly used approach to management was structure-centric: the hierarchical bureaucracy. This approach was highly visible in such leading corporations as IBM, AT&T, and Exxon, and was in use in most of the largest U.S. and European corporations. Today, it is still used in some corporations and in many governmental and nonprofit organizations, but in recent years it has lost favor and market share because it leads to high costs and inflexible performance. Realistically, it is likely to continue to lose market share. I mention it because it is still in use; however, at this point, I think it is reasonable to put the hierarchical bureaucracy approach aside entirely; it simply is not an effective way to organize and manage most businesses.

EXHIBIT 1. LOW-COST OPERATOR.

- McJobs: "unstimulating, low paid, with few prospects" (as defined by the *Oxford English Dictionary*)
- Minimum fringe benefits
- Little training and development
- Tight job descriptions
- Top-down decision making
- Low job security
- Extensive use of part-time and temporary employees

But the bureaucratic approach is not the only way to be structure-centric. The last decade or two have seen the rise of the low-cost operator. This management approach clearly falls within the structure-centric approach to organizing, but it has several features that make it more effective than the hierarchical bureaucracy (see Exhibit 1).

The defining feature of the low-cost operator is a focus on gaining competitive advantage through low wages and benefits rather than through the performance of talent. The low-cost operator generally ignores the advantages talent can create by outperforming the talent in competitor organizations (though sometimes its marketing efforts might aim to create a different impression). Bottom line, it argues for winning either by having labor as a neutral with regard to performance and cost (and achieving low costs in other areas, such as materials and supplies) or by having lower labor costs than competitors.

The most visible low-cost operators are retailers such as Wal-Mart and many of the fast-service restaurant chains, including McDonald's and Burger King. Ultimately, these companies do not try to win by having better service or more innovative and productive employees. They aim to keep their labor costs low and win customers through low prices. They don't try to achieve their low costs by having highly motivated employees. Instead, they focus on keeping their labor costs low by paying low wages, maintaining low staffing levels, and, as much as possible, containing benefit costs.

It is tempting to say that the low-cost operator approach is never the best way to manage because it fails to develop and utilize employees' full potential. An HC-centric model is certainly more appealing to those of us who value learning and aspire to a high standard of living for everyone in our society. However, the reality is that in some industries the low-cost operator model may be the most profitable one to use if it is well designed and executed.

Wal-Mart has frequently made the argument that it uses the low-cost approach because of the demands of its customers for low prices. Its CEO has said it has no choice, that low labor costs are the only way it can have low prices. A major reason why it can pay low wages and still fill jobs is that it is willing and able to hire low-skilled people. It also demands relatively little of employees in terms of innovation, product knowledge, and customer-service orientation. Certainly its employees need a minimum level of performance in all these areas, but since Wal-Mart does not try to distinguish itself by offering exceptional customer service, it does not need to compete with HC-centric organizations for the best talent.

Low-cost retailing and fast food are not the only industries in the United States and other developed countries where low labor costs can be a competitive advantage. Some others include farming, cleaning and janitorial services, and many types of food processing. All of these share a key characteristic: the work they ask their employees to do is relatively simple, repetitive, and low-value-added. When this type of work exists—and where the work cannot be altered to allow an individual employee to add more value—it is hard to look at talent as a way of gaining competitive advantage. And when talent isn't a potential source of competitive advantage, it is hard to argue that people should be well paid, offered opportunities to develop, and involved in decision making of any significance.

The key issue is really the amount of value that individuals can add. Just as in the old assembly lines in the automobile industry, where individuals did the same simple tasks every thirty to sixty seconds, today people simply have trouble adding much value in some businesses. In many instances, all an organization needs is a "warm body" with the ability to do a relatively easily learned task over and over again. When this is true, attempts to attract, hire, and train the best talent are usually money wasted. Even when good employees perform as well as they can, it makes little or no difference in organizational performance.

When businesses are dominated by simple, low-value-added work, they can do one of three things to keep labor costs low. First, as discussed, they can become very good at minimizing labor costs by paying low wages and providing minimal or no benefits. Second, they can automate and mechanize work so that they require more highly skilled employees. When this happens, talent can actually become a source of competitive advantage because people can use their problem-solving abilities and their knowledge of the work process to add more value to the product. Third, they can offshore the work because it can be done much more cheaply in low-wage countries that have an abundance of unskilled labor.

BMW

BMW is a recent example of a company that has decided to compete based on the talent in its manufacturing organization.

Auto companies have a long history of redesigning production processes to make the work more interesting and challenging. A lot was written in the 1960s and 1970s, for example, about Volvo's team-based manufacturing facility in Kalmar, Sweden. And during that same period, numerous joint labor-management employee-involvement programs were introduced in the U.S. auto industry. Perhaps the most visible project in the United States was Saturn, in which the United Auto Workers and General Motors tried to establish a cooperative relationship that would simultaneously create better working conditions for employees and higher-quality cars.

Some of these efforts enjoyed success, but none of them succeeded in making the HC-centric approach to management the dominant management approach in the auto industry.

Enter BMW. BMW's business strategy includes providing purchasers with a wide variety of choices in terms of how their cars are equipped. The variety of products produced is so great, in fact, that the same exact car is produced only once every nine months. The company also places a premium on producing a quality product. This combination of variety and quality is not easily achieved in products as complex as today's automobiles. It is likely to be even more difficult to achieve going forward. It requires

---

(*Continued*)

advanced technology in the manufacturing process as well as employees who are highly skilled and flexible.

Recognizing this, BMW's newest manufacturing facility in Leipzig, Germany, opened in 2005, is radically different from traditional auto plants. To begin with, the process for staffing the new plant (initially, and continually) places a strong emphasis on getting only the highest-quality workers. To create and sustain a plant that can thrive on such a complex manufacturing model, BMW uses a rigorous employee selection process that is unusual in the industry.

Applicants are screened for their ability to thrive in a team environment and cooperate with others. In addition, applicants are screened for their ability to learn and problem solve. Those who get interviewed go through elaborate day-long drills that are designed to screen out individuals who can't work in a team environment.

The plant's physical layout is also markedly different from that of other automobile manufacturers. It has an open structure that helps establish the connection between administration and production, as well as flexible work structures.

Finally, the company provides virtually unprecedented job security. And that is part of the reason why, for many Germans, getting a job at BMW is the ultimate accomplishment. The company's human resource department receives more than two hundred thousand applications annually.

Offshoring has received a lot of attention in the last few years, and it is important to note that it is not just low-skilled work that is being offshored. Increasingly, higher-skilled work is being off-shored, because people who can do complex knowledge work and are willing to work for much lower wages than people in the United States and Western Europe are available in Russia, India, China, and other developing countries.[1] There are doubts about how much longer they will be available at a low cost because the supply is limited. Nevertheless, at this point, offshoring is a viable option, and even if it becomes more expensive, it will continue to be used as a source of skilled labor.

It may sound like I am saying that most companies that cannot automate or offshore their work have no choice, and simply must use the low-cost-operator approach. That is not the case. I think that only a relatively small number of companies have no choice in the matter. In many cases, the low-cost-operator approach looks like the best choice simply because the cost of its use is not accurately computed.

Often when consdering their human capital costs, organizations focus too much on labor cost per hour and fail to consider some of the additional costs that come with low wages. I believe that if most organizations did a cost analysis of the impact of low wages on their total cost and compared the results to the total costs of the HC-centric approach to management, they would find the HC-centric approach is right for them. A prime example of this is the retail world, where Wal-Mart's low wages and minimal benefits may not be the best way to obtain low costs. When Wal-Mart's costs are fully accounted for (see box), they are not necessarily lower than the costs at a higher-wage company, Costco, which takes a more HC-centric approach to management.[2]

Low Wages Aren't the Best Option

Wal-Mart has the highest profile, but it is just one of many companies that are trying to gain competitive advantage by paying low wages and benefits. Many senior managers feel that they must pay low wages to meet customers' demand for low prices. Wal-Mart's CEO argues that he has "no choice." But are they correct? Recent studies show that they may not be.

Low wages generate a variety of negative employee behaviors that add to the overall cost of doing business. Although rarely calculated, these costs often turn out to be substantial. For example, employees at low-wage companies have significantly higher turnover rates: Wal-Mart's is nearly 50 percent, and many fast food, retail, and service companies have much higher rates. Researchers who have calculated the total costs of such turnover

---

(*Continued*)

find that it is the equivalent of one or two months' salary for unskilled workers who leave and must be replaced, and more than a year's salary for skilled ones.

High rates of absenteeism are also common at low-wage companies because their employees don't lose much pay when they fail to show up for work and don't care if they lose their jobs. Absenteeism has a negative impact on productivity because it often creates the need to use inexperienced replacement employees. In addition, because workers rarely give notice that they won't be showing up, low-wage companies must overstaff so they won't be caught short-handed. If enough workers aren't on the job to serve customers, or if customers can't find the same employee who helped them on their last visit, absenteeism drives business away and reduces customer loyalty.

Added to the hidden costs of low wages is the readily measurable one of employee pilferage. In retail establishments, shrinkage due to employee theft is higher when wages are lower. While it's not clear how much of this is due to employees' justifying their criminal behavior because they are poorly paid, and how much results from the fact that people willing to take low wages are more prone to theft, what is undeniable is that the cost of pilferage directly hits a company's bottom line.

Low-wage companies also spend considerable amounts keeping unions at bay. Realizing that union organization means higher wages and more expensive benefits, low-cost employers hire consultants to develop anti-union tactics, conduct "educational" sessions for their employees, incur legal and court costs associated with fighting unions, some even shut down operations to avoid a fate they see as worse than lost business.

The most significant negative consequence of a low-wage strategy may well be the quality of the workers who apply for such jobs. Low-wage companies tend to end up with employees who are below average in ability and who require close supervision that is costly.

Precisely because of the high costs created by low wages, research shows that the companies with the lowest overall operating costs often are not those that pay the least. For example, pilots at "low-cost" Southwest Airlines actually take home more on average than do their counterparts at "high-cost" United Airlines. The difference between these two unionized airlines is found in the way they manage their people. Southwest has effective training and job designs that motivate employees and make it possible for them to work effectively with minimal supervision.

Costco pays its workers $17 an hour on average, while its competitor, Wal-Mart's Sam's Club, pays only $10. Eighty-five percent of Costco employees enjoy company-provided health insurance, as compared to less than half at Sam's Club. Significantly, these high wages and benefits have not come out of the pockets of Costco shareholders. In fact, Costco has outperformed Wal-Mart on the stock market over the last five years. Costco's stock has risen 55 percent; Wal-Mart's has fallen 10 percent. Costco generates slightly more sales than Sam's Club with 38 percent fewer employees, and its employees have much lower turnover and better interactions with customers. They require less supervision and engage in less pilferage. Costco is able to combine good wages with low costs because its employees are organized in ways that reward them for their ideas and effort.

So the evidence is clear: most companies don't have to make the hard choice between high employee wages and low prices. Their real choice is between a traditional approach to management and a high-wage, high-involvement approach. And that's good news for shareholders, customers, and employees alike.[3]

Retail is not the only type of business in which low wages do not necessarily lead to the lowest costs. Japanese auto manufacturers have shown this to be true in the manufacturing arena, Starbucks has shown it for food service, SAS has shown it for computer services, and Southwest has shown it for airlines. Indeed, there is every reason to believe that as offshoring continues to grow, and more technology is employed in the workplace, fewer and fewer organizations in the United States and in other developed countries will be able to compete successfully by using the low-cost-operator approach.

HC-CENTRIC MANAGEMENT

Two particularly visible and popular approaches to HC-centric management are being used by organizations today. Both of them depend on the effective utilization of talent as a key differentiator and source of competitive advantage. Where they differ is in how they treat talent and how they expect to gain competitive advantage from it.

In a recent book I coauthored with Jim O'Toole, we identified these two HC-centric approaches as the high-involvement approach and the global-competitor approach.[4] The high-involvement approach is the older of the two.

HIGH-INVOLVEMENT MANAGEMENT

The high-involvement approach to management can be traced back at least to the early 1950s. It was then that a few companies began experimenting with self-managing work teams and other approaches to moving power to lower levels in the organization so that individuals could participate in important decisions about how work is done and take responsibility for their performance.

The high-involvement approach places a great emphasis on the nature of the work that individuals do. It argues for work that allows individuals to make decisions, gives them feedback about the effectiveness of their performance, and challenges them to develop and use their skills and abilities.[5] It also emphasizes the importance of having employees who have the ability to self-manage, who are well trained, and who can reasonably expect to have careers with the organization.

Much of the writing about the high-involvement approach to management focuses on the importance of leadership. It usually goes on to emphasize the importance of a democratic or participative management style. Group decision making led by a leader who is good at listening, building consensus, and incorporating individuals' input is seen as critical to an effective high-involvement approach to management.

Recent writing about high-involvement organizations has increasingly emphasized the importance of shared leadership.[6] This approach is a natural next step in the evolution of high-involvement management. It argues that high-involvement organizations shouldn't depend on a few individuals with exceptional leadership skills providing a charismatic environment that galvanizes the rest of the organization. Instead it argues that many individuals can and should be expected to take on leadership roles when situations present themselves. Shared leadership means that individuals throughout an organization take the lead when they have the appropriate knowledge and expertise. As discussed in Chapter Nine, in many ways it converts leadership from an individual activity to a team sport.

Employment stability is another important feature of high-involvement companies. High-involvement companies believe in a long-term, mutually beneficial relationship with their talent. High-involvement organizations commit to the training and development of their talent, and to retraining people as the nature of the work and technology changes. Consistent with a commitment to the existing workforce, most promotion is from within. High-involvement organizations also place a strong emphasis on egalitarianism. There are few signs of status differentiation in high-involvement organizations; managers and workers park together, eat together, and engage in social events together.

High-involvement organizations place a strong emphasis on their talent sharing the financial performance of the organization. Typically most employees own stock in their company and may also participate in profit sharing or gain sharing bonus plans based on the financial performance of their particular work area or even work team. Not surprisingly, high-involvement organizations are in large part committed to communicating financial results to all employees. They often have financial literacy programs designed to educate the workforce with respect to the financial performance of the company.

Perhaps the defining feature of high-involvement organizations is that they value a long-term loyalty relationship with their workforce and make a major effort to build commitment to the organization and a sense of community in the organization. They also emphasize a commitment to high job and financial performance. This is usually done in the context of building commitment to the organization and creating a win-win relationship with employees.

Figure 3 graphically captures the underlying management philosophy of the high-involvement organization in contrast to a traditional bureaucratic one. It shows that the traditional organization typically has a hierarchical structure with large amounts of power, information, knowledge, and rewards at the top and

FIGURE 3. POWER, INFORMATION, KNOWLEDGE, AND REWARDS.

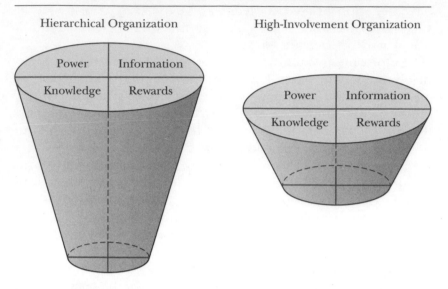

Hierarchical Organization   High-Involvement Organization

relatively little at the bottom. In contrast to this is the flatter structure of a high-involvement organization. Interestingly, the amount of power, information, and knowledge at the top is not necessarily less in a high-involvement organization; in fact, it may be greater. The signature feature is the processes, structures, and reward systems that locate large amounts of information, knowledge, power, and rewards at the lowest levels of the organization. When this is combined with a long-term commitment to individuals, and to their development by way of interesting work and a sense of community, the result is an environment in which employees truly care about the organization's success and profit.

When a high-involvement organization is well designed and well managed, a type of virtuous spiral emerges. As shown in Figure 4, high organizational performance occurs because of giving information, knowledge, and power to all members of the organization. As a result of this, individuals are rewarded more and motivated better, and the organization becomes a more attractive place to work. This in turn leads to higher levels of performance and a continuing spiral of improving performance and increasing desirability of the organization as a place to work.

FIGURE 4. DYNAMIC VIRTUOUS SPIRAL.

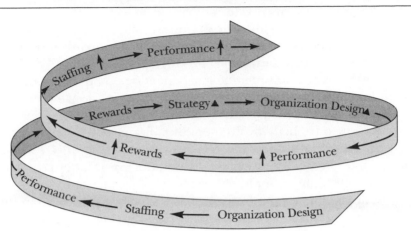

This relationship between individuals and organizations can last decades when it is supported by the right business strategy and a well-designed organization.

Exhibit 2 presents the major characteristics of a high-involvement organization. Individual organizations may not have all these characteristics, but they do represent somewhat of an integrated whole. Most of them need to be in place if a high-involvement organization is to perform effectively. They all point toward individuals' playing major roles in organizations and having their rewards tied to the success of the organization. These characteristics also clearly differentiate high-involvement organizations from

EXHIBIT 2. CHARACTERISTICS OF HIGH-INVOLVEMENT ORGANIZATIONS.

- Enriched work designs
- Participative decision-making structures
- Shared business information
- Committed to education and development of people
- Career oriented
- Rewards for organization performance
- Community
- Shared leadership
- Committed to talent management

structure-centric organizations. None of them are typically present in structure-centric organizations whether they are low-cost operators or traditional bureaucratic organizations.

High-involvement organizations are found in many industries. They enjoyed a particularly strong growth spurt during the 1980s and early 1990s.[7] High-involvement management is perhaps most popular in midsize and small firms, but it certainly is not limited to them.

It is always more than a little precarious to identify organizations that are long-term high-involvement organizations—in the world of management, nothing seems to last forever. Despite this, I would like to note a few of my favorites. For decades now, Harley-Davidson has been a leading example of how high-involvement management can be applied in a unionized manufacturing organization.[8] In the retail industry, Whole Foods has grown rapidly over the last decade and has made effective use of the high-involvement approach to management. Procter & Gamble is a global organization that pioneered high-involvement management in its manufacturing plants in the 1960s and continues to use many of the principles of high-involvement management throughout the corporation.

Finally, I cannot help but mention Southwest Airlines and its multiple decades of success. This company clearly differentiates itself based on its human capital and its high-involvement practices. Nucor Steel, Costco, Starbucks, and UPS are additional firms that can be counted among the larger U.S. corporations that have adopted most, if not all, of the characteristics and practices associated with high-involvement management. I mention these corporations not as a complete list but as illustrations of the fact that high-involvement management can work in a variety of industries and work settings.

GLOBAL-COMPETITOR APPROACH

The global-competitor approach to management is relatively new. Like the low-cost operator model, this approach was developed in part as a response to the global competition that corporations face today. It is also very much a product of the rapid technological developments that have occurred in the last several decades and the need for organizations to constantly develop and apply new technologies.

Global competitor organizations are the glamour companies of the current era. They often are enormous in size and global in reach. A quick look at the technology industries and many of the more complex service industries, like financial services, reveals that virtually all the leading firms in these sectors have adopted the global-competitor approach. Many media and entertainment companies have also adopted this approach.

Because global-competitor corporations offer their customers the latest technology and services, they often need complex organizational structures and the ability to innovate. They know that knowledge and talent are their primary sources of competitive advantage. Like high-involvement organizations, they realize that they can compete successfully only if they have the best talent available and have talent that is committed to high performance and continuous improvement.

Global competitor organizations are constantly searching for talent and are constantly concerned with upgrading their talent. They take a "travel light" approach to talent. To be agile, they minimize their long-term commitments to employees. Rather than being strongly inclined toward building talent, they are much more likely to do a cost-benefit analysis or a return on investment analysis and decide to buy or build talent on the basis of the results.

Not surprisingly, global competitor companies that utilize rapidly developing technologies are particularly likely to buy talent rather than to build it. Global competitor organizations often hire relatively senior managers from the outside. This is a major difference from the high-involvement approach, which tends to lean consistently toward building rather than buying needed skills and knowledge.

Because global-competitor organizations often do buy talent, their employment contracts—or *deals,* as they are sometimes called—tend to differ from those in high-involvement organizations. High-involvement organizations typically have a single employment contract emphasizing employment stability and the willingness to invest in talent development; global competitors typically offer multiple contracts.

You will often find a small core group of employees in a global competitor who have employment relationships like the ones offered in high-involvement companies. These core people are the long-term members of the organization. The organization invests in their development, and they share in the financial success of the organization.

But global-competitor organizations also often have a second larger group of employees who are subject to buy-build decisions when it comes to employment. These individuals don't have a high level of employment security. They are, however, expected to be strongly committed to their work and typically do have interesting and challenging work to do. They also often share in the financial success of the organization through profit sharing and bonuses.

Unlike high-involvement organizations, global-competitor organizations place much less emphasis on their talent developing a commitment to the organization's success. Their focus is on individuals doing their jobs well.

Many global-competitor organizations make extensive use of contract employees and temporary employees. They find this is an effective way to quickly acquire talent that can provide important areas of expertise. It also avoids their having to make a long-term commitment to someone with a skill set that may quickly become obsolescent or out of sync with the organization's needs.

Global-competitor organizations are willing to go anywhere in the world to find the right talent at the right price. They do this even if it means reducing jobs in their home country and laying off existing employees. For example, over the last several decades, many of the largest U.S. semiconductor firms have moved most of their manufacturing offshore to Asia (for example, to Malaysia, China, and Vietnam). Increasingly, software firms are moving their production work to India, Russia, and other countries where talent is available at "the right price."

Global-competitor organizations make no apologies for offshoring jobs. It is a natural consequence of their need for good talent at the lowest price available. It is a kind of creative destruction that they see as necessary to stay at the leading edge in their industry.

In many respects, the relationship between global-competitor corporations and their employees is transactional, but that does not necessarily make it ineffective. Employees are expected to contribute their skills and to perform at high levels. Because this employment contract is clear to them and they are rewarded for their performance, they do provide what is expected of them. In combination with the core employees, they create a knowledge-able and flexible pool of talent for the organization.

Apple, Microsoft, and Intel have used the global-competitor approach almost from their inception, while IBM moved to it in the 1990s. IBM is a particularly interesting story, because it once could accurately be described as a structure-centric organization, using a largely bureaucratic approach to management. It was a very well-managed structure-centric organization, and as a result performed well for decades. But its leaders realized in the early 1990s that this approach was no longer viable, given the emergence of a variety of tough competitors, the need to respond to a global marketplace, and the need to shift its product offerings toward services.[9]

During the 1990s, IBM essentially threw out much of its traditional loyalty-based approach to talent management, which included job security, defined-benefit pensions, and promotion from within. The company then took a different tack, adopting a global-competitor approach in order to gain flexibility and continue to develop its knowledge and talent in ways that would allow it to respond effectively to global markets and new technologies.

Exhibit 3 presents the major features of a global-competitor approach to management. The list has some overlap with the characteristics of a high-involvement organization, but is clearly quite different in the kind of employment relationship firms establish and how they manage their talent.

EXHIBIT 3.   CHARACTERISTICS OF GLOBAL-COMPETITOR ORGANIZATIONS.

- Interesting work
- Global talent pool
- Offshoring
- Outsourcing
- Employment depends on performance and skills
- Pay for performance
- Just-in-time training
- Career self-management
- Long-term core group of employees
- Pay what it takes to attract and retain talent
- Willing to buy talent

Although the most visible users of the global-competitor approach are large technology firms (for example, IBM, Microsoft, Sun Microsystems, Cisco, and Intel), many other companies use this approach as well. Most large financial service firms, including Citicorp, Merrill Lynch, and UBS, use the global-competitor approach, as do most large accounting and consulting firms.

As with the high-involvement approach, global-competitor organizations are quite different from both types of structure-centric organizations. They are designed to treat talent in ways that will allow it to make a major contribution to their success. They also are very much focused on creating an environment that will attract and retain outstanding talent. In that sense, they are like high-involvement organizations, but they differ in the methods they use to motivate talent and to be sure of having the right talent at a particular time.

Global competitor accounting firms and professional service firms typically make little use of contract employees and have a "promote from within" policy. They recognize the need to have some continuity in areas such as customer interfaces. Entertainment firms and sports teams, on the other hand, use an extreme version of the global-competitor approach. They use many temporary and contract employees and they constantly try to upgrade the quality of their workforces by hiring new talent.

Interestingly, if you look inside many of the best low-cost operators, you will find a little global-competitor organization. This usually is the part of the organization that does the key management work and creates and maintains the organization's core competencies. Wal-Mart, for example, uses a global-competitor approach in its purchasing and logistics functions, despite being a low-cost operator. Company leaders know that they need the best talent in these areas and that they cannot obtain it by taking the low-cost-operator approach. Not surprisingly, Wal-Mart and many other low-cost operators also do not take the low-cost approach when it comes to their senior managers.

MAKING THE CHOICE

In considering the choice between HC-centric and structure-centric, it is important to distinguish between talent-critical and talent-intensive organizations. A company is not necessarily talent critical or pivotal simply because it has a large number of employees and a large portion of its costs associated with labor. That makes it talent intensive, but not necessarily talent critical.

Further, just because an organization's performance depends on how well a few individuals perform relative to its competitors, it is not a talent-critical organization. (No one wants a second-rate CEO or head of research and development in a technology company. Having the best individuals in a few key positions is an important focus in most organizations; it is not a characteristic that makes an organization talent critical.) A company is talent critical only if its strategy calls for it to gain a competitive advantage as the result of a large percentage of its talent outperforming the talent in other organizations as a result of its quality and the way it is managed.

Adopting a strategy that calls for talent to be the critical difference maker is appropriate when an organization operates in a business where two conditions exist. The first is that the performance of an organization's talent is determined by how it is selected, developed, managed, retained, and organized. The second is that the performance of an organization's talent is a strong determinant of organizational performance. A particularly strong case can be made for an organization being talent critical when its talent is counted on to provide hard-to-duplicate types and levels of performance.

In most cases, talent critical organizations should employ an HC-centric approach. The same is not necessarily true of organizations that are talent intensive. They may perform best by taking the low-cost-operator approach. The one exception is when talent is scarce. It may be that in order to attract and retain the amount of talent they need, talent-intensive organizations are best off adopting the HC-centric approach even if they are not talent critical.

In making the choice between HC-centric and structure-centric management, the following questions can help guide senior managers in deciding whether their companies should adopt (or retain) an HC-centric approach to organizing.

- Do the majority of employees require high levels of knowledge to do their work?
- Is innovation critical to sustained organizational effectiveness?
- Is being able to innovate and change an important capability?
- Is employee turnover costly?

- Do employees continue to improve and get better at doing their jobs over a long period of time?
- Does the business serve customers best when it has long-term employees who understand customers' needs and develop relationships with them?
- Does satisfying customers require individuals in various parts of the organization working together effectively and seamlessly to create a product or service?
- Is the work people do difficult to supervise and manage because it is complex?
- Does the person doing the work often have more knowledge about how to do it than a manager?
- Is it difficult to measure individual performance and hold individuals accountable for their results?
- Is there a scarcity of people with the skills needed to do most of the work in the organization?
- Does the knowledge that is essential to an organization's key capabilities and competencies continue to expand and develop?
- Is a high percentage of the organization's assets made up of intangibles?
- Is (or can) much of the simpler, more repetitive work of the organization be outsourced?
- Are employees more difficult to replace than equipment?
- Is virtual supervision of people common?

If the answer to most of these questions is yes, then an HC-centric approach is the right one for an organization. Which raises the next question: which HC-centric approach is best?

CHOOSING AN HC-CENTRIC MANAGEMENT APPROACH

HC-centric organizations have a choice: they can adopt the global-competitor approach or the high-involvement approach. Both potentially can be successful in businesses that are talent-critical. Both can lead to competitive advantages that result from the performance of talent.

The fact that organizations have a choice between the high-involvement approach and the global-competitor approach raises a key question: when does one fit better than the other? The answer is that it depends first and foremost on the type and rate of change that an organization faces. The more an organization expects to face rapid change, particularly change that requires it to change or at least improve its core competencies, the more it should adopt the global-competitor approach.

The major advantage of the global-competitor approach over the high-involvement approach is the ability to bring in new talent and quickly update or change the technological expertise of the workforce and the core competencies of the organization. Although buying talent, the mode of global-competitor organization, has some dysfunctions, it is hard to argue with the point that it allows for more rapid change, and in some cases, for more cost-effective change, than does an internal talent development approach. The global-competitor approach also is particularly appropriate when an organization is expanding rapidly and when that expansion is international in nature.

High-involvement organizations take more time to build. Selecting the right employees and integrating them into the communities characteristic of this type of organization does not happen quickly. Thus, the high-involvement approach can limit the speed with which an organization can grow and develop. Interestingly, the high-involvement approach seems to be easier to install in countries that have a democratic political tradition. This approach just seems to align more with democratic societies.

The high-involvement approach fits particularly well when organizations want to do relationship selling. When an organization wants to establish a continuing relationship with its customers, continuity in the sales force and in the members of an organization is an important asset. This argues strongly for having a stable group of employees with the kind of organizational commitment that the high-involvement approach to management creates—at least with respect to the sales and service force, but often also with respect to the whole organization. Employees working in this kind of environment are more likely to be able to deliver a sales relationship that will keep customers over a long period of time.

Organizations that want to develop a customer focus are prime candidates for the high-involvement approach. Having a customer focus usually requires cross-function and cross-department cooperation and a willingness to sacrifice for the good of the whole.[10]

IBM and Marriott are just two examples of companies that are trying to become more customer-centric and are finding that developing this capability pushes them to adopt more and more of a high-involvement approach to management.

Organizations that have stable products are very good candidates for high-involvement management. This type of business often has customers who know a great deal about the organization and its products and expect to interface with a salesperson who has at least comparable stability and knowledge. Indeed, it is ideal to have a salesperson who has greater product knowledge. This is only likely to be achieved if the organization puts an emphasis on long-term employment. In this type of business, product improvement and operating efficiency gains often require good product knowledge. Rather than needing employees to develop new organizational competencies and capabilities, they require employees who know the products and the customers.

SAS, the computer software company, is a great example of an organization that practices high-involvement management because it fits its business niche. It sells software programs that are regularly updated and are used by organizations for decades. Not surprisingly, SAS has decided that continuity in terms of product knowledge and relationship selling are very important to it. Continuity allows for easy updating and upgrading of products, but perhaps more important, it leads to customer interfaces with employees who know both the customer and the products. This is a powerful competitive advantage in a product space that is evolutionary rather than revolutionary.

Organizations offering products and services that require high levels of internal coordination and cooperation are particularly good candidates for the high-involvement approach. The resulting commitment to long-term employment and to individuals' being committed to the organization leads to high levels of internal cooperation and collaboration.

COMBINING APPROACHES

Some organizations have integrated the global-competitor and high-involvement approaches; they use features of each in establishing their approach to management. Effective management is all about making good choices. Sometimes the best choice is a combination of the two HC–centric management approaches that fits a particular organization's strategy, rather than an off-the-shelf installation of either one.

One note of caution is in order here: the pieces need to fit together to create a meaningful whole. Each of the approaches has a certain integrity and coherence. Mixing them can create a confusing message about the identity of the organization. One test of whether mixing makes sense is how the combination relates to the organization's strategy. If it is a good fit, it probably will make sense to most employees.

The key point is that managers need to understand the pluses and minuses of each approach, and where they fit; they also need to be able to apply that information in picking and developing a management style that fits the business mode of their organization. The key elements of the business model that are important to consider are rate of change, type of technology, rate of growth, geographic presence of the organization, and the type of competencies and capabilities that the organization needs to have in order to be effective.

AFTER THE CHOICE

The first step in creating an effective HC-centric organization is about determining which HC-centric approach best fits the organization's business model. Once this choice has been made on the basis of the factors discussed in this chapter, it is about effective implementation and use of the chosen approach's practices, policies, and structure. Thus, in the chapters that follow, I describe the most important features of HC-centric organizations and how organizations should operate when they use the high-involvement approach and the global-competitor approach.

CHAPTER THREE

DESIGNING ORGANIZATIONS

Designing an organization is challenging regardless of whether it is HC-centric or structure-centric. Reduce even the simplest of organizations to its bare essentials, and it's still complex, requiring multiple systems, processes, structures, and practices.

Creating a highly *effective* design is especially challenging because no single feature (no practice, process, structure, or system) can be viewed as a stand-alone "best practice," no matter how good it is. Ultimately, only the complete picture counts. An organization is only as effective as the degree to which its practices, processes, and structures fit and work with each other. Put another way, an organization may have all the "best" practices, but if those practices do not work together to produce behaviors that support the business model, they will not produce an effective organization.

The key to designing an HC-centric organization, then, is creating a totality of systems, practices, processes, and structures that work together to support the effective acquisition, development, deployment, retention, and performance of talent. This requires many practices and structures that are different from those typical of an organization that does not look to human capital for its competitive advantage. This chapter addresses the major features of organizations and discusses the way those features differ between HC-centric and structure-centric organizations. Later chapters add more detail on the key features of HC-centric organizations and focus more on the difference between designs for the high-involvement and global-competitor approaches.

THE STAR MODEL

The Star Model, shown in Figure 5, is often used to identify the key elements of organizations.[1] It shows five star points, all of which are connected to one another. The connections between strategy, people, structure, processes, and rewards indicate that these elements must work together to create an effective organization. So if a company's leaders are considering a shift from a structure-centric approach to an HC-centric approach, one thing should be clear at the outset: Creating an HC-centric organization is not a matter of simply making a tactical change in some of the boxes. In fact, it is a matter of altering all the boxes. This is the major reason why many organizations find it difficult to change from being structure-centric to being HC-centric.

Figure 6 shows a revised version of the Star Model that I have found useful in my work with companies that want to become HC-centric. It does not change the names of four of the points on the star, but it adds a "competencies and capabilities" box and it alters the placement of "strategy." These changes highlight the importance of competencies and capabilities and the role they should play in strategy formulation and implementation. It also

FIGURE 5. CLASSIC STAR MODEL.

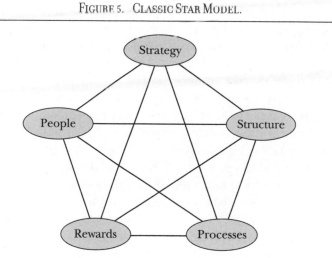

FIGURE 6.   HC-CENTRIC STAR MODEL.

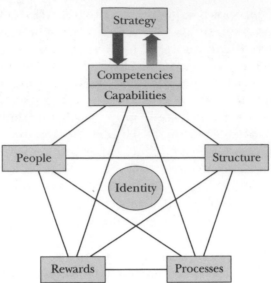

adds "identity" to the model, emphasizing the importance of a firm's culture and external image.

Although each point merits discussion in its own right, what is important at this point is the model as a whole, and the ability to think about the model as a whole. All too often individuals who make organization design decisions do not think about the design in a big-picture way. Faced with the demands of the day and their jobs, they focus on one or another part of the model.

If there's an issue regarding compensation, they deal with that. If there's an issue about job design, or about the need to infuse the organization with a new talent, they focus on that. This is understandable. Unless you're creating an organization from scratch, it's hard to consider all facets at once. But to make the kinds of fundamental changes necessary to move an entire organization away from a structure-centric mode and into an HC-centric mode—or for that matter to create a new organization that takes an HC-centric approach—a big-picture perspective is critical. Thus, as we consider each point on the star, remember that it needs to fit with the other points.

STRATEGY

Strategy defines which products, services, and markets an organization will focus on and how it will compete. It states an intent that should guide choices about how the organization creates value and about how it is designed.

Strategy must take its cue from the environment in which the organization does business. For example, American, United, Delta, Southwest, and Jet Blue are all in the airline business. And so, as a group, their strategies over time are more likely to look like each other's than to resemble the strategies of companies in, say, a consumer products business. But that doesn't mean they will have the same strategy or perform at the same level.

Research indicates that an organization's performance depends in large part on how well its strategy attends to the demands of the environment and how well it executes its strategy.[2] The large difference in the performance of airlines, then, reflects the degree to which their strategies fit the environment and how well they execute them. In this case, Southwest has performed well for several decades because it had the right strategy and excellent execution. The same cannot be said for its major competitors United and American, or for the defunct People Express (which had the same strategy as Southwest but poor execution).

An organization's strategy may or may not be based on a mission or purpose. Many organizations have been and will continue to be successful without having a sense of purpose that gives meaning and direction to their actions. But achieving success without a sense of meaning is much more likely for a structure-centric organization than it is for an HC-centric organization. The difference is that HC-centric organizations depend on people, and people are more likely to be committed to an organization that has a purpose they believe in and support than to one that doesn't. Thus having a meaningful purpose can make the difference between a successful HC-centric organization and an unsuccessful one. As a result, it can be the key to an HC-centric organization's outperforming a structure-centric organization.

HC-centric organizations can adopt many types of purpose.[3] The first type that comes to mind is those based on important social values such as doing good and acting with fairness and respect. For example, Starbucks and Southwest have purposes that include treating employees and customers with respect and dignity. Genentech and Medtronic have purposes that provide meaning by focusing on improving and extending people's lives. Avon is committed to providing women around the world with an opportunity to have an income and improve their quality of life.

An alternative to a purpose that appeals to human values is one that focuses on such business challenges as creating high-quality products and services, and winning. For example, Toyota has made "the relentless pursuit of excellence" its purpose, while many sports teams have made winning championships their purpose. Apple, Sony, 3M, and Ideo all have purposes that focus on innovation.

Having a meaningful purpose is one part of having an excellent HC-centric organization. However, if pursuit of that purpose is not a focus of the other points on the star, the impact will not be positive; indeed, it may be negative. The failure to honor purpose in how the organization operates can and will lead to cynicism and mistrust. Thus, HC-centric organizations need to be sure that they do what they say when it comes to how the business strategy is executed and how the organization is designed and operates.

COMPETENCIES AND CAPABILITIES

Having the right competencies and capabilities is basic to strategy execution.[4] That is why, in Figure 6, arrows indicate a mutual influence process between the "competencies and capabilities" point on the star, and the "strategy" box. When an organization competes on what it can do, the link between strategy and competencies and capabilities is critical.

Here's how the link works: *competencies* refers to the technical expertise and knowledge base that underlie the products and services a company offers. Every successful organization has one or more competencies: Monsanto, for example, has the biotechnology of plants, Shell has deepwater exploration, Microsoft has software engineering, and 3M has chemical processes. The knowledge that forms the basis of competencies often exists only in the brains of a few employees, but that doesn't diminish either its reach or its importance. It is needed in order to create the patents and intellectual property that lead to winning products and services.

An organization's *capabilities* are the things that the organization can do. A capability, for example, might be the ability to operate a global network of customer-service engineers who serve the same customers, the ability to bring a product to market quickly, the ability to innovate, or the ability to manage customer relations.

Capabilities do not reside with one individual or a small group of gurus. Instead, they are the product of the collective knowledge and ability of employees to work together to execute the activities that the organization's strategy calls for in terms of products and services. For example, Toyota's quality capability includes its work processes, the assembly skills of its manufacturing employees, and the design skills of its engineers.

When I asked Andrea Jung, the CEO of Avon, why Avon has been so much more successful than other direct-sales organizations, she cited two capabilities. The first comes as no surprise: brand management. The second was a bit of a surprise to me. She said it was the capability to do business on a global basis. She went on to note that because of this capability, Avon has been able to create successful operations in many countries, while most other direct-sales organizations are only successful in their home country (for example, Mary Kay).

An effective organization typically needs both state-of-the-art knowledge with respect to its core competencies and capabilities that allow it to execute its strategy with respect to product or service development and delivery. If either is lacking, it is hard for an organization to have a competitive advantage. This is true for both structure-centric and HC-centric organizations.

A major reason for adopting an HC-centric approach is to gain a competitive advantage by having superior competencies and capabilities. The HC-centric approach is particularly likely to be a good fit when an organization wants to have capabilities that require a knowledgeable, involved, highly motivated, and change-ready workforce. Thus if innovation, for example, is an important capability for an organization, success is much more likely with an HC-centric approach to management.

Strategy needs to drive competencies and capabilities, but existing capabilities and competencies—as well as the potential to develop new competencies and capabilities—need to drive strategy. In other words, they all need to be considered simultaneously to ensure a good fit. In considering the development of new competencies and capabilities, it is important to focus on the availability of talent since it is the basis of both and may be scarce or not available at all.

The following observation by Jim McNerney, the CEO of Boeing, nicely captures the relationship between strategy and capability: "It's all about understanding what organizations can and can't do. . . . It's not about strategy. . . . It's not easy, but I'm saying, that is more commonly done well than the assessment that a leader has to make about execution—whether it can be done."[5]

A strategy that cannot be implemented is a faulty strategy, just as a strategy that doesn't direct the organization to develop the appropriate competencies and capabilities is a poor strategy. Thus competencies and capabilities and strategy are intertwined and need to be an important part of every strategy discussion.

The way in which the connections among strategy, competencies, and capabilities are manifested differs from organization to organization. Consider GE, which has an interesting approach to competency and capability management that fits its strategy of being in multiple diverse businesses. Given the wide variety of businesses it operates (from running television networks to building locomotives), it doesn't make sense for the corporate office to manage its core *competencies,* as there are simply too many, and the expertise needs to be in the business units anyway.

However, GE has identified some key *capabilities* that it wants all its businesses to have, and these are managed by the corporate office. Quality is one capability that GE has focused on for over a decade; talent management has been a focus for over fifty years. In these and in financial management, corporate headquarters takes steps (for example, training, knowledge sharing, mandatory processes, and practices) to ensure that all divisions of GE are world class and operate in a similar manner.

IMPLICATIONS

In structure-centric, hierarchical organizations, strategy is typically formulated by senior management, often with outside consulting help (from firms such as Booz Allen, or Bain, or McKinsey) that gathers data about market conditions and opportunities. Often there is little focus on the human capital of the organization and its ability to develop new competencies and capabilities, nor is there a great deal of focus on the current status of its competencies and capabilities.

One clear implication of the connection between strategy and competencies and capabilities in HC-centric organizations is the need to involve individuals from throughout the organization in the strategy formulation process. It takes the consideration of multiple perspectives to provide the best information, not just about the external environment and what customers want but also about the internal environment and the ability of an organization to execute a particular strategy. These perspectives are also critical in implementing a strategy, particularly if it calls for the development of new competencies and capabilities.

Involving people from all parts of an organization in strategy formulation helps ensure that a strategy is practical; it also helps ensure that the commitment to implementation is widespread in the organization. Last but not least, it is consistent with the high-involvement approach to HC-centric management.

Broad-based involvement in strategy is not easy in large organizations, but with effort and innovation it can be done. IBM provides a good example of one approach. IBM has developed an innovative Web-based approach (called "WorldJam") to getting input from employees on strategy and new product ideas. WorldJam sessions are led by senior members of IBM and focus on a variety of key issues faced by the corporation.

Essentially, WorldJams are electronic "town hall meetings" during which employees are asked to respond to issues online. IBM's technology enables organizers to pick out themes, ideas, and grudges from their online dialogue. Based on that input, managers then make decisions about development of new capabilities and products, and about the improvement of existing ones. In the best-case scenario, these meetings surface new solutions and identify and spur the development of new products.

A second implication of the relationship between strategy and competencies and capabilities concerns the relationship between an organization's management approach and strategy. Whether an organization adopts a global-competitor or a high-involvement approach should influence and be influenced by strategy decisions. For example, global competitors can be quite nimble when it comes to developing new competencies and capabilities because they have fewer restraints on them as far as buying the new talent necessary and terminating existing talent. For the same reasons they may prove more agile when it comes to entering into new business and developing new ways of doing business.

STRUCTURE

The most visible feature of organizations and the one that usually gets the most attention when organizations are being designed is structure. No doubt, structure is a very important determinant of an organization's performance, but it is only one determinant—and it must be designed so that it fits with the other points on the star.

HC-centric organizations look radically different from structure-centric organizations when it comes to the type of jobs they offer as well as the type of organization charts or designs that they use. Structure-centric organizations emphasize hierarchy, and they tend to have well-defined and described jobs with clear accountabilities and responsibilities. In many cases, they also segment work into small parts of a total service or production process and, as a result, individuals end up with highly repetitive, low-skilled jobs.

Structure-centric organizations typically have relatively steep hierarchies, in part because the segmentation of work results in individuals doing only a small step in a product or service process. This in turn creates a need for a hierarchy to integrate and coordinate what is being done by individuals. It also may require close supervision, because individuals rarely have much motivation to perform well in jobs that are highly repetitive and lack a sense of wholeness.[6]

Structure-centric organizations are often organized around R&D, marketing, sales, production, and staff functions such as finance and human resources. Alternatively, large structure-centric organizations often are organized around business units or customer groupings. Each of these units then has a functional structure.

More complex structure-centric organizations may use matrix structures that involve multiple reporting relationships. They rarely, however, have true team-based management structures and do not include teams that are relatively self-managed. They pay little attention to the motivational characteristics of the work itself.

HC-centric organizations, whether high-involvement or global competitors, need to be the polar opposite of structure-centric organizations when it comes to structure. HC-centric organizations start from the premise *that the key feature of the structure is its ability to motivate and direct the behavior of a knowledgeable workforce.* Thus they place much less emphasis on hierarchy and control and much more emphasis on the motivational characteristics of the work that individuals are asked to do. They also emphasize enabling individuals to self-manage when it comes to coordination and working with others.

HC-centric organizations usually have a flat organizational structure with few supervisors. Team-based structures are very common in high-involvement HC-centric organizations. They have a number of advantages, including giving individuals flexibility about what to do and how to do it.

Well-designed teams have the potential to give individuals a much clearer look at the performance of the organization and how their work impacts financial success and customer satisfaction. Teams often can produce a whole product or offer a whole service, and as a result, give individuals feedback as to how well they are performing. They also can provide the kind of customer contact that leads to a focus on results. Effective teams can coordinate their work and make close supervision unnecessary.

W. L. Gore is one HC-centric organization that takes very seriously the idea of having an emerging structure. It encourages an organic approach to the development and change of structure that is driven by the identification of new products. It avoids formal hierarchies and structures. Gore's structure is particularly appropriate for an organization that chooses the high-involvement approach to management. It assumes that employees will be with the organization long enough to develop a deep commitment to its values and its approach to organizing.

W. L. Gore

W. L. Gore has an HC-centric approach to organizing that is designed to foster innovation. The best description of it is on Gore's Web site:

Corporate Culture

How we work at Gore sets us apart. Since Bill Gore founded the company in 1958, Gore has been a team-based, flat lattice organization that fosters personal initiative. There are no traditional organizational charts, no chains of command, nor predetermined channels of communication.

Instead, we communicate directly with each other and are accountable to fellow members of our multi-disciplined teams. We encourage hands-on innovation, involving those closest to a project in decision making. Teams organize around opportunities and leaders emerge. This unique kind of corporate structure has proven to be a significant contributor to associate satisfaction and retention.

We work hard at maximizing individual potential, maintaining an emphasis on product integrity, and cultivating an environment where creativity can flourish. A fundamental belief in our people and their abilities continues to be the key to our success.

How does all this happen? Associates (not employees) are hired for general work areas. With the guidance of their sponsors (not bosses) and a growing understanding of opportunities and team objectives, associates commit to projects that match their skills. All of this takes place in an environment that combines freedom with cooperation and autonomy with synergy.

Everyone can quickly earn the credibility to define and drive projects. Sponsors help associates chart a course in the organization that will offer personal fulfillment while maximizing their contribution to the enterprise. Leaders may be appointed, but are defined by "followership." More often, leaders emerge naturally by demonstrating special knowledge, skill, or experience that advances a business objective.

Associates adhere to four basic guiding principles articulated by Bill Gore:

- Fairness to each other and everyone with whom we come in contact
- Freedom to encourage, help, and allow other associates to grow in knowledge, skill, and scope of responsibility
- The ability to make one's own commitments and keep them
- Consultation with other associates before undertaking actions that could impact the reputation of the company

Here is how Gore describes the organization to prospective employees in order to develop its employer brand:

Working at Gore

At Gore you'll find direct communication, a team orientation, and one title—associate—that's shared by everyone. It's an unusual corporate culture that contributes directly to our business success by encouraging creativity and opportunity.

Gore's "Lattice" structure gives associates the opportunity to use their own judgment, select the right projects, and directly access the resources they need to be successful. For more than 40 years, the talent, determination, curiosity, and inventiveness of our associates have contributed to the introduction of new products at a pace that few global corporations can match.

Has the Gore approach to organizing been effective? I think the answer is yes. Since its founding in 1958, it has grown to an organization with eight thousand associates, sales of over $2 billion, and frequent recognition as one of the best places to work. Since Gore has been successful, it is reasonable to ask if its source of competitive advantage is copyable. The answer is yes and no! The general approach to organizing and achieving competitive advantage is, but the details of what its people do simply don't apply to most organizations. Even copying the general approach is not easy because it takes special skills and leadership to make it work. Indeed, one of its strengths is the fact that it is hard to copy. W. L. Gore can say what it is doing without being concerned that someone will quickly or easily match its source of competitive advantage.

HC-centric organizations should not be solely or predominantly structured around functions (marketing, manufacturing, and so on) unless they are very small. Functional structures create too much distance between individuals and the results of their work. All too often, individuals in functionally structured organizations become more concerned about their particular function than about the product or service that is being offered. This typically happens because they lack contact with the external environment and with the customers that are being served. HC-centric organizations avoid this by using multi-functional teams that are in touch with the external environment.

Here's a good diagnostic question to ask of any employee: How many degrees of separation are you from the external environment? Often, in structure-centric organizations, the number of individuals between any given employee and a customer is at least five or six, whereas in a well-designed HC-centric organization, the answer should be no more than two or three.

One possible organization structure for an HC-centric organization is the small-business-unit model. Small-business units have the advantage of providing a customer focus that allows the talent in an organization to understand how their knowledge and skills affect the organization's products and services. In situations where customers want more than a single product from a company, HC-centric organizations may need to go to a customer-centric organization that is complex in its design.[7] Numerous customer-focused teams may need to be created that integrate the various services and products being sold to particular customers.

Finally, the jobs that individuals do and the tasks that they perform in HC-centric organizations should be loosely defined and open to change. Instead of tightly written job descriptions, individuals in an HC-centric organization may simply develop with their managers a list of goals or objectives to be accomplished within a particular time period, say, six months or a year. They are expected to problem solve and determine what methods, procedures, and skills they need to use to meet their goals. If they are on a team, their goals may simply be team goals, and it is up to the members of the team to decide how the team will operate and what each individual needs to do and learn to meet the team's goals.

The avoidance of detailed job descriptions has two positive effects. First, it makes work more interesting and more challenging, and therefore more motivating. Perhaps more important, it allows individuals to come up with the best work methods and procedures and to structure their work activities to fit the situation. In a knowledge work environment, where valuable talent is deployed, in most cases they are the ones who know the most and have the best sense of what needs to be done and how to do it. Thus avoiding detailed job descriptions and rigid mandates about what to do makes a great deal of sense.

IMPLICATIONS

All too often, managers assume that the best way to implement a strategy is to change the nature of jobs and reporting relationships. Time after time, the *Wall Street Journal* and other leading business publications report that XYZ Corporation has launched a new strategy, and as a result has restructured itself. These restructurings generally change the number of management levels, create new divisions, or perhaps outsource some function or support area. The options are limitless.

The problem, however, is that these structural changes often ignore or fail to deal effectively with talent issues. They assume that successful change comes primarily from being able to come up with a new, better organization structure. This is a particularly dangerous assumption in knowledge work organizations. In them, much of the intellectual capital of the organization rests in individuals, the systems that they work within, and the relationships that exist. Thus change efforts need to focus on all the other points of the star, not just the strategy and structure boxes.

Simply changing reporting relationships and jobs runs the risk of failing to develop the competencies and capabilities needed to implement a new strategy. It also runs the risk of causing valuable talent to leave and, as a result, seriously decreasing the effectiveness of the organization.

PROCESSES

The information and decision processes of an organization cut across its structure. They can be thought of as the nervous system of an organization, since they are designed to gather data and control action. Without effective information and decision processes, there is no organization, only chaos. In many respects, they are the glue that holds an organization together, allowing it to act in a coordinated way. What is appropriate in terms of measurement, communication, and decision-making processes are very much determined by the anatomy or structure of the organization. The information and decision processes of an organization need to fit its structure.

It is hardly surprising that organizations structured to be HC-centric need very different information and decision processes from organizations that are structure-centric. Structure-centric organizations, in essence, require a big-brain, control model of decision making and information management.

Information systems need to be centralized in both their design and their management. They need to gather data from the external environment and from the internal activities of the organization, and provide them to senior management. They then can make key decisions about what the organization will do and how it should operate.

What is measured by the organization typically reflects its approach to how value is added. In the case of a structure-centric organization, key issues are financial control and production or service management. Thus most of the measurement processes in the organization focus on when and how well tasks are performed and how much it costs to perform them.

The budgeting process is tremendously important in a structure-centric organization. It emphasizes both what is to be done and what doing it is expected to cost. Sometimes monthly, weekly, daily, even hourly reports are generated about the financial and operational performance of parts of the organization, or in some cases the key individuals in the organization. This is the way top management knows how the organization is performing, and when and how it needs to change that performance.

It is a bit simplistic but not totally inaccurate to think of a traditional organization as managed on the basis of parts of the organization sending information to senior management and getting back directions, instructions, and evaluations of their performance as well as information about what they need to do in the future. It is essentially a one-way communication process, or perhaps, more accurately, a two-way one in which information goes to the upper levels of management and directions come back. There is relatively little room for, or patience for, back-and-forth or lateral communications.

The communication and decision processes in an HC-centric organization are very different from those in a structure-centric organization. The difference starts with what is measured.

Yes, expenditures need to be measured, but they don't need to be measured and controlled by a budget. Yes, it is important to measure the financial condition of the organization, but it is also important to measure the condition of its core competencies and capabilities. Yes, the condition of machinery is important, but so is the condition of the organization's talent. Yes, coordination is necessary, but it does not need to be done on a hierarchical basis. Yes, control is important, but it doesn't need to be based on rules and regulations. It can be based on values and a shared commitment to the organization's strategy and mission.

Finally, decisions need to be made, but they do not necessarily need to be made at higher levels of management. If people throughout the organization have the information and knowledge necessary to make decisions about how they should perform, they can make them.

Perhaps the best way to think of an HC-centric organization from a decision and information process point of view is to think of information as not just being sent up an organization but moving across and between different parts of an organization. This, inevitably, leads to many decisions being made at what a hierarchical organization would regard as its "lower levels," an approach that fits the anatomy of an HC-centric organization. It doesn't have the amount and type of hierarchy that a structure-centric organization does. As a result, it has to use non-hierarchical information and decision processes; otherwise, it would be unable to function because the senior management group would be overloaded with decisions.

Moving decisions to individuals throughout the organization leads to a change needing to be made in who receives business information. Individuals throughout the organization need to make informed decisions and manage their performance, so they need much more information than is required by their counterparts in a hierarchical organization.

When talent is critical, as it is in an HC-centric organization, it makes a great deal of sense to carefully measure its condition and utilization. Therefore, in addition to data about how the financial capital and physical assets are being used, in HC-centric organizations it is very important to measure the condition of an organization's talent.[8] Indeed, the measures of talent should be at least as valid and extensive as those that measure financial capital.

What should be measured about the condition of an organization's talent? Of course, measures are needed on how people are performing, but measures are also needed of how motivated people are, how skilled they are, and what their intentions are with respect to their careers. In short, a whole host of measures are needed that indicate the condition of the talent of an organization.

This is a reach in the eyes of many, but I am going to say it anyway because I think it is right: "all" that is being asked when it comes to talent is for organizations to gather the same quality of data and spend the same amount of effort analyzing it as they do for data about equipment and financial capital. HC-centric organizations need to know where their important talent is and what it is doing, and they need to spend a considerable amount of time deciding how to allocate it, how to develop it, how to attract it, how to retain it, how to motivate it, and how to achieve a high return on the investments they make in it. This is true whether they operate as a high-involvement organization or as a global–competitor organization.

One final point about HC-centric organizations and measurement: it ties directly back to the "competencies and capabilities" point on the star. The information processes in an organization need to measure not just the condition of the human capital but the condition of the organization with respect to its key competencies and capabilities. Knowing what skills individuals have is an important piece, but it does not show the whole picture.

The whole picture requires looking at the ability of the organization to execute key capabilities such as customer focus, speed to market, innovation, and quality, and to use its competencies and capabilities to improve its products, develop new ones, and make research and development breakthroughs. These need to be monitored in an HC-centric organization with the same vigor and care that structure-centric organizations monitor budgets and return on capital investments.

The focus on measuring competencies and capabilities in an HC-centric organization does not mean that financial measures can or should be neglected. Quite the contrary: they are important, particularly when it comes to providing feedback to members of the workforce.

In an HC-centric organization, individuals throughout the organization need to get data about how the organization is operating and what its financial results are, so that they can understand the impact of their performance and engage in better self-direction and self-management. Without financial information, it is impossible for individuals to direct their behavior and learn about the outcomes of their efforts.

Implications

HC-centric organizations need performance management systems that are far superior to the ones usually present in structure-centric organizations. Performance management systems in structure-centric organizations tend to be unpopular and seen as a bureaucratic exercise.[9] They fail to do a good job at providing feedback to individuals and setting reasonable motivating goals for individuals. Traditional organizations can get away with this because they have carefully defined performance parameters and responsibilities for most jobs that act as controls on employee behavior.

In HC-centric organizations, performance management systems need to be very effective. These organizations lack many of the traditional practices that control, direct, and motivate behavior (for example, detailed job descriptions) in structure-centric organizations. They need a performance management system that develops talent, sets motivating goals, produces agreement on what needs to be done to accomplish key goals, and is flexible enough so that an individual's goals, objectives, and behavior change as the strategy of the organization evolves.

Rewards

The design of the reward system needs to be carefully aligned with the talent needs, the information processes, and the structure of an organization. These factors, more than the other parts of an organization's design, determine how an organization's reward system should be structured. An organization's strategy, and its competencies and capabilities should be the critical determinants of what is rewarded.

Structure-centric organizations typically have well-developed hierarchical reward systems. The pay of individuals is based upon the job that they do, their seniority, and (in some cases) their performance. The amount of pay is primarily determined by the nature of their job and its market value. Individuals are given small merit increases based on their performance against job standards. Individuals are promoted based on their performance and seniority and receive increases when they move up the hierarchy in an organization.

In a structure-centric organization, the amount of compensation and rewards that people receive is directly related to how high up they are in the structure. This is logical because higher-level employees are much more important than lower-level employees in determining the performance of an organization; they make key strategy decisions and direct the work of others. They are also typically the individuals who receive the most stock, perquisites, and fringe benefits in an organization. They have big offices, personal assistants, the right to travel first class or on private jets, and so on, all things that indicate that they have greater decision-making authority and higher-level positions.

The reward system sends a very clear message in a structure-centric organization: where you are in the structure is what matters most in determining your rewards. If you want more rewards, you must move up the structure to get them.

HC-centric organizations do not have the structures and processes that fit the kind of pay programs used by structure-centric organizations (such as well-defined jobs and a clear hierarchy). But even more important, they need to send a different message about the role of individuals. They need to communicate to individuals that they are in an organization that focuses on talent and human capability. The reward system can best do this by supporting the development of the organization's talent as well as rewarding high levels of performance.

The logical starting point for an HC-centric reward system is the individual, not the job. The skills and competencies that individuals need to have should drive the reward system.[10] A focus on an individual's skills and competencies not only fits the core identity of the HC-centric organization, it reinforces the growth of individuals. Instead of starting from a job description and deciding what a job is worth, an HC-centric reward system needs to start with the person and determine what the individual is worth based on their skills, knowledge, and competencies.

Given the relatively flat structure of HC-centric organizations, it does not necessarily follow that individuals should receive significant pay increases only when or even when they move up the hierarchy. Indeed, since hierarchical moves may be relatively rare, and the focus is on talent, it makes a great deal more sense to focus pay changes on when individuals learn new skills and improve their competencies. When this occurs, a "promotion" may be very much in order, and along with the promotion, additional pay may be warranted.

Structure-centric organizations not only have large differences in pay from top to bottom, they have large differences in benefits and perquisites. In the case of large corporations, many CEOs make more than six hundred times the pay of the lowest-paid employees, and some CEOs make more than $100 million a year. In HC-centric organizations, a more egalitarian approach to rewards is appropriate. It fits the reality that talent throughout the corporation is critical and that the responsibility for performance is shared.

As in structure-centric organizations, it makes sense to reward performance in an HC-centric organization. But it often does not make sense to focus the reward system on individual performance. Instead of just rewarding individual performance, team, business unit, and organization performance need to be a focus. Two of the most compelling reasons for this are practicality and the identity of HC-centric organizations.

Making Pay Public in Whole Foods

From humble beginnings in Austin, Texas, Whole Foods has grown rapidly into one of the most successful and innovative food retailers in the United States. In part, this company's competitive advantage stems from a commitment to a high-involvement approach to management. Whole Foods departments are organized by teams, which are largely self-managing. Each team makes hiring decisions and has control over the merchandise sold in its department. In addition, the teams regularly receive financial data on their department's performance, and are given bonuses based on their effectiveness.

(Continued)

At Whole Foods, employees know what their fellow employees throughout the organization are paid. Yes, pay is public in Whole Foods, and always has been, from the very top of the organization to the very bottom. CEO John Mackey believes that information empowers people and that team members need to be able to discuss business openly with other team members. So Whole Foods has always had published wage guidelines and full disclosure of individual salaries. New hires are told up front that salaries are made public and a salary report is produced annually that lists each team member's gross compensation for the calendar year.

As a result, Whole Foods employees believe it when they are told that no one at the company makes more than fourteen times the average hourly pay of a full-time team member. Publishing salaries is a great way to assure team members in Whole Foods that management is making good on its promises with respect to salaries and pay for performance. Making pay public also fits with helping employees understand and take responsibility for the costs and revenue of the company. (In 2006, when Whole Foods had disappointing financial results because of slower-than-expected sales growth, CEO Mackey announced that he would reduce his annual salary to $1.)

Open salary information policies are still rare in U.S. corporations but fit well with a high-involvement culture. They allow for informed decision making and foster a culture of trust and open communication. An open salary policy fits very nicely with the argument that human capital is the critical resource, and as a result, the way in which people are treated and managed is everyone's concern.

Practicality is a serious matter. In the typical HC-centric organization, it may not be possible to do a good job of measuring individual job performance, simply because of the team structures used and the often rapidly changing nature of what individuals are doing. Without the static nature of structure-centric organizations, annual individual contracts for merit increases or bonuses often simply do not fit well. What fits are bonuses based on team performance, particularly if teams have significant responsibility for product creation, product delivery, or both. Also a good fit are gain sharing, profit sharing, and ownership plans that base rewards on the business performance of the organization.

Profit sharing and stock ownership plans are particularly good fits in HC-centric organizations that do knowledge work and are relatively small in size. An effective stock ownership plan can create a sense of common identity across the organization and draw individuals throughout the organization into a sense of inclusion.[11] Stock plans are a particularly good fit in high-involvement organizations because they lead to a commitment to organizational performance and long-term membership.

Of course, structure-centric organizations can also use profit sharing and stock ownership plans, but they are never going to find them as effective as they are in a well-designed HC-centric organization. The so-called line of sight from what an individual does to how the organization performs is rarely strong enough in a structure-centric organization to establish a motivational pull on an individual employee. The reasons for this are straightforward: an individual often doesn't have the information about or the influence on organizational performance that is needed to create the motivation for extra effort. This is not true in a well-designed HC-centric organization. Because individuals have information about the business and how they can influence it, bonus plans, profit sharing plans, and ownership plans can be quite motivational.

Further, in an HC-centric organization, talent is clearly seen as the difference maker: it drives organizational performance and, as a result, individuals throughout the organization can see how their performance impacts organizational performance. It follows logically that because individuals make a difference, they should be rewarded based on organizational performance. With a structure-centric organization, it is the structure, systems, and senior management performance that are seen as making the difference and as key to the organization's effectiveness. As a result, it is not as important to reward individuals at all levels for how well the total organization works.

Implications

HC-centric organizations should have reward programs that encourage learning and development as well as contributions to organizational performance. The best way to encourage learning is to base pay on the market value of individuals, not jobs, and to reward skill development. When it comes to rewards for performance, it makes sense for each individual to have at least some rewards based on how the organization performs. As discussed in Chapter Five, this means making use of equity-based pay systems, and in the case of high-involvement organizations, organization performance–based reward programs.

PEOPLE

The final point on the star—"people"—should get much more attention in the design of an HC-centric organization than it does in a structure-centric organization. This is true of both high-involvement and global-competitor organizations. However, this is the point on the star where high-involvement and global-competitor organizations differ most, because they have very different employment deals in the areas of talent development, rewards, and careers. They need to attract and retain different individuals and therefore need to have somewhat different talent management policies and practices.

All HC-centric organizations are obsessed with talent. They realize that their competitive advantage rests on their ability to attract, develop, retain, and manage people who fit their business strategy by providing the competencies and capabilities it calls for. Structure-centric organizations also pay attention to people, but it is usually in order to find people who fit the jobs that are open and to figure out how to attract, retain, and motivate them. It often appears that people issues are an afterthought in structure-centric organizations. Instead of the organization being designed for talent, the organization is designed for execution, and then a search is begun for talent that fits the organization's design.

It is tempting to write a long list of all the desirable characteristics that people should have in any HC-centric organization. Clearly, they should be reliable, willing to learn, motivated— I could go on and on. But that might obscure the key point of the Star Model: the people who are hired in the organization must fit the other points on the star. And that can only be accomplished by paying an incredible amount of attention to the hiring process, and the other key talent management systems in an organization.

All the talent management systems in an HC-centric organization must be targeted at obtaining, developing, retaining, and motivating people who will give the organization a competitive advantage as a result of their performance. Where does the ultimate responsibility for an organization's talent rest? Having the right talent management systems falls into the functional area of HR, but clearly the HR function cannot by itself ensure that the organization has the right talent. Indeed, they should not necessarily even be the part of the organization that takes the lead in talent management. In most HC-centric organizations, the lead in talent management should rest with senior management.

As discussed in Chapter Seven, HR's role should be to provide expertise on how to manage human capital and to help with the implementation and design of the talent management programs of the organization. But managing talent effectively is not just a matter of having good systems for performance management, selection, development, and so on. It, like having an effective organization, is a matter of multiple talent management systems and practices fitting together into a coherent whole that positions people in an organization to fulfill the business strategy. And so, although HR can inform, influence, and coordinate talent, it cannot and should not go it alone or for that matter be in the lead. Simply stated, this is too important to leave to HR; it must be done by managers throughout an organization.

The key elements of a complete talent management system include an employer brand, a recruitment and selection process, a training and development process, a performance management system that is tied effectively to the reward system, and an information system that includes data on satisfaction, motivation, talent development, talent utilization and performance. As I mentioned earlier, there also needs to be a process for assessing an organization's competencies and capabilities.

Because of their differences, global-competitor and high-involvement organizations need somewhat different talent management practices and systems. For example, high-involvement organizations need talent development systems that build long-term relationships with employees. Global competitors need systems that focus on obtaining the best talent that is available in the global labor market.

IMPLICATIONS

To attract the right individuals, HC-centric organizations need a clear statement of what their value proposition is for employees. That is, they need a statement that is grounded in actual practices, that says why someone should work there, what the conditions of employment are, and how long individuals can expect to work there. There needs to be a clear policy about what continued employment depends on and what consequences less-than-satisfactory performance will bring. The value proposition of every HC-centric organization needs to establish it as a leading place to work.

In the case of a global-competitor organization, the value proposition should include being a good place to work and a good place to have worked. Developing this perception is critical to being able to attract and retain the best talent for as long as it is needed. Having a clear value proposition is a critical part of what it takes to attract and retain individuals who will perform effectively in an HC-centric organization. They need to value the rewards offered them. If they don't, motivation and retention problems are inevitable. Since high-involvement and global-competitor organizations offer somewhat different rewards, they need to attract and retain different employees. For example, someone who wants a career with one employer is a much better fit for a high-involvement organization, while someone who likes change and is not worried about job security is a better fit for a global competitor.

All HC-centric organizations need to be known as places that nurture, value, and love good leaders. Simply stated, it is impossible to operate an effective HC-centric organization without outstanding leadership. And this doesn't simply mean a few charismatic leaders at the top of the organization; rather, it means leadership throughout the organization that is able to translate its mission, vision, and strategy into behaviors and rewards for individuals. Given the relative flatness and non-hierarchical structure of HC-centric organizations, it is particularly critical that leaders provide a sense of direction and motivation that will act as a substitute for hierarchy.

IDENTITY

At the center of the Star Model in Figure 6 is "identity." I have chosen to use *identity* here rather than the more common term, *culture*, because I think it better captures this critical feature of an HC-centric organization.[12] Culture usually refers to the internal values and norms of an organization that define how things are done and what is important. It is almost always measured by asking the members of the organization what it is.

By *identity*, I mean the fundamental personality of the organization with respect to how it treats people, what it values, what the right ways to do things are, and what are acceptable and unacceptable behaviors. It is clearly a psychological concept, in the sense that although it has an objective reality, it is subjective and exists in the eyes of people in the organization and those who know the organization, that is, its customers, investors, and competitors.

In an HC-centric organization, there should be a relatively high agreement among all those who know the organization about what the major features of its identity are. This is likely to happen only when all the points on the star are integrated, consistent, transparent, and well known to everyone. Much of the identity of an organization is, in fact, a direct result of what the features of the points on the Star Model are and how they fit together.

Both structure-centric and HC-centric organizations can and often do have clear, strong identities. However, they differ significantly in the major features of their identity. The key identity features of structure-centric organizations include *bureaucratic, stable, rigid,* and in some cases *efficient.*

In an HC-centric organization, the points on the star need to fit together in a way that articulates an identity that is clear about the importance of human capital. It must say that talent is the key to the organization's competitive advantage. The specific details of how talent will provide that advantage and what kind of talent is valued will vary somewhat from organization to organization because it will depend a great deal upon the business strategy of the organization and whether it is a high-involvement organization or a global competitor. But there should be no question that an HC-centric organization has as an important part of its identity a leading role for talent when it comes to gaining competitive advantage.

Implications

The identity of an HC-centric organization should have clear principles concerning how members of the organization are treated. It is easy to say that as a general principle people should be treated fairly, but an HC-centric organization needs to be clear what *fairly* means and to do what it says when it comes to how it treats people. Although global-competitor and high-involvement organizations differ in how they treat people, they both need to state clearly how they treat people and what they mean by fair treatment.

The second point that HC-centric organizations need to have as part of their identity is high expectations for the performance of the organization and its members. Human capital cannot be a source of competitive advantage in an HC-centric organization unless it performs at a level that is superior to performance in competing organizations. Thus, low-performers and poor working relationships simply cannot be tolerated.

Design Differences

Every point on the star is different for structure-centric and HC-centric organizations. The two approaches have different strategies, structures, processes, reward systems, and people. Because their design is different, their performance is different. As discussed in the chapters that follow, implementing an HC-centric design is not simple; it requires a number of practices, procedures, and systems that are new and require skilled managers. Each chapter focuses on an organizational design feature that is critical to the effectiveness of an HC-centric organization, and discusses how the feature must operate in order to establish talent as a source of competitive advantage.

CHAPTER FOUR

MANAGING TALENT

HC-centric organizations excel only when they have outstanding talent. To have outstanding talent, they need an outstanding talent management system—one that attracts the right talent and helps them understand exactly what to expect from their work experience with the company. The best talent management systems also provide employees with the kind of developmental experiences that build the organization's key capabilities and core competencies. Last but not least, they retain the right talent.

Put another way, effective talent management systems don't just acquire and introduce highly qualified people to the organization—they ensure that the fit is right between employee and employer. They also monitor and manage an individual's relationship with the organization effectively for as long as it is in the best interest of the organization to have the individual as an employee.

It is not an overstatement to say that effective HC-centric organizations are obsessed with talent management. This is one area where Jack Welch has it right when he says that talent management deserves at least as much focus as financial capital management.[1] It deserves that amount of focus at all times, not just when an organization is trying to acquire talent or to implement change.

HC-centric organizations always face tough competition for the talent they want. They need the kind of talent that is in demand regardless of whether the economy is strong or weak: top percentile talent. Warnings of future talent shortages and more competition don't cause them to change their approach to talent management, because they always face stiff competition for the talent they need. They treat times of talent availability (economic downturns) as opportunities to upgrade their talent.

Many would-be HC-centric organizations do not devote an adequate level of effort to talent management because their senior managers don't truly understand the return on human capital investments. This is a common failing. Surveys of CFOs and other executives suggest that less than 20 percent of U.S. companies know what return they get on their human capital programs.[2]

No one argues with a focus on human capital when the organization is a professional sports team. Nor do they argue with it when it is a movie studio or entertainment business. But when the organization is a retail store or manufacturing operation, it is a different matter. This is true even though a strong case can be made for focusing on talent, because *the organization sees human capital as the differentiator.* If, for example, the major source of competitive advantage an organization has is the way customers are dealt with, then focusing on the talent that delivers the right sales experience is a must do. It makes as much sense as it does for a baseball team to focus on putting the best talent on the field—even if it is more difficult to link the investment explicitly to a financial return.

Not surprisingly, in the case of sports teams, those teams that are perpetual winners spend more money on talent and typically have better scouting and player development systems than do other teams. In sports, different approaches can be successful. The New York Yankees, for example, are classic *global competitors* who buy talent, whereas teams such as the Oakland A's and Cleveland Indians have championed the *build strategy* and have been able to pay lower wages and still win, although not as frequently as the Yankees. The Oakland A's, with a low budget, win because they do an excellent job of talent management and development.[3]

High-involvement organizations emphasize building and developing talent. To do this they develop a long-term relationship with their employees. In essence, they believe that in their business the best way to achieve competitive advantage through human capital is to invest in building a long-term, mutually beneficial relationship with their employees.

Global-competitor organizations come from a different perspective. They feel that because the environment and the need for skills are changing rapidly in their business, they must be able to shift their talent mix quickly, effectively, and at a low cost. This means making a relatively small investment in development and having a more transactional relationship with most of their employees.

Even global-competitor organizations recognize the need for a core group of employees who have a longer-term relationship with the organization and who provide a sense of continuity and a focus on performance. They, in essence, are the keepers of the corporate identity and knowledge bases. Although they take different approaches to talent acquisition and development, high-involvement and global-competitor organizations are similar in that they focus very clearly on talent as their key source of competitive advantage.

MANAGEMENT PRIORITIES

Unquestionably, the effective management of talent has to begin at the very top of the organization. The senior management team needs to spend a significant portion of its time focusing on talent management. Just how big a portion is hard to specify precisely, since it does need to vary depending upon the type of talent being managed, whether the organization has a buy or build strategy, and a host of other factors. However, a good rule of thumb is that senior managers, in particular, should spend 30–50 percent of their time focusing on talent management. In professional service firms (for example, law, accounting, consulting, and the entertainment industry), a higher percentage is likely to be appropriate. As one executive commented to me while I was writing this book, "Any organization that is more focused on managing its financial capital than its human capital is brain dead."

Consider the example set by General Electric. Even before Jack Welch became CEO of GE, the company was known for senior management commitment to talent management. This commitment is a big part of what has made the company so successful, and it continues to be strong. As CEO Jeff Immelt notes in GE's 2006 annual report, GE has a leadership development process that creates the strengths and capabilities that drive competitive advantage.

GE is famous for its Session C meetings, in which senior managers from the company discuss the development of the firm's talent. This same process is replicated at lower levels in the organization, so that during the course of a year, serious discussions take place about most of the human capital in the company. Leaders at all levels in GE believe that this type of concentration on human capital is necessary if the company is to truly establish its talent as a source of competitive advantage.

Bank of America provides another example. CEO Ken Lewis owns the talent management processes and consistently holds business unit heads personally responsible for meeting the objectives that they set in the talent development and management area. Every summer, he meets individually with the top twenty-four executives at the bank to review the organization and its talent pipeline.

Lewis's in-depth sessions with these executives explore talent and people issues and how they will be handled for the business growth and development strategy that the bank has in place. The executives are expected to come to these sessions with metrics and databases that point to the key strengths and weaknesses in their unit's talent pipeline. They are expected to make specific commitments regarding the development of talent and show their plans for talent movement. They are also asked to demonstrate explicitly how their talent moves will be aligned with the business strategy. For example, if they propose growth for their business, they are expected to show that they have the talent or can acquire the talent to support that growth.

Competitive Advantage at Goldman Sachs

The global investment banking and securities firm Goldman Sachs has always viewed itself as a cut above the rest of Wall Street. It takes great care to select, promote, and ultimately make partners of the brightest people it can find.

At Goldman, the talent management process begins with an incredibly rigorous selection process that can last weeks. Job candidates from the best schools talk to multiple interviewers before a hiring decision is made. The interviewers consider it an honor to have a chance to participate in the selection process.

The selection process for becoming a partner is arduous. It is managed by a committee chaired by senior partners. Members of the selection teams are trained in what the firm is looking for; they're also taught how to question their fellow partners about candidates in a consistent way.

One of the things selection team members are told to ask about is performance on specific assignments and about contributions outside their departments. The idea is to ensure that only those people who will be effective "culture carriers" of the very strong and distinctive Goldman Sachs culture are made partners. It's not uncommon for the people on the selection committee to interview a dozen partners before coming to a decision about any individual candidate for partnership. (This is in addition to considering the candidate's performance reviews, getting feedback from peers and subordinates, and interviewing the candidate.)

Since the mid-1990s, the selection process has used a system called "cross-ruffing" as part of its process to vet candidates. Cross-ruffing has partners from different departments review candidates. For example, investment banking partners review candidates from trading departments, trading department partners review candidates from investment banking, and so forth. This is to be sure that individuals who make partner are in fact broadly seen as outstanding performers.

Goldman Sachs expects the partnership process to help it retain talent in the face of heavy competition from other financial institutions. Increasingly the firm has tied partner compensation to individual performance rather than to firm performance in order to be sure its best performers are highly paid.

Goldman Sachs has fewer than four hundred partners at any given time, and typically, they each earn in the vicinity of $5 million to $10 million a year. In 2006, top traders were said to have made as much as $100 million, while the average per-employee pay in Goldman was $623,418. Not surprisingly, this pay-per-employee level is the highest on Wall Street.

Goldman Sachs provides another clear example of an organization obsessed with talent management. At this firm it is an honor for senior managers to be asked to be part of a selection process for new employees. And senior managers who do participate place great emphasis on the process, sending the message throughout the company that talent is a high priority from day one.

THE EMPLOYER BRAND

Every organization is known for certain things when it comes to how it treats its employees. This "employer brand" is a key part of what attracts talent to a company. All too often, this brand is the result of happenstance and the uncoordinated actions of the organization with respect to its employment decisions and policies. For HC-centric organizations random branding is simply not tolerable.

The right employer brand is a critical asset and a competitive advantage for an HC-centric organization. It needs to be developed deliberately. An employer brand needs to speak to what individuals can expect when they join an organization and it needs to help individuals determine whether they are a good fit for the organization.

Global-competitor organizations, in particular, need to manage their brand carefully; they need a regular infusion of new and often hard-to-recruit talent. If their employer brand is boring and unattractive, so too will be their talent and performance.

There are a number of ways to develop an effective employer brand. One way is simply to state it over and over again in all recruiting and other materials that go out from the organization. When individuals actually apply for a job, either online or in person, they should be given an introduction to the organization that emphasizes what life will be like if they join. It should be a realistic preview that tells it like it is. This type of preview not only can help set realistic expectations, it can drive away individuals who are not a good fit and who would not stay long if they did get hired.[4]

Linblad Expeditions, the adventure travel company, doesn't make the error of painting an unrealistic picture of the jobs it has. It sends a DVD to job applicants showing two shots of crew members cleaning toilets! (This video is also available on the company's Web site.) In another segment, an employee warns that at Linblad, you "have to work your butt off." Why paint such a negative picture of the work at Linblad? The answer is obvious: to scare off individuals who won't be happy working for Linblad.

The employer brand should be featured in all communications about job openings. For example, in its employment ads, United Technologies points out just how much it has spent on educating its employees. According to one ad, "Since 1996 we've spent more than half a billion dollars sending employees to any accredited college or university." United Technologies allows employees to obtain a degree in any field they choose and gives them company stock when they get a degree ($10,000 for a bachelor's degree).[5] Incidentally, according to CEO George David, the program has been very successful, because it has created a better workforce— more thoughtful, more alert, more confident, and more loyal.

Another way to convey an employer brand is to provide job applicants with copies of company attitude survey results so that they can get a realistic view of how employees feel about working for the company. In the case of some HC-centric companies, it makes sense to feature the brand in ads for products and services. This is particularly powerful when the employer brand is aligned directly and explicitly with the company's branded offerings to customers. Southwest Airlines provides an example; the employee experience is often featured in its TV commercials because it involves upbeat employees who enjoy giving good customer service. The employee experience can also be featured on a company's Web site, with videos that show employees talking about what it is like to work for the organization and what the company means to them.

Each year, more organizations apply to be listed among the best employers in surveys that identify the top companies to work for. This is obviously a positive, but it is important to understand the distinction between being seen as a generally good place to work and having the right brand. To recruit and retain the right talent, HC-centric organizations must be sure that the qualities that make them a good employer will attract the kind of talent that they need.

For example, if an HC-centric organization is trying to achieve competitive advantage through technical leadership, then the brand needs to emphasize that the company is a good place for techies to work. If it is trying to establish itself as a customer-focused organization, then the best approach may be to emphasize that it is a good place to work for people who like to have fun and that it is a cool place to work. Starbucks provides an obvious example. It is seen as a good place to work partly because it pays well and gives most of its employees health care benefits—but most of all, because it offers a friendly, pleasant work environment.

PERQUISITES

Some managers equate a good employer brand with perks. Consider many of the extras that were common in information technology companies during the dot-com boom of the late 1990s (see Exhibit 4). As the dot-com list shows, the supply of perks that organizations can offer their employees is almost infinite. The key question, of course, is whether offering them actually contributes to organizational effectiveness.

At first glance, some items on the list do not appear likely to lead to greater organizational effectiveness. But before dismissing them, it is important to consider how they might impact organizations in the following areas:

- *Retention:* As discussed later, it is clear that the total reward package an organization offers does have a strong impact on retention. The key issues with respect to retention are whether the reward package retains the right employees, and whether the organization is getting a good return on the cost of the rewards it is offering. This is difficult to determine, but a starting point is certainly to ask individuals how much they value the various perks and to, of course, monitor employee turnover.

EXHIBIT 4. SPECIAL EXTRAS IN DOT-COMS.

- Electronic game room
- Computers and Internet access at work
- Home computers and Internet access
- Stock for spouse
- Pet-friendly work place
- Pet insurance
- Pet day care
- Health club
- Chef take-home meals
- Sabbaticals
- Beer blasts

- Twenty-four-hour free food for family
- Online shopping discounts
- Concierge service
- Laundry for gym clothes
- Equity in venture capital fund
- Oil change in parking lot
- Dental service in parking lot
- Dry cleaning
- No dress code
- Baby blankets for new parents
- Forty-two kinds of drinks

- *Attraction:* Visible perks clearly can attract people to the organization. The key here is whether they attract the right people. For example, rewards such as parties and lucrative retirement packages may in fact attract individuals who are less interested in performance and more interested in making friends or being personally secure.
- *Employer brand:* Visible rewards can clearly distinguish an organization as a good place to work. Again, the key issue is whether they create the kind of brand that the organization wants. For example, extensive use of stock options by organizations can create a brand of an organization as being a place where you can get quite wealthy. Giving individuals free time to explore exciting research projects can create the perception that the organization is a place where innovation is common and individuals can use their creative skills.
- *Work-life balance:* By providing personal services at work, organizations can give people more time to work and to spend in nonwork activities. For example, by providing car washes and a concierge service, organizations can help deal with the many errands and complexities involved in day-to-day life. Providing on-site medical care is another time-saver that can allow people to work more, spend more time in activities they enjoy outside of work, or both.
- *Sense of community:* A number of perquisites can create a greater sense of community in the workplace. Parties are one obvious way to do this, but so are charity events, community service activities, and athletic teams.

The bottom line on perks is this: it is easy to go overboard and spend money on perks that make very little contribution to organizational effectiveness. Still, it is possible for seemingly extravagant perks to be cost-effective in an HC-centric company *if* they contribute to reductions in turnover, attract good employees, create a sense of community, improve the employer brand, and so on. The key issue with every perk is whether in fact its cost can be justified in terms of these outcomes. Some of the dot-coms got it right—by aligning their perks with the employee behaviors and lifestyles that they knew would suit their organization. Others did not, and as a result, they wasted their money.

Google

Google is regularly rated as the number one company to work for in the United States. Part of the reason it gets such high ratings is the extensive perk system that it has created. When it comes to perks, Google is a 1990s dot-com on steroids. In fact, it's hard to know where to start, when talking about all the extras that employees at Google get.

For example, the company's food service operation is unmatched; it includes eleven free gourmet cafeterias in the Mountain View, California, headquarters.

But that's just the tip of the iceberg. As a Google employee, you can get a $5,000 bonus if you buy a hybrid car. If an employee refers a friend to work at Google, and that friend is hired, Google will pay the employee a $2,000 reward. Google gives employees who have a baby $500 to help with take-out food during the first four weeks at home. Five on-site doctors are available to provide employees with check-ups and medical care free of charge. And, like many of the dot-coms launched in the 1990s, it also has a weekly Friday party with a band.

Google pays its employees extremely well. Many of them are millionaires as a result of the company's high-flying stock. Yet Google continues to give employees stock options, and has also made it possible for them to sell their options before they mature.

The inevitable question with respect to all that Google offers its employees is causation. Does the success of Google allow it to treat its employees as its most important resource or is it successful because it treats employees as its most important resource? In many respects, it may be both.

Google clearly is an organization that has developed a virtuous spiral when it comes to performance and reward. Because it has done well, it is seen as a great place to work and attracts great people. Because it attracts great people, its performance continues to improve and reach new highs, which in turn allows it to reward its employees well and to attract outstanding individuals.

In some ways, the key causal factor in the Google equation is the belief on the part of its founders that people are the key to success, and that treating them as the organization's source of competitive advantage will in fact lead to high performance. This belief has led to a combination of a successful organization and an extraordinarily talent-focused approach to management.

To make good decisions about perks, organizations need to make a reasonable determination of the payoff to them of reducing turnover, freeing up employee time, having a large number of job applicants and the other outcomes likely to result from perquisites. It is clear that some behavior that results, such as reductions in turnover, can in fact have a very positive impact on the cost structure of an organization. Turnover often costs organizations as much as a year or more of the employee's salary because of the extensive recruiting and learning costs that are involved in replacing someone who leaves.[6]

FIT

As part of its effort to attract the right type of software engineer, Google has worked hard to establish its employer brand among potential employees. One of the more interesting things the company has done is to place ads in a number of technology journals and magazines that feature its Google Lab Aptitude Test (GLAT).

The GLAT contains a number of questions that, over the years, Google has found useful in predicting who will be a good engineer for the company. By putting the GLAT into the public domain, Google allows individuals to self-assess and see whether they are a good fit for the organization. In essence, it is a different kind of realistic job preview that helps brand Google as an employer. What kind of questions are on the GLAT? Here is a sample: *What number comes next in this sequence: 10, 9, 60, 90, 70, 66?* Sorry— I don't know the answer, but if you do, contact Google. You may be right for them! The GLAT also contains some humorous culture test items. Here is one of my favorites:

Which of the following expresses Google's overarching philosophy?

A) "I'm feeling lucky"
B) "Don't be evil"
C) "Oh, I already fixed that"
D) "You should never be more than 50 feet from food"
E) All of the above

Google has also opened a software facility in Kirkland, Washington, just six miles from Microsoft's headquarters in Redmond, Washington. Why pick that location? The answer is simple: To poach employees from Microsoft and to show just how important it thinks recruiting the best talent is.

ACTIONS THAT HURT

It shouldn't be necessary to point out that an organization's executives need to be extremely careful about how their actions affect their employer brand, but it is. Unfortunately, many executives still make the kind of decisions that are extremely damaging to their organization's employer brand. As a result not only do they make it more difficult to hire good people in the future, they spread dissatisfaction, mistrust, and embarrassment among their existing employees. Consider the following two examples:

Northwest Airlines has never had a great relationship with its employees. In 2006 it made it worse. Management sent out a booklet to employees subject to a layoff, advising them how they could save money after being laid off. Among the things included in the "101 Ways to Save Money" booklet were buying jewelry at pawn shops, getting auto parts at junkyards, taking shorter showers, and finding valuable things in the trash by "dumpster diving"! Employee outrage followed distribution of this would-be helpful booklet. Management apologized for issuing it, but the damage had already been done.

Radio Shack, another customer-service organization, followed through on an announcement that it planned to cut four hundred jobs by sending e-mails to the employees selected for layoff several days later. Knowing that e-mail pink slips were coming, many employees became obsessed with checking e-mail for several days until they found out whether they were or were not among the individuals being laid off. In addition, those who were laid off left angry because no one actually talked to them.

A notable contrast to the way Radio Shack and Northwest Airlines handled their layoffs is the approach Cisco Systems took when the dot-com bust hit. Cisco managers were very concerned about maintaining the company's excellent reputation as an employer because they knew that they might want to re-hire the individuals the company was forced to lay off; what's more, they hoped to be able to attract the best talent when business picked up.

Cisco took a number of steps to be sure that it would continue to be seen as a good employer even though it had to reduce its workforce. For example, the company offered sabbaticals to some of its employees and offered to pay partial salaries to laid-off employees who went to work for charities and community ventures. It also helped subsidize the continuing education of former employees who wanted to advance their skills or change careers. Not surprisingly, when it became time for Cisco to start hiring again, it had no problem attracting a very talented applicant pool.

Attracting Customers

Developing an effective employer brand not only can attract the right employees, it can also attract customers. Consider Singapore Air and Southwest Airlines. They both use their brand as an employer to attract customers as well as employees. As mentioned earlier, Southwest's recruiting efforts and general advertising campaigns explicitly emphasize the fun and the freedom that comes with being an employee and the special relationships that its employees have with customers.

The Southwest approach is designed to attract employees who have the skills and the desire to provide good customer experiences. It also sends a positive message to customers about who will be serving them and how they will be treated. Finally, the approach conveys an important sense of transparency; if the company is willing to be public about the quality of its relationships with employees, it must be confident that those relationships are truly strong.

Singapore Air has taken a similar approach with its in-flight service personnel. The image of the Singapore flight attendants that is marketed to consumers is one of attractive women offering exceptional service, something that seems to attract male business travelers. The airline's marketing also attracts women applicants who fit the image of the Singapore flight attendants who are shown in their advertising.

Wal-Mart's Efforts

I can't leave the topic of employer brand without commenting on the moves Wal-Mart has made to increase its attractiveness as an employer. Wal-Mart has a serious problem with its employer brand, partly because of its failure to offer medical coverage to many of its employees but also because of its at times arbitrary, capricious, and unreasonable personnel policies having to do with overtime, part-time work assignments, scheduling work hours, and a host of other working conditions issues.

In 2006 Wal-Mart introduced a new program that requires the managers at its more than four thousand stores to meet with ten rank-and-file employees every week in order to hear what's on their minds. It is supposed to show workers that Wal-Mart appreciates them and that Wal-Mart has an ongoing commitment to listening to and addressing their concerns. It may be a first step, but it falls a long way short of what Wal-Mart truly needs to do to develop a positive employer brand. Perhaps the most important thing its managers can do is actually listen to what employees have to say and make changes.

The Wal-Mart program also includes several new perks as a way of acknowledging employee contributions. One is a special Wal-Mart polo shirt that is given to employees after twenty years of service. Unfortunately for Wal-Mart, offering employees polo shirts after twenty years of service runs a big danger of being seen as tokenism. Given Wal-Mart's emphasis on low cost, it is probably able to buy the shirts for less than $2.00, and that is not a very significant recognition for somebody who has been working for the company for twenty years. On the other hand, if, at twenty years, it gave employees stock or something that has both symbolic and financial value, the company might in fact be able to begin to change its employer brand.

Employment Contracts

An employer brand is an intangible. However, many tangible practices and behaviors contribute to it. A key practice that can contribute to an effective brand is the development and communication of an employment contract. Developing a formal statement of what they offer employees and what they expect from them is an effective way for companies to attract the right employees and form a positive relationship with the individuals who are hired. To be clear; I'm not talking about a legal document; I am talking about a statement that is designed to tell employees what the organization expects of them and define what individuals can expect from the organization.

EXHIBIT 5.   HIGH-INVOLVEMENT LEARNING CONTRACT.

Employer	*Employee*
• Provide ongoing opportunities and support for education and training inside and outside the organization.	• Invest in own competence development.
• Structure daily work and career paths to apply existing competencies and build new skills.	• Use competencies to help achieve organizational objectives.
• Encourage and reward individuals who develop and use skills effectively.	• Help build competencies of coworkers.
• Assist individuals to find new work opportunities internally (or if demand for existing competencies decreases, externally).	• Contribute to organizational learning.

The contracts of high-involvement and global-competitor organizations need to differ in a number of areas, because they manage talent differently. The contracts of high-involvement organizations should offer stability of employment, support for development, rewards based on organizational and often individual performance, a career, and a workplace community. Exhibit 5 sketches the type of learning contract that high-involvement organizations should offer.

High-involvement organizations should not offer job security, because with change, those individuals who are unwilling or unable to learn new skills may not be retained. They need to stress that continued employment depends on individuals' performing at a high level and being willing to learn and develop. They also need to state that employees are expected to make a high-level commitment to the organization and to be highly involved in understanding the organization's business, work processes, and customers. High-involvement organizations may make some use of contract and temporary employees to protect the employment stability part of their employment contract with their regular employees, but they rarely have multiple contracts.

The global-competitor employment contract should differ from the high-involvement one primarily in terms of its approach to training and careers. It needs to emphasize that individuals are responsible for their careers and that they are expected to maintain their employability; that is, they are expected in most cases to keep their skills current and to change them as the business of the organization changes. Like the high-involvement organization contract, it should put a strong emphasis on performance and state that continued employment depends on an individual's performing at a high level.

Often not stated formally in a global competitor's employment contract is the existence of an inner core of employees who have more of a high-involvement contract; that is, they have a long-term relationship with the organization and receive more support for development. These individuals are usually key technology leaders and individuals who are expected to achieve or have achieved high-level management positions. Depending on the nature of the business, this group may constitute anywhere from a small percentage up to 30 or 40 percent of the workforce.

As noted earlier, global-competitor organizations usually make extensive use of contract employees and temporary employees. This adds even more flexibility to the organization and fits well with the global-competitor approach of buying rather than building talent.

INDIVIDUALIZED DEALS

Organizations have always operated with multiple employment relationships. Hourly workers clearly have had and still do have a different relationship with their organizations from that of salaried employees. But this difference is based on the types of jobs, not on their holders' needs, desires, and skills. In an HC-centric organization, having different employment relationships for employees with different needs, desires, and skills makes a great deal of sense.[7] It is an effective way to attract, retain, and motivate employees who are critical to the organization's effectiveness. This is equally true for global-competitor and high-involvement organizations.

In HC-centric organizations individualized employment deals make sense because they are a powerful, cost-effective way for organizations to attract and retain the very best talent. Because individuals differ greatly in their personal lives, ages, their preferences, and so on, it's impossible to create a single employment deal that works for all the employees of large organizations. The obvious solution is to give enough choices so that organizations can offer employment deals that fit a variety of individuals.

Potential choices include when to work, where to work, the type of compensation, the type of work, the amount of work time, the type of career, and the fringe benefits received. These are all among the key elements of the work relationship that potentially can be individualized. Of course, the kinds of choices individuals should be offered depends very much on the nature of the organization and the type of employees it needs.

Career Customization in Deloitte & Touche

For over a decade, Deloitte & Touche has been a leader in providing individuals with employment flexibility. And in the past few years, the firm has proven itself to be on the cutting edge of understanding what it means to be an HC-centric organization.

Initially the company gave employees flexibility in where they worked and in arranging their schedules. Although meeting with generally positive reactions, these flexible work arrangements fell short of meeting the needs of the workforce for individualized careers and the organization's needs for a high-performance workforce. It was a partial solution that created administrative complexity and failed to address the major career choices that employees face.

In 2005, Deloitte & Touche began testing an approach it calls "mass career customization."[8] This approach represents an integrated career model that allows individuals to design a career that fits their needs. It recognizes that employees may want to change their career choices as they mature and as their interests change, and it creates a shared responsibility for careers between the individual and the organization. The expectation on the part

---

(*Continued*)

of Deloitte & Touche is that it will help retain the right talent by providing individuals with meaningful career options that will allow them to not just balance the demands of work and personal life but integrate them into a meaningful lifestyle.

Based on the success of the mass career customization program in several eighteen-month trials, Deloitte & Touche plans to cover all of their 42,000 employees with their mass career customization approach by the end of 2008. The results of the trials show positive results in areas of employee job satisfaction and retention. Interestingly, the pilot tests so far have found that rather than individuals predominately choosing to dial down their career efforts, employees are frequently choosing to dial up their commitment to their career. They want to increase their professional commitment to their career by returning to full-time hours if they have been on a reduced schedule, seeking promotions, and striving for higher rewards and compensation.

The Deloitte & Touche approach provides individuals with choices in four areas: pace, workload, location, and role. It allows individuals to make choices in each of these areas, and as a result, end up with a relationship to their work and the company that is truly customized.

The four areas are the critical drivers of the kind of work individuals do, as well as the work-life balance that they establish. *Pace* refers to the rate of career progression; *workload* reflects quantity of work; *location* refers to where the work is performed; and *role* refers to the kind of position and responsibilities that someone takes on. Taken in combination, they represent the key elements of an individual's relationship to their work and Deloitte & Touche.

Mass career customization appears to be a particularly good fit for Deloitte & Touche, because it is, when all is said and done, a knowledge-work, project-based organization. This type of organization has a constant need to retain and develop knowledge workers and to match them with the work that needs to be done. Knowing what individuals desire and want from their work, and what they are capable of doing, is an enormous aid when it comes to matching them with the project work that needs to be done at any point in time. It also is important in responding to the increasing diversity of the workforce. Of course, there is no guarantee that most individuals will be able to customize their careers in ways that satisfy them even with mass customization.

There are limits to how many can be promoted, and work has to be done even if no one wants to do it. But the leaders of Deloitte & Touche believe a good individual and organizational fit is much more likely to happen when individuals are given choices.

Creating individual deals for employees seems to be particularly appropriate for global-competitor organizations. It is a way for them to capture the best talent for the time they need it. In the case of high-involvement organizations, it should be an important feature of their employment contract, but it should not interfere with the desire of high-involvement organizations to create a sense of community and involvement in the business. Too much individualization runs the risk of creating a type of free agent transactional work relationship that works against a high-commitment, high-involvement culture.

One important disadvantage of creating individualized work relationships is the complexity of the deals. Complexity not only creates administrative problems, it can create fairness problems. Administrative complexity is much easier to handle today than in earlier decades, because of modern information technology and the type of sophisticated human resource and management systems that are available. The fairness issue is a different matter.

Perhaps the most effective thing an organization can do to cope with the fairness issue is to make it clear at the time of hiring that the employment contract is an individually negotiated one. When this is added to the stipulation that the contract reflects the market realities for each individual, at least individuals know what they are getting into when they join an organization that individualizes employment deals.

Will individuals stop making and talking about unfavorable comparisons? Probably not, but such comparisons and conversations are not necessarily all negative. Managers should listen for indications of true inequities in comparison to what individuals would get elsewhere, and they should act when necessary. This is an important part of retaining the best employees. If the organization keeps to an external reference point and is sure that individuals have deals as good as they can get elsewhere, or better, it is unlikely employees will leave even if they feel internal equity is lacking. What an organization must avoid is a constant renegotiation of contracts whenever someone else in the organization gets what is perceived to be a better deal.

CRITICAL SKILLS

To attract key talent, a company must first figure out what kind of talent it needs. As noted, Google seeks people who identify with the GLAT. But how does Google decide what goes on the GLAT? How should any company think about the particular skills it needs to excel?

Fundamental to effective talent management in an HC-centric organization is the identification of strategy-critical skills. It is not enough to simply say that individuals need to be able to do certain things. HC-centric organizations need to go far beyond this and match their skill staffing requirements to their strategic plans. The competencies and organizational capabilities identified in the strategic plan need to be translated into skills that will guide the staffing of the organization.

It is particularly important to identify the skills likely to be differentiators in terms of the successful execution of the business strategy. For example, if the key differentiator is technical excellence in a particular area, then the organization may have to do extraordinary things to be sure it gets the best and most competent technical talent in that area.

If, however, the key differentiator and source of competitive advantage is the ability to deal with customers, it may not be a matter of having a small number of technical experts so much as having a workforce selected for and extremely well trained in interpersonal and customer-centric skills. The point is that the organization needs to translate the competencies and capabilities that it expects will provide a competitive advantage into specific skills that are identifiable and need to be present in the workforce.

Identifying the skills and positions critical to the strategy is the first step in identifying the critical talent pools that an organization should focus its efforts on. The second step is to look at the degree of skill and performance variance among people who hold strategically critical positions. Those positions where there is considerable variance are the ones that require the most attention and focus. The reason for this is relatively straightforward: variation usually means improvement is possible. If everyone tends to perform the job well, it is not likely to be an area where improvement is possible, and thus it does not warrant special attention and management.

Talent scarcity is the third factor that affects the criticality and the degree to which certain jobs and types of talent warrant special focus. Positions where talent is scarce deserve special attention when it comes to talent management. They may require extra recruiting efforts, higher compensation, and even a slightly different employment contract.

An effective approach to talent management takes an overall look at the positions in the organization and rates each one on the criteria of skill scarcity, performance variance, and strategic impact. The highest-rated jobs, called "pivotal" jobs by my colleague John Boudreau, deserve the greatest attention.[9] These positions deserve extra effort when it comes to recruiting, development, and retention. Management needs to make individuals holding these jobs a particularly high priority in their recruiting, reward, and development activities. These individuals also should be taken into account when an organization establishes its brand as an employer. It may be worth creating a brand that identifies the organization as a particularly good place for individuals with critical skill sets to work.

Sometimes an analysis of an organization's critical skill sets and jobs turns up some surprising results.[10] For example, Federal Express found that improving the performance of its drivers would have more impact on corporate performance than improving the performance of its pilots. Pilots are more skilled but have been readily available over the last decade, and their performance does not differ greatly. The best pilots generally tend to perform at about the same level as most other pilots.

Service delivery drivers have a surprisingly demanding job that requires good decision making about scheduling and customer relations. A poor driver can easily alienate a customer and cause a shipment to miss a scheduled delivery. As a result of its analysis of pivotal jobs, Federal Express has put a great deal more emphasis on talent management for its drivers.

Westfield Corporation, an international manager of shopping malls, has found that the concierge position is a critical part of attracting people to malls. Concierges help shoppers navigate Westfield's large, complex malls. Because they deal frequently with the public and often are asked to solve a wide variety of difficult problems, individual concierges have quite variable performance. It also turns out that when done well, the concierge job makes a very positive impression on customers. Based on this information, Westfield now focuses on recruiting the right individuals for these jobs and pays a premium wage to attract good talent.

In the sports world, football teams have increasingly come to recognize that one of their offensive tackle positions is pivotal. Usually it's the left tackle, because with a right-handed quarterback, the left tackle is the critical provider of pass-rush blocking. A right-handed quarterback cannot easily see a rush coming from his left side, and as a result, if the left tackle fails to successfully pass-block for the quarterback, the quarterback is often unable to escape the rush of a defensive lineman and is sacked. The consequences of a sack are not just the loss of yardage but also the potential loss of the team's most valuable—or pivotal—player, the quarterback. In the case of a team with a left-handed quarterback, the situation simply reverses and the right tackle becomes the critical member of the offensive line.

It also turns out that the skill set necessary to be successful as a pass-blocking tackle is relatively rare. It takes size, strength, mobility, and a considerable amount of athleticism. Now that pro teams have recognized the importance of the position, tackles are the highest-paid players on the offensive line, and usually are among the highest-paid players on the team. They also are frequent first-round draft picks.

PICKING THE RIGHT PEOPLE

Any HC-centric organization's employee selection process needs to do two important things. First, it needs to identify the right talent. Second, it needs to create the right first impression in the mind of potential members of the organization.

It is beyond the scope of this book to go into the details of which selection processes will provide a valid and accurate assessment of individuals. A great deal of the selection process needs to be customized to the organization doing the hiring and the position being filled. It is not beyond the scope, however, to say that the process needs to take a comprehensive look at individuals, and in particular, a look at their past behavior. When all is said and done, past behavior is the best predictor of future behavior. Indeed, it is often a better predictor of future behavior than the impression people make in an interview or how they present themselves on paper.

There are good reasons for psychological testing, particularly when new employees need training to do a job. Intelligence, when all is said and done, is the best predictor of an individual's ability to learn new things, and in many cases to do a job.[11] Thus, in organizations that emphasize a build approach to talent management and have a high-involvement approach to management, it often makes sense to assess an individual's intelligence. If people are expected to work in a group environment, as they often are in a high-involvement organization, interviews and simulations of group situations are a good way to gather data about whether someone will fit.

Particularly in case of a high-involvement organization, there is no substitute for a rigorous selection process. The selection process must give the impression that working for the organization is a special opportunity, and that it hires only a select few. This is a critical part of the hiring message for any organization that wishes to gain competitive advantage through its human capital.

The importance an organization ascribes to talent acquisition can be communicated in many ways. One of my favorites is Microsoft's process. Microsoft uses multiple intensive interviews during which applicants are asked brain-teaser questions. The first interviewers exchange information with each other and provide suggested questions to the next interviewers. Some of the questions asked are intended to see how individuals think; no one is expected to know the right answer to "Why are manholes round?" or "How many gas stations are there in Seattle?"

Microsoft adds an interesting twist to the interviewing process: it has at least one outsider, a person who will not work with the applicant, meet and assess the applicant. Microsoft does this to avoid too much groupthink in the hiring process and to obtain a broader perspective on who gets hired. Part of the rationale is to avoid developing pockets of divergent culture because different parts of the organization engage in their own hiring and selection activities.

Hewlett-Packard and Microsoft have started using virtual job fairs and interviews. Job applicants can create an online avatar (a computer-generated image) to represent themselves. Applicants can navigate their avatars through the virtual space and use them to communicate with a company representative (also an avatar). HP, Microsoft, and other technology firms also use Web sites (for example, Facebook, YouTube) to attract technology-oriented job candidates. It is not clear that virtual interviews with avatars can help companies make good selection decisions, but there is always the possibility that they will provide information that would not appear in a traditional interview. If nothing else, it is a way to gain information about how tech-savvy job applicants are.

Another organization that does a great job of using its selection process not only to identify good employees but to communicate a sense of its organizational culture is Goldman Sachs. It has a highly performance-oriented global-competitor culture, with a strong emphasis on teamwork. Because it is a leading financial services organization that pays top wages, it has no trouble attracting job applicants.

As mentioned earlier, the most important part of the firm's selection process is a large number of interviews with individuals throughout the firm. Each applicant is subjected to days of interviewing, during which one of the major topics is the culture of Goldman. Applicants are told that it is very team oriented (employees always say "we," not "I") and that it is not just an espoused culture, it is the way people behave once they join the firm. It is also made clear that individuals who want to succeed in Goldman Sachs have to put forward a high level of effort and to be extremely work-focused.

Although Goldman Sachs may be an extreme when it comes to a thorough selection process that communicates to potential employees the difficulty of getting a job there, many other organizations also do this effectively. Most of them have built the reputation of being a premier employer over the years, but others, such as Google, Costco, and Starbucks, are more recent arrivals on the scene. Starbucks and Costco are particularly interesting because they are in the retail business sector, which is often known for lax hiring standards and high levels of turnover. Part of the reason Costco and Starbucks have outperformed their competitors is the extensive selection process they use and the feeling of employees that these companies are special places to work.

Not every organization can benefit from the type of extensive selection process that Goldman Sachs and Microsoft use. There is always the risk that too extensive a system will in effect discourage even qualified applicants because the value proposition of the organization simply isn't and can't be compelling enough to make a long selection process tolerable. Goldman Sachs and Microsoft are leaders in their businesses that have been in virtuous spirals for years and therefore have a special recruiting advantage when it comes to attracting highly talented individuals. Nevertheless, organizations with less visibility and dominance in their fields often can use a rigorous selection process, if the process itself has value for the individual.

One way to make the selection process valuable to applicants is to promise them feedback about their strengths and weaknesses and how they are evaluated by the firm. For individuals interested in learning and self-development, this can be quite attractive. In firms that use the high-involvement approach, these are just the kind of individuals that the organization should be recruiting.

I do not know of any organization that does this, but one option is to offer all job candidates an hour-long session with a career counselor at the end of the entire selection process. This should be optional, but for some individuals, it could be a useful incentive for going through an extensive selection process that might take more time and effort than they would otherwise be willing to devote. It might also attract just the kind of individuals an HC-centric organization should hire.

An increasingly popular and effective recruiting strategy is to offer internships. In most cases, companies offer these to college students, but increasingly they are also offering them to high school students. It is a wonderful opportunity to both provide promising recruits with a realistic preview of what it's like to work in the organization and, of course, to test the students out with respect to whether they would represent good long-term employees of the organization. In many respects, it's a low-risk way to hire important human capital. Goldman Sachs, for example, puts a big emphasis on internships and sees this kind of job as the critical driver of its new college and MBA graduate recruitment effort.

DEVELOPMENT OPPORTUNITIES

An important consideration in talent management is the issue of whether the organization is committed to talent development. If it is, then it needs to focus on the balance between classroom education and job experience. One of the distinct talent advantages that a build-oriented high-involvement organization has is in this very area: it can afford to take a longer-term view of talent development and use job experiences as a way to develop its human capital.

Although a job experience approach can take longer than educational coursework, it is usually much more effective.[12] This is particularly true when it comes to developing people who will have general management responsibilities. There is nothing like experience as a teacher. Of course, not just any experience will do; it needs to be based on a systematic program of development that considers the nature of the job, the type of management style that the organization wishes to develop, and the existing skills of the individual.

GE provides an interesting example of a company that uses an experience-based approach to developing its management talent. It rarely if ever hires a senior manager from outside the organization because it feels that it is too risky. Without seeing someone operate in GE, insiders feel they can never be sure that an outsider will be successful. As a result, they place a strong emphasis on providing job-based career development opportunities for GE's managers.

One of the most effective practices that GE uses in developing general managers is to give high-talent individuals relatively small "popcorn stand" management responsibilities. Because GE has a number of businesses, some of which are small in the context of GE's overall operations, it can use these smaller businesses as development and testing sites for its highly talented managers. If a manager makes mistakes or proves to be a poor candidate for senior management, GE has the opportunity to find this out at a relatively low cost. Losing money on a "popcorn stand" is simply not that big a deal for GE, but losing money in a major business certainly is.

For years GE used its locomotive business as a "popcorn stand." It was not closely connected to the key businesses in GE and it was not a key contributor to GE's revenue. Thus it provided a great learning and testing opportunity for management talent. Bob Nardelli ran this division and, in fact, ran it so well that it actually began to make a significant contribution to GE's profit. He moved on to a bigger job in GE before becoming CEO of Home Depot when he failed to get the CEO job at GE. Recently he got back into the transportation business when he became CEO of Chrysler.

ENABLING CAREER SELF-MANAGEMENT

In all HC-centric organizations, individuals need to take responsibility for their own development and career. In a high-involvement organization with a focus on talent development, this is less necessary than it is in a global-competitor organization, with its focus on buying talent and constantly adjusting its talent mix. But it is still an important consideration.

Effective career self-management by individuals is ultimately in the interest of both individuals and organizations. It is obvious why effective self-management is good for individuals; it may be less obvious why it is good for organizations. For organizations it is simply better to have individuals who make the right decisions about developing themselves and feel good about their careers than to have employees who are confused and making poor career decisions. In the worst-case scenario, organizations that assume the burden of managing employees' careers for them in a rapidly changing world can end up with individuals who are difficult to employ effectively but are hard to dismiss.

An organization can do a number of things to help individuals self-manage their careers effectively. As discussed further in Chapter Five, a major focus on talent appraisal is an important part of it. Particularly when the feedback from the talent review sessions is effective and timely, it can give individuals a clear idea about what their future in the organization can be, what kind of skills they need in order to achieve their career goals, and what they can do to develop their skills.

Simply having appraisal sessions and providing feedback is not all that organizations can and should do, however. One obvious addition is to provide employees with good information about the direction the organization is taking with respect to its technology and business model. This information can help individuals make decisions about how to develop themselves, what jobs make sense for them, and what kind of careers they can plan on in the organization.

One of the world's largest accounting firms, Pricewaterhouse-Coopers, provides its accounting staff with just the kind of career direction information that enables effective career management. Based on a study by Susan Mohrman and George Benson at the Center for Effective Organizations, they provided their audit staff with data showing how their income is likely to be affected by the number of years they work for PwC.[13]

Among the interesting conclusions of the PwC study was that if individuals stayed with PwC for a year or two beyond the typical stay, it could result in significantly higher pay in their next job. Remember, this is in the context of an organization that is a global competitor and expects to have a high turnover rate among its professional staff. Very few initial hires ultimately reach partner in this up-or-out career world. For many individuals, the issue is not whether to leave but when to leave.

The data showed that from both the organization's and the individual's perspective, many people decided to leave too early. All they needed to do was stay an extra year or two and they were likely to get a much better-paying job once they left PwC. Once they became aware of this, employees did in fact stay longer. It also turns out PwC was able to benefit from their staying because it led to improved customer service and an increased return on the investment made in the individual. In short, staying longer was a clear win-win situation.

Hewlett-Packard and Cisco are among the companies that have established excellent career centers to help people analyze and plan their careers. These centers provide counseling as well as a tremendous amount of information about the availability of jobs both within and outside the company. In addition to providing information, career centers are an ideal way to give employees access to assessment technology. Tests of all kinds can help people understand where they are in terms of their interests, skills, motivation, and abilities, allowing them to realistically evaluate their career choices.

As the use of company intranets grows, it is increasingly possible to implement virtual career centers. Organizations can put considerable amounts of assessment technology and career information on a career Web site to give people personal tutoring, advice, and feedback without their ever having to contact another individual. Deloitte Touche Tohmatsu has done this and reports that it has gotten a very positive response from its employees.

An intranet-based development system also fits nicely with the increasing use of 360-degree feedback appraisals. In these appraisals, people are asked to nominate others who can give them feedback about their performance. The nominees receive an e-mail asking them to assess the individual seeking feedback; the replies are then fed back to the requesting individuals to provide a sense of how others see their performance and skills.

Pratt & Whitney, the aircraft engine division of United Technologies, has developed a particularly impressive Web-based approach to helping employees develop their skills. It includes regular updates on what skills the organization thinks it will need in the future and what skills are becoming obsolete. It includes push technology that alerts employees who are in danger of becoming obsolete. Finally, it serves as a resource for employees who want to learn new skills. It lists all training and degree programs available to employees and the names and addresses of employees who can act as resources in key learning areas.

ENABLING WORK CHANGES

Key to the development of individuals is the ease of movement within an organization from one assignment to another. This can be self-managed only when an organization has a well-developed posting system for job openings and a willingness to support internal transfers. Many of the new human resource information systems (HRISs) that organizations are using do include job postings. However, it is not enough to just post the job; the posting needs to include a great deal of information about the characteristics of the job, including the skills and competencies needed and what the application process involves. The posting should also provide good information about the rewards, challenges, and demands of the position.

A number of companies, including IBM and some professional service firms, have developed sophisticated systems that provide job information to employees. They also allow managers looking for talent to search the organization and identify people with the right skill set. Web-based systems make it especially easy for the internal movement of employees to be dynamic and interactive.

Current employees provide profiles of their background, interests, and skills, which are then stored in the system. When jobs open, their characteristics are matched to the database of profiles, allowing the technology to make a first determination about whether someone might be a good fit. Push technology can then be used to inform the individuals of the job opening. This has the obvious advantage of providing current employees with a strong assurance that their organization wants them to stay, values their skills and experience, and will help them develop a virtuous career spiral. It also sends a message to employees that the organization takes talent utilization and the concerns of individuals seriously. As a result, it contributes to a company's identity as an HC-centric organization.

Web-based systems can also help meet the staffing challenges of managers who must fill open jobs. They can use the technology to search the profiles of skills and competencies and identify any employee who fits a job opening they need to fill. This is a quick and efficient way for the people doing staffing to obtain a list of qualified internal candidates.

The willingness of organizations to let individuals make internal moves is the last and sometimes most difficult piece that needs to be put in place so that individuals can reasonably self-manage their careers. There are a number of reasons why it is difficult for individuals to make internal job transfers, but often the major factor is the lack of management support. The transfer of a valuable employee inconveniences the manager in whose work area the individual currently works. Any move causes disruption, and as a result, managers sometimes hide their most talented people or go out of their way to discourage movement. This type of behavior is not acceptable in an HC-centric organization. Just as financial capital has to be utilized effectively, human capital has to be put to its best use.

RETAINING THE RIGHT TALENT

This discussion of talent management will not be complete until I once again consider talent retention. As I mentioned earlier, losing talented individuals is a significant cost for every organization. It is often less costly, however, for structure-centric organizations than it is for HC-centric organizations. Structure-centric organizations invest much less in developing the skills, competencies, and knowledge of their employees. In addition, because structure-centric organizations are likely to have simpler, more structured jobs, they can often hire from a broader labor market and can often get people quickly up to a reasonable performance level without making a huge investment. Further, because they don't expect a great deal from the individual, they don't have to go through a selection process that is as elaborate and expensive as the one an HC-centric organization must use.

For HC-centric organizations, employee turnover can be very expensive. This is particularly true of high-involvement organizations, which typically make an even greater investment in individuals than do global-competitor organizations. In addition, they use a management style that assumes people are going to be in the company for a long period of time.

Numerous studies have been done to estimate the costs of turnover. They vary significantly on just how much they conclude turnover costs, but one finding is rather consistent. The higher the salary individuals receive, the more expensive it is to replace them.[14] Thus, replacement costs are often estimated by taking a multiple of a salary. It is also generally agreed that the larger the salary, the greater the multiple should be. For example, in replacing relatively unskilled individuals, often the cost is one or two times the monthly salary. However, in the case of a senior executive, the cost is more likely to be ten or fifteen times monthly salary.

I know of no good analysis that shows how the cost of turnover differs between HC-centric and structure-centric organizations, but I would estimate that HC-centric organizations find it at least twice as expensive to replace highly paid individuals and perhaps one and a half times as expensive to replace lower-paid individuals. In any case, there is little question that turnover is expensive and that HC-centric organizations should be constantly monitoring their turnover rate, focusing on why individuals leave, and developing approaches that retain the right individuals.

It is particularly important that organizations retain their high-performance and critical talent employees. This often takes special effort and a special focus. The following are keys to successfully retaining all employees but, in particular, to retaining the critical talent in an organization.

KNOW THE MARKET

The research on why employees quit shows that in most cases people leave for a straightforward reason: they have found a more attractive alternative elsewhere.[15] The implication of this for an organization that wishes to retain its employees is obvious: it must know the market. It must know who its competitors are, what those competitors are offering, and how it can gain a competitive advantage over those competitors when it comes to retaining talent.

MEET OR BEAT THE MARKET

Once an organization knows what its competitors are offering, the next step is obvious. It needs to meet or beat that offering. An organization may not be able to meet or beat every feature of what's being offered by competitors, but it ought at least to have a total employment package that is as good as that offered by its major competitors. This, of course, is particularly important in the case of pivotal and high-performing talent.

One important additional point needs to be made here. The critical issue in meeting or beating what a competitor has to offer involves not how somebody in HR assesses the situation but how individuals assess their internal opportunities against their external opportunities. Thus organizations should take every opportunity to find out how their employees view the labor market, their satisfaction with their current situation, and what other organizations are offering.

SELL THE EMPLOYMENT CONTRACT

Since individuals react to what they perceive to be the employment deal and opportunities a company offers, it's important that they be fully informed about what their employer offers. All too often, individuals leave an organization unaware of what career opportunities exist, what is planned for them in the future, and what the nature of the employment deal is at their organization.

Many organizations spend a great deal of effort educating new and potential employees on all the opportunities they offer. However, they forget to let their current employees know what a bright future potentially exists for them if they stay with the organization. Perhaps the best way to summarize this point is as follows: organizations constantly and regularly need to re-recruit existing employees. This, of course, is particularly true of the outstanding employees, because they are the ones most likely to be hearing from external recruiters.

KNOW THE INDIVIDUAL

There is no substitute for knowing what individuals want and value. Literally thousands and thousands of studies have addressed what employees value about work and how important features like pay, promotion opportunities, the work itself, and supervision are to them. Without question, the most consistent finding of these studies is that individuals differ in what they value. Some value money more than the work itself, some value promotion opportunities more than job security, and so on. What individuals value is determined by a plethora of factors, including age, gender, past experiences, and lifestyle. If an organization knows what someone values most, it can tailor the retention package to fit what that individual wants.

To some degree, organizations can create a more homogenous set of employees by their recruiting practices and their employment contract. Recruiting processes and employment contracts that highlight the rewards that come from working for an organization attract individuals who particularly value those rewards. Organizations can also select individuals based on what they value.

Nevertheless, it is always dangerous to assume that all, or even most, employees in an organization place similar value on the rewards an organization gives them. It is important to find out what individuals want and to be sure to create a work environment that offers it to them. One recent study found that organizations may not be aware of why their employees would leave. In this study, top-performing employees reported that the number one reason they would consider changing jobs is money; promotion came in a distant second. Their employers, however, felt promotion was number one, while pay was a distant third.[16] It turns out that HR managers were particularly likely to underestimate the importance of money and overestimate the importance of social relations.

Studies vary greatly in whether they find that individuals most frequently leave for more money, better career opportunities, better work-life balance, or other factors; what they don't vary in is the finding that if individuals are dissatisfied with what to them is an important feature of the work environment, they are likely to leave. Thus it is important that organizations know what their employees value and do everything they can to be sure that they are offering their critical employees rewards that will retain them.

FOCUS ON HIGH-PERFORMANCE TALENT

It makes sense to focus retention efforts on highly performing talent. As noted, the most expensive talent to replace is high-performance talent. The organizational performance loss is greater when they leave, and they tend to command a higher market value. Retaining the best talent is critical to developing a virtuous spiral that results in better and better talent and increased organizational performance.

Two steps must be taken in order to retain high performers. The first is to identify them. I deal with this in the next chapter when I discuss performance management systems. The second is to be sure that they are rewarded at a high level. The key here is tying rewards to performance through an effective performance management system and a reward system that delivers significantly greater rewards to high-performing individuals. At the very least, high-performers should be paid more and have better career opportunities than others in the same organization.

WHAT IS NEEDED

Talent management is the most important process in HC-centric organizations. Decisions about people should be made with the same rigor, logic, and precision that are applied to decisions about capital investment, products, technology, and physical assets. To do anything less than this is to risk creating an organization that cannot perform effectively.

The following are the most important talent management features of an HC-centric organization:

- How well talent is managed is measured, and managers are held accountable for their talent management performance.
- A strong employer brand clearly identifies the organization as an attractive place to work for individuals who want to—and can—be a source of competitive advantage.
- The employment contract differs for a high-involvement organization and a global-competitor organization. In the case of the former, it emphasizes long-term employment and a commitment to the organization. In the case of the latter, it emphasizes the employee's responsibility for personal growth and development and that the organization will help with the development but not guarantee employment stability.
- The reward package that individuals receive fits their preferences and needs.
- Critical skills for a competitive advantage are identified, and individuals with those critical skills are hired or developed, regardless of what it costs.
- The selection process is used to identify who has or can learn the skills that the organization needs. It is also used to determine whether a prospective employee will fit well in an HC-centric organization and to on-board individuals.

- In the case of high-involvement organizations, development opportunities for individuals are carefully planned and made available.
- Career self-management is enabled through information systems and creating the opportunity for individuals to change their work assignments on an as-needed basis.
- A major emphasis is placed on retaining high-performance talent.

Chapter Five

Managing Performance

In an HC-centric organization, "talent management" is important, but "performance management" is even more so. Talent management is the critical factor in determining the potential performance of individuals, groups, and organizations, but the ability to *manage performance* is often the major differentiator between organizations that produce adequate results and those that excel. Without a focus on performance management at all levels of an organization, it is hard to see how it can find competitive advantage through its talent. Simply stated, in an HC-centric organization an effective performance management system is not optional, it is a must-have.

It is far from easy to get performance management right in any organization. The corporate world is littered with companies whose employees regularly game their performance reviews to their advantage.[1] People at all levels go through the motions of formulaic performance reviews with astonishing insincerity and have little to show for it. There also are numerous examples of situations where individuals thought they were doing the right thing only to find out they were mistaken. Finally, in many organizations, performance reviews simply aren't done either because of employee resistance or because managers "dry lab" (fake) them.

An effective performance management system needs to accomplish four things. First, it needs to define and produce agreement on what type of performance is needed. The bedrock of any performance management system should be agreement on what needs to be done and how it should be done. Without a clear definition of what kind of performance is desired, it is impossible to develop and motivate individuals who can meet or exceed performance standards! It also is key to guiding the performance of individuals so that it supports the organization's strategy and plans.

Second, it needs to guide the development of individuals so that they have the skills and knowledge needed to perform effectively. To be effective, a performance-management system needs to help employees gain the skills and knowledge they need if they are to perform effectively.

Third, it needs to motivate individuals to perform effectively. Even the best talent will perform at a high level only if motivated to do so. When it comes to performance, high levels of both talent and motivation are needed.

Finally, it needs to provide data to the organization's human capital information system. It needs to be a primary source of information about how individuals are performing and what skills and knowledge exist in the workforce. This information is a critical input to succession planning as well as to strategic planning.

In this chapter I look at the first three objectives, then discuss performance management system design and pay-for-performance systems. Chapter Six will take up the fourth objective, providing talent management information.

DEFINING PERFORMANCE

Every performance management system in an HC-centric organization should include the explicit identification of what needs to be achieved and how performance will be measured. HC-centric organizations don't have bureaucratic control systems and detailed job descriptions, thus, without an effective performance management system there may be ambiguity about what each individual should do and what constitutes effective performance.

Best Buy: Work Time Isn't Always Face Time

More and more managers are being asked to manage employees with whom they don't have regular contact. This is a result of telecommuting, globalization, and a host of other issues that require or allow people working for the same organization to be located in many different places. IBM and Sun Microsystems, for example, are among an increasing number of companies where close to 50 percent of employees have no regular office space; instead, they telecommute and use hoteling offices (designated offices available for day use) depending upon where they are at a particular time.

When physical separation exists, managers and employees need to find a way to organize and manage work that is effective for them. This is particularly important when the issue is performance planning and management.

Best Buy, which is heavily committed to distance management, has a project called Results-Only Work Environment or ROWE. Employees in participating departments are allowed to work virtually anywhere and anytime as long as they successfully complete their assignments on time. Ultimately, Best Buy expects to have about three-quarters of its employees at corporate headquarters using the program.

Best Buy introduced its ROWE program because of its senior leaders' commitment to being a high-involvement organization and their feeling that allowing employees to plan and manage their work assignments was consistent with their high-involvement management approach.

The key to having an effective virtual management relationship is performance management. Expectation setting is the critical activity. Best Buy has invested heavily in training its managers on how to set expectations in a virtual work relationship. Since often managers cannot observe the work of employees until the final product is produced, they have to manage schedules for product completion and product delivery. This requires setting realistic goals and holding individuals to delivery on their commitments. For many managers this is difficult to do because they are used to observing work in process and "making suggestions" as to how it can be done better or more quickly. Watching work get done, of course, also provides some comfort to the manager that, in fact, work is being done correctly and that it will be delivered.

The program at Best Buy has been producing positive results. It has resulted in retention of some key talent that the organization most likely would have lost without it and has resulted in higher performance levels because of the increased setting of clear expectations and goals for employees.

What is needed for an effective performance review is more than agreement on what an individual will accomplish during a period of time; it requires agreement on how performance will be measured. In most cases, it is also important to establish how the agreed-upon performance will be achieved and what measures will be used to assess whether it was achieved in the agreed-upon manner. This is particularly important when managers are being appraised and the organization has a strong commitment to high-involvement management. Leaders who get results "at any cost" can destroy the credibility of the high-involvement approach. The best measures of performance focus on specific behaviors and goals. They avoid attempts to measure traits such as *reliable, honest,* and *hard-working.*

DEVELOPING EMPLOYEE SKILLS AND KNOWLEDGE

From a human capital management perspective, it is particularly important for an organization to develop good measures of each individual's skills, knowledge, and competencies. Without these indicators it is difficult to know what the human capital resources of an organization are and therefore what type of performance it is capable of. At the very least, such knowledge can help a company decide how employees can contribute to a strategy, how much training needs to be done, and what kind of hiring is necessary to yield the skill mix the organization needs.

Information about skills and competencies is also critical in diagnosing the cause when business strategies run into difficulty. It may well be that the strategy is not flawed; the organization simply doesn't have the capability to execute it. The skills of the individuals charged with executing the strategy may be at the core of an organization's performance problem.

Last but not least, a skills assessment is an important source of information about what development activities individuals should engage in. This can help individuals understand what skills they need, provide them with a development plan that allows them to acquire those skills, and set the stage for their being rewarded when they develop new needed skills. Evaluating the skills of individuals and giving them advice on their development, then, should be a critical part of every appraisal process.

Dell's founder, Michael Dell, provides a good example of taking assessment seriously as a development tool. His own appraisal includes a survey that collects data from a broad range of employees. A few years ago the results showed that a large number of employees felt that Dell was impersonal and was emotionally detached from the workforce. What happened next says a great deal about Dell's efforts to continuously improve his performance and that of the organization.

Dell immediately faced his top management team and offered a frank self-critique, acknowledging that he is very shy and that this can make him appear aloof and unapproachable. He vowed to change and followed up by showing a videotape of the talk to every manager in the company. Further, he put some desktop props in place to help remind him and others of the change he was committed to. For example, he put a model bulldozer on his desk to remind him not to ram ideas through before testing them with others.

In addition to the behavior changes that may result from Dell's efforts, the symbolism of his being appraised and trying to change is very important. It sends a message to the entire organization that improvement is expected and should be standard operating procedure for everyone in the organization, not just the lower-level employees.

MANAGING MOTIVATION

Motivation is the performance capstone—without it, good performance will not occur. Individuals can have all the right skills, knowledge, and expertise and still be poor performers if they are not motivated.

To say the literature on employee motivation is extensive is an understatement. The body of research on the subject is enormous and continues to grow. The findings range from the obvious to the very complex. Fortunately, research makes it very clear what performance management systems need to do to motivate individuals to perform well. They need to create agreement on what needs to be done and to clearly tie valued rewards to performance.[2]

While much has been written about how a carrot-and-stick approach to motivation can actually de-motivate employees, the research evidence shows that rewards based on performance can motivate people to excel.[3] What's important to understand is that the nature of the reward is critical—as is the way in which the reward is related to performance.

Offer the wrong carrot, and employees will feel insulted, misunderstood, or just apathetic. Motivation requires offering rewards that individuals value and that are clearly tied to their performance.

In any discussion of motivation it is important to distinguish between internal rewards and external rewards. Individuals give internal rewards to themselves (things like feelings of competency, achievement, and self-esteem) because they feel they have accomplished something or achieved something that they wanted to.

External rewards are tangible things that individuals value; they can be given directly by others (such as praise) or by organizational systems (such as pay). How motivated individuals are to perform is essentially the product of the degree to which receipt of the rewards (internal and external) they value depends on how well they perform.

HC-centric organizations need to do everything that they can to make sure that the receipt of both the internal and external rewards valued by their employees are directly related to how well they and the organization perform. This of course is where the performance management system comes into play. It needs to be designed so that individuals are rewarded according to their performance and it needs to deliver the appropriate kind and amount of rewards to individuals based on their performance.

Rewarding performance sounds simple, and seems as if it should be relatively easy to do but nothing could be further from the truth. It is complicated not just because performance measurement is difficult but because of the variation in what individuals value and the difficulty of establishing a clear line of sight from how individuals perform to the receipt of rewards they value.

The research on goal setting goes a long way toward establishing what the performance management system needs to do in order to tie the reception of internal rewards to performance.[4] When managers set goals, they need to keep in mind that the difficulty of the goal is a key determinant of performance. Easy-to-achieve goals tend to lead to poor performance, but so do goals that are too difficult. When goals are set too low, individuals settle for low levels of performance. When goals are set too high, people give up because they do not believe they can succeed, or they cheat to give the impression of success. Goals that are perceived to be achievable but challenging should be the objective because they are the most motivating and produce the highest levels of performance.

The nature of the work that individuals do is a second factor that has a major impact on internal motivation.[5] When individuals use skills they value, produce a whole or meaningful part of a product or service, and receive performance feedback, their work is motivating.

In order for individuals to reward themselves for performance, they need feedback about their performance. Often the results of their performance are obvious (in baseball the batter can see a home run leave the park), but in some cases workers can see the results of their behavior only if the measurement processes of the organization provide relevant feedback.

What is required for external rewards to be motivating is that they be large enough so that individuals feel the effort they are putting forth to achieve them is worthwhile. Rewards also have to be clearly tied to performance in ways that lead individuals to feel that they will actually be delivered if the appropriate level of performance is achieved. This occurs only when individuals trust the organization with respect to making good on its commitment to rewarding performance. This is why a culture of truth telling and transparency is needed for a performance management system to be effective. Without truth telling, trust will not develop and individuals will not believe that performance on their part will lead to the rewards they have been promised. Without transparency it is often difficult for individuals to see how their performance will affect their rewards.

PERFORMANCE MANAGEMENT SYSTEM DESIGN

Virtually every organization has a performance management system that is intended to have a positive impact on how well individual employees are performing. Yet performance management is an area where organizations seem to be constantly changing their practices, usually in response to dissatisfaction with the existing system.

Four major factors make it difficult to create an effective performance management system. First, design options abound; as a result, there are many opportunities to make design mistakes. Second, in most circumstances, both the evaluator and evaluated are uncomfortable with the process and have not received adequate training in how to do it. Third, in many situations, accurate and effective performance measurement must be based on a host of inputs and complex judgments. Fourth, time pressures work against the necessary level of engagement by all parties.

At this point I think it is useful to give an overview of the design features that separate good performance management systems from less effective ones. My list of characteristics is based on decades of research (my own and that of other researchers) intended to identify what distinguishes effective performance management systems.[6]

In this case I am defining system effectiveness as producing a clear understanding of what performance is expected from an individual and measuring whether the individual accomplished what was expected. The system needs to do these two things in a way that leads to motivation and skill development.

These design features apply to both global-competitor organizations and high-involvement organizations. They are the fundamental features that need to be incorporated in any performance management system in organizations that wish to achieve competitive advantage through their talent:

- The organization conducts appraisals top-to-bottom.
- Appraisal delivery is evaluated for effectiveness.
- Goals are set in advance.
- Frequency fits rate of organizational change.
- How goals are accomplished matters.
- Input from person appraised is part of the process.
- Objective performance measures are used.
- Measures are strategic.
- Ratings are meaningful.
- Pay for performance and development discussions are separate.
- The organization has (or is building) a skills database.
- Ongoing performance feedback is the norm.
- Team performance is managed and measured.

Now that I have introduced them, let's look at each of them in detail.

THE ORGANIZATION CONDUCTS APPRAISALS TOP-TO-BOTTOM

Appraisals need to start at the top of the organization. All too often the senior executives in an organization are not appraised and do not appraise their subordinates. The result is that performance appraisals become something senior executives tell middle management to do to lower-level employees. Needless to say, this sets up a negative dynamic in the way people think about and conduct appraisals.

Among other negatives, employees see no senior management role-modeling of how to do appraisals, and senior managers are not held accountable for their performance. As a result, not only does performance management become a dysfunctional event, it fails to translate the business strategy into deliverable goals and objectives throughout the organization.

The solution is simple to identify: The CEO and board need to use the process as a way to translate the organization's strategy into action. The performance appraisal process needs to start with the board of directors doing a thorough and rigorous appraisal of the CEO, and it needs to cascade down from there.

Siebel Systems Performance Management System

In the late 1990s, CEO Tom Siebel recognized that the way Siebel Systems managed workforce performance was no longer adequate. He was afraid that the "strategy execution" gap—the difference between what people knew they should do and what they were actually doing—was too big. The company needed a solution that would enable it to execute its strategy consistently across global locations.

Building on their industry-leading capabilities in customer relationship management (CRM) software, Seibel's managers developed an "employee relationship management (ERM) system" called "*my*Siebel." Deployed in December 2000, it was an important part of performance management until Siebel was acquired

---

(Continued)

by Oracle in 2006. The *my*Siebel system provided planning and performance management, training, content management, workforce collaboration, and employee support. It streamlined many processes within the company, including performance evaluation, communication of objectives, and expense reporting. Siebel executives credited the implementation of *my*Siebel with a substantial improvement in employee satisfaction. Here is how the system worked:

The week after the end of each quarter, the executive committee—the top fifteen senior managers—spent three days in a retreat analyzing the results of the prior quarter and establishing objectives for next quarter. By the seventh calendar day of the month following the offsite, Tom Siebel's personal objectives and those of his direct reports were posted on the performance management module of *my*Siebel. By the fifteenth, these objectives had been translated into objectives for the functions and business units that reported to the VPs and were posted on *my*Siebel. By the twenty-first of the month, every employee had posted and received feedback on their quarterly objectives. These objectives served as the key metrics that would be used to evaluate their performance over the next three months.

Every employee could view the objectives of any other employee, including those of Tom Siebel himself and other members of the executive committee. This allowed people to understand how others were allocating their time and attention.

The individual performance evaluation process ran parallel to the objective-setting process. The managers were all responsible for evaluating their own direct subordinates by the fifteenth of the first month of each new quarter. The review and feedback had to be posted to the *my*Siebel performance management module. But unlike the posting of objectives, which were accessible to everyone inside the company, performance evaluations were visible only to the managers to whom the employee reported. Accordingly, only Tom Siebel, as CEO, could access everybody's performance evaluations.

Bonuses were tied to the achievement of the quarterly objectives. For people involved in the delivery of products and services, a large part of their objectives and compensation were tied to sales targets and customer satisfaction scores. For salespeople, part of the bonus was held back and paid out over the course of the year based on quarterly customer satisfaction scores. A sales-person could lose some of this bonus if satisfaction was low. (These bonuses could be as much as 40 percent of an individual's pay.)

The process of performance management was supported by the information system architecture. The information system pushed information to employees and allowed them to pull the information they needed. After logging on, each employee had a personal "home page" that contained a different corporate announcement or story every day. This pushed current communications and corporate agenda items to the employee. It also contained an area that suggested training opportunities for given work and career paths. Each employee was expected to complete five Web-based training modules per quarter. The system also allowed employees to pull corporate data and information. It included detailed information about corporate strategies, products, and customer information, performance data, and competitor and market information.[7]

Before Siebel, the CRM software company, was acquired by Oracle, it developed a system that did an excellent job of using performance management to support the implementation of the company's strategy. Because Siebel was in a fast-changing business, computer software for managing customer relations, the appraisal system set new goals and targets every quarter. The goal-setting process for the performance management system began with the CEO and cascaded down the organization. Individuals throughout the organization set their own goals based on those set by individuals above them, and then each quarter their performance was reviewed against their goals.

APPRAISAL DELIVERY IS EVALUATED FOR EFFECTIVENESS

It is important to evaluate how well appraisals are done by managers. This makes a significant statement about their importance to the organization, gives managers feedback about how well they conduct appraisals, and motivates them to do a good job of appraising performance. A systematic evaluation of appraisals should include three elements: an audit of the quality of the written documents and evaluations produced in the process, a gathering of survey data on how the individuals who are appraised feel about the appraisal event, and measures of the timeliness of the appraisal meetings and reports.

GOALS ARE SET IN ADVANCE

Organizations need to establish specific and quantifiable goals for acceptable levels of performance. Managers and their subordinates need to sit down before the performance period begins and establish what measures will be used in the evaluations and what levels of performance are challenging but achievable. Research suggests that the more interactive the goal-setting activity, the more likely people are to accept the goals, be motivated by them, and see performance appraisal as a fair and reasonable process.[8]

FREQUENCY FITS RATE OF CHANGE

How often the performance objectives of an individual need to be updated depends on the rate of change in the work the individual does. It is easy to fall into an annual schedule, but in many cases this is not often enough. Given the rate of change in today's business environment, rarely if ever is it too frequent, performance objectives can be obsolete in days, not years. Siebel updated its employees' objectives every three months; it felt it had to update them often in order for the objectives to be meaningful and in order for the employees to be doing what they should be doing.

The managers at the Manchester, Vermont–based sporting, home goods, and clothing company Orvis review each individual's key performance measures every month. This is a big investment of time, but a wise one. Sometimes the goals do not need to be changed, but Orvis is always monitoring the environment, and the monthly reviews ensure that the company does change goals when the environment demands it.

HOW GOALS ARE ACCOMPLISHED MATTERS

In an HC-centric organization it is very important that managers be appraised on how they have gotten their results. For example, appraisals should include whether a manager has developed a successor, is a source of leadership talent for other parts of the organization, and role-models the type of leadership behavior the organization wants.

HC-centric organizations run the risk of preaching talent-focused leadership while rewarding managers solely on the basis of financial and operating results. Often this leads to a number of counterproductive outcomes, such as managers' resorting to demanding, autocratic, or punitive leadership to get good short-term results.

GE was one of the first organizations to tackle this management issue squarely. To be rewarded and valued at GE, managers must both produce good results and demonstrate managerial and leadership behaviors that are consistent with the company's leadership brand.

GE uses a version of the two-by-two matrix, shown in Figure 7, to make sure its managers both get the right results and get them in the right way. Anything less is likely to lead to dismissal. It is important to note that GE doesn't immediately fire individuals who exhibit the right managerial behaviors but get poor results—it works with them and gives them a chance to improve. This is not true of managers who exhibit poor behaviors but get good results. GE removes them from their managerial jobs to prevent further damage, placing them elsewhere in the company or firing them. In the case of poor results and poor behavior, dismissal usually is swift and certain.

FIGURE 7. LEADERSHIP PERFORMANCE MATRIX.

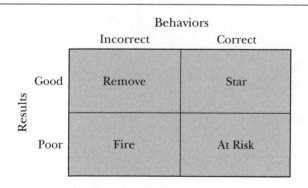

INPUT IS PART OF THE PROCESS

HC-centric organizations should ask the people who are being appraised to provide input at the end of the performance appraisal period. They should be able to present their version of how well they have performed their work assignments against their preset goals. My research supports the value of giving people this opportunity before their appraiser reaches a performance judgment.[9] It leads to more accurate appraisals and to individuals' believing they have been fairly appraised.

OBJECTIVE PERFORMANCE MEASURES ARE USED

Many appraisals fail because the performance measures consist of ratings using vague terms such as *excellent,* or poorly defined general traits or personality dimensions such as *reliable, communication skills, customer focus,* and *leadership.* These traits are difficult to judge and almost always lead to communication breakdowns and misunderstandings between appraisers and the individuals being appraised. They also fail to provide the type of assessment required for the organization to have valid metrics concerning the condition of its talent.

Organizations need to adopt a balanced scorecard of behavior- and outcome-based measures that quantify, or at least clearly identify, what performance and behavior are being judged. For example, rather than assessing the general dimension of reliability, the appraisal should focus on whether critical work has been completed on time and whether preset goals were met.

Here is a simple example of how agreement between rater and ratee can be increased when the appraisal focuses on observable behaviors and the business outcomes they produce. Assume that growth is an important business objective for a company; given this, the behaviors that lead to growth need to be identified and each person assessed against those behaviors.

For instance, the sales staff in a company might be appraised on such behaviors as the proportion of sales that come from new products, the number of suggestions for product innovation, or the opening of new sales territories and customer accounts. These types of specific measures establish the strongest link between the organization's business strategy and the appraisal process. They also provide objective data on which to base an appraisal.

MEASURES ARE STRATEGIC

One of the most difficult challenges in performance management concerns what to measure in a team environment where individual performance should be focused on contributing to team performance. The general manager of the Oakland A's, Billy Beane, has demonstrated the importance of looking beyond a few simple measures of individual performance in baseball.[10] When Beane took a look at the hard numbers for the performance of individual players and correlated them with the percentage of games teams won in a season, he found many of the conventional measures of individual excellence were not as predictive of team wins as one would assume. But one relatively obscure statistic—on-base percentage for hitters—stood out as a good predictor of team performance. This has led to on-base percentage becoming a much more popular measure in the world of professional baseball.

Basketball is another sport where teams are beginning to look very differently at metrics. Traditional measures such as scoring average, assists, and rebounds certainly are one way to measure an individual's contribution to the team—but only a partial way and maybe not the best. For example, instead of scoring average per game, or even per minute played, a better indicator of individual performance often is points per shot attempt. This takes into account not only shooting percentage but whether the shot is a 2- or 3-point effort and whether the individual gets and makes foul shots.

Perhaps an even better indicator of an individual's contribution to a basketball team is how the team fares while the individual is on the floor. It turns out that some individuals consistently show a positive number during their time in the game, while other individuals consistently show a negative number when they are in the game.

The new metrics being used in baseball and basketball, of course, don't translate directly to most business situations. But the principle of using solid data to determine what makes for an effective performer does. Particularly important is establishing a relationship between the performance of a team, group, or organization and the performance of an individual. Organizations need to know and state what it is that individuals should contribute and how much of it they are contributing. This needs to be an important part of their performance review and influence staffing and reward decisions.

Further, it is important that determination of the key measures of individual performance be based on more than just the opinion of informed individuals; they need to have an empirical analytic basis that examines the relationship between individual performance and the performance of the organization. This is the genius of Beane's analysis of baseball. He undertook what amounted to a scientific investigation of the sport to determine how the performance of individuals relates to organizational performance.

The result of Beane's rethinking the evaluation of players and the staffing of his team has led to the Oakland A's being a successful baseball team even though, as noted earlier, they have a very low budget for salaries. This dramatically makes the point that having individuals do the right things is more valuable than having highly paid talent, and perhaps even what is considered to be the best talent in the eyes of individuals who have not done their analytic homework.

RATINGS ARE MEANINGFUL

Structure-centric organizations, in keeping with their stability-oriented, bureaucratic structures and practices, tend to use performance measurement schemes that go way beyond the precision that is necessary or justified by the process. Some organizations rank-order hundreds, or in some cases thousands, of people from first to last, numbering them from one to whatever the total number of individuals is in the part of the organization that is being appraised. This effort is like trying to measure the length of an object to the closest thousandth of an inch using an ordinary straight ruler; the information needed to compare people so precisely just isn't available.

Not only does ranking create bad data, it sends the wrong message about how the organization values its talent. Instead of showing a concern for individuals and fairness in assessing them, it sends the message that the organization values structure and rules.

Another seriously flawed rating practice is forced distributions. Some organizations (for example, GE, EDS, and Accenture) require their managers to identify a certain percentage of employees who are failing, often 5–10 percent, and a certain percentage who are doing particularly well, often 15–20 percent. Jack Welch used this practice at GE, and he has argued that others should use it as well.[11] He also goes on to say that in his view, organizations should fire the employees who fall in the bottom category. Now that Welch has retired, GE no longer fires the bottom 10 percent, but it does still use the forced-distribution approach.

The forced-distribution approach ignores the reality that some work groups have no poor performers and others have no good performers. It causes managers to disown the appraisal event and say essentially, "I was just following the rules" when they deal with a "poorly" performing employee. Further, it moves the organization significantly away from a virtuous spiral environment.

Instead of employees' asking how they can improve organizational performance, the method fosters internal competition and survival of the luckiest or most political. It also can lead to the departure of valuable human capital that does not want to live in an internally competitive environment or that is evaluated as performing poorly simply because it is part of a high-performance group. In a *Wall Street Journal* interview, Steve Bennett (who left GE to become CEO of Intuit) provides the best summary evaluation of the GE forced-ranking system: "I think that's really dumb. I would never do forced rankings."

Given the problems, why do companies use the forced-distribution approach? The answer is simple but not particularly flattering to many managers. It represents an easy way to solve a classic problem: rating inflation. Just as some university professors tend to give high grades to everyone, some managers find it easier to be generous with high ratings, and, as a result, many organizations suffer from top-heavy performance appraisal scores. Instead of dealing with the problem as a failure of leadership judgment, some companies adopt a dysfunctional bureaucratic solution, mandating a result. Because it is a leadership problem, the best solution rests in creating effective leadership rather than in the top-down bureaucratic mandate of a forced-distribution system.

Managers need to be held accountable for the ratings they produce. It has to be clear that ratings must be justified by operating results that are correspondingly high. It often helps to set up cross-organizational meetings in which managers have to justify their ratings to their peers and top executives. Capital One and Intel call these "cross-calibration" meetings. Both companies have used them effectively to control rating inflation and to develop consistency in how managers use their rating scales. Overall, the best solution to rating inflation is not a bureaucratic rule: it is a set of behaviors and processes that are put in place and modeled by the leadership of the organization. In other words, senior executives need to be leaders, not bureaucrats.

All HC-centric organizations do need to rigorously assess the performance of their members and ask whether they are better off retaining and developing individuals or replacing them with talent from the outside. Whether the decision is to retain or replace is one where high-involvement organizations and global-competitor organizations may differ. Global-competitor organizations put more focus on replacement, while high-involvement organizations focus on what can be done to develop individuals who don't have the right skills.

In most situations, a three-tier rating system (some version of "walks on water," "swims," "drowns") typically provides all the information needed to handle pay increases and to identify candidates for promotion and dismissal. In certain instances, a fourth category ("too new to judge") is needed for employees who are new to the job and just learning how to perform it. PECO Energy Corporation is one company that uses only three categories: "great," "OK," and "needs improvement." This simple system provides all the information the company feels it needs to manage its employees. It replaced a five-point scale that produced ratings that were more complicated but not more useful.

PAY FOR PERFORMANCE AND DEVELOPMENT DISCUSSIONS ARE SEPARATE

Organizations need to separate the discussion of pay for performance from the discussion of development needs and activities. This means that the appraiser and the person being appraised should hold two separate discussions—one that covers past performance and the resulting pay increase or bonus, and a second, separated by at least a week, that reviews the future development and career situation of the individual. The reason for this is simple: when rewards are at risk, they tend to dominate attention and what individuals take away from an appraisal discussion. As a result, the development discussion does not get the time and attention it deserves; all too often, the discussion that it does get is overlooked or forgotten.

THE ORGANIZATION HAS (OR IS BUILDING) A SKILLS DATABASE

Information about the skill assessment of individuals needs to become a matter of record in the organization. The best way to do this is by having an intranet-based system that profiles each individual in the organization. It should include information about their skills, competencies, plans to develop new skills, and work histories. In the best of all worlds, it would also include the type of career customization information that Deloitte & Touche is now collecting from its talent.

One example: Like an increasing number of HC-centric organizations, SAS, the very successful privately owned software company, has an extensive skills database that helps managers analyze the fit between the skills the organization has and the skills it will need in the future. This helps them manage change as well as assess how likely it is that SAS can make specific changes.

ONGOING PERFORMANCE FEEDBACK IS THE NORM

All too often, the major success factor missing from the efforts of organizations to manage the performance of their members is ongoing feedback. The importance of regular, immediate feedback is captured by the following employee comment: "It doesn't do me any good to learn what I did wrong eight months ago." Immediate feedback is needed to correct performance problems.

Years of research on performance management systems have shown that designing the correct system is only part of what is required for effective performance management. In addition to the right assessment scales and the right goal-setting processes, individuals need ongoing feedback about their performance and the expectations the organization has of them. This not only makes the formal performance appraisal process work more effectively, it improves the ongoing performance of individuals.[12]

Despite the obvious positive impact of ongoing feedback, all too often managers save up their feedback and advice for a formal performance review meeting. This can be particularly inappropriate and dysfunctional when an annual review cycle is used. It is not as bad when quarterly reviews or monthly reviews are used, but even there, ongoing regular feedback outside of review meetings is desirable and makes the formal performance appraisal system more effective.

Managers have any number of reasons not to give ongoing feedback to individuals who work for them and with them, but perhaps the major one is personal discomfort. Giving feedback, particularly negative feedback, can lead to unpleasant situations and conflict. But the alternative of not giving feedback is far worse.

Clearly, one key to getting managers to give feedback to individuals is strong leadership from the top. Years ago, I was struck by some comments that Andy Grove, the then president of Intel, made. He said, "We are paid to manage organizations. To manage means to elicit better performance. We managers need to up our resolve and do what we are paid to do." This is just the right attitude for CEOs and in fact for managers throughout any HC-centric organization.

It may not always be fun, but giving ongoing feedback is one of the most important things any manager can do in an HC-centric organization. When people are counted on to make a significant difference in organizational performance, nothing is more important for a manager to do than to guide and direct their performance.

All too often managers say they just don't have enough time to do appraisals and give feedback. I find this excuse particularly inappropriate. In a managerial job, what should be more important than ensuring that the individuals who work for a manager are performing well? Nothing! If something else is more important, then the job is not a management job.

TEAM PERFORMANCE IS MANAGED AND MEASURED

Most performance management systems focus on individual performance. But some of the most important performance measurement systems in HC-centric organizations should be those that focus on groups or teams who have responsibility for a particular business process, customer, or geographical area. When teams are assessed as a whole, the members of the team are motivated to deal with the team's performance problems, which may include poorly performing team members and poor working relationships. When only individuals are appraised, team performance issues often are not addressed.

Measuring team performance is particularly important and difficult when a team has a high level of interdependence, that is, when individuals on the team need to work together closely to produce a product or a service. In these cases, it is critical that the team as a whole be assessed and that the appraisal focus on both its performance level and its capability level.

In many respects, the same principles that apply to measuring individual performance are appropriate for appraising team performance. For example, it is very important that the results of any assessment be given to the team so that it has the chance to improve its performance.

Depending on the situation, it may or may not be desirable for the manager or team leader to assess the performance of the members of a team. Doing so can take attention away from the performance of the team as a whole, and this can be dysfunctional in a situation where the work requires a high level of cooperation and teamwork. It also tends to decrease the extent to which teams are motivated to solve their performance problems, particularly those caused by poorly performing individuals.

Organizations often have team members assess each other. This can be quite powerful both as a team-building activity and as a motivator of performance improvement by individuals. It also can help guide and motivate skill development. But—and this is an important *but*—peer assessment requires the right measures and methods. It is not something that should be "just done." This is particularly true when the peer appraisals are used to determine rewards. "Gaming" the results is a real possibility if rewards for individuals are based on peer ratings.

In most cases, it is not possible to generate a profit-and-loss statement for a team. Instead of being responsible for a whole business, a team is usually responsible for part of a business or a particular customer segment. Nevertheless, it usually is possible to get at least some financial performance numbers as well as production or customer service performance numbers for a team. Obviously these are desirable; they help team members see the team's impact on the performance of the organization. Financial data also make it easier to set performance goals for the team and to reward the team based on its contribution to the overall performance of the organization.

Getting Pay for Performance Right

Pay systems warrant discussion at this point, because of their tie to performance management. This is one case where what fits a high-involvement organization does not necessarily fit a global competitor. As discussed in Chapter Three, both certainly need pay-for-performance systems as well as pay for skills systems. However, for a number of reasons they may need to use somewhat different approaches to paying for performance and skills.

High-Involvement Organizations

The key issue in the design of any pay-for-performance system is how much performance-based pay should depend on collective performance, that is group, unit, or total organization performance, and how much on individual performance. Collective pay-for-performance systems tend to have less motivational impact because they lack the clear line of sight that a well-executed individual pay-for-performance system has.[13] That said, team bonuses, profit sharing, and broad-based stock plans can be especially effective in high-involvement organizations. Organizations managed with a high-involvement approach can do more than any others to create a line of sight for individuals between their performance and organizational performance.

A clear line of sight can be developed because of the combination of open business information, knowledge about the business, and the power to influence the business that exists throughout high-involvement organizations. In addition it makes sense to emphasize collective pay for performance in high-involvement organizations because the culture is one of community and shared responsibility.[14]

The exact mix of collective pay for performance, that is stock versus profit sharing versus small group incentives, needs to be based on an organization's design. In small organizations, organizational performance usually is relatively influenceable and transparent, so it can be used to determine the amount of reward an individual gets, and hence it makes sense to have company-wide profit sharing and bonus plans. In very large organizations the line of sight for an organizational pay-for-performance approach is inevitably going to be weak even with the high-involvement approach, so it makes more sense to have business unit-based bonuses, team incentives, and in some cases gain sharing pay plans.

Every high-involvement organization should have one feature: minimal hierarchical differentiation. High-involvement organizations should have only one class of employees—first class. Cisco, Google, and many other technology firms are great examples of what this looks like in practice. It means everything from relatively few if any special perks (such as dining rooms and reserved parking spots) for senior executives through the same benefit and pay plans for all employees.

The reason for having an egalitarian environment is clear. High-involvement organizations are based on the idea of everyone being the important human capital of the organization. Giving some individuals special parking spaces, a better benefit plan, and special stock plans contradicts this and says that some individuals are more important than others. This is not a message that leads to a sense of one for all and all for one.

Because of the long-term employment relationship and participative decision making that exists in a high-involvement organization, it is very important to have broad-based stock ownership. Properly structured stock plans can act as a powerful retention device and increase organizational commitment.[15]

Since high-involvement organizations emphasize long-term employment relationships, their reward systems need to do the same thing. This is best done by giving employees stock that vests after a number of years of employment, stock options that can be exercised after a period of years, and retirement plans that accumulate value over the employee's career.

Rewarding individuals for increasing their skills in ways that are useful to the organization should be a key practice in high-involvement organizations. Because high-involvement organizations have a long-term commitment to individuals, it makes sense for them to work with their talent to develop career tracks and training programs that build their skills in areas that support the organization's business strategy.

As people acquire new skills, it is important to reward them with higher pay for multiple reasons. First, it recognizes that their market value has gone up. Second, it is a way to motivate additional skill development. Finally, it affirms that in an HC-centric organization, skills are what determine the value of talent, not what kind of job it holds or how long it has been employed.

GLOBAL COMPETITORS

Because the employment contract in global-competitor organizations is different from the high-involvement contract, the rewards system needs to be structured somewhat differently. This is especially true when global-competitor organizations have several different types of employees.

As noted earlier, global-competitor organizations often have core employees and regular employees, as well as contract and temporary employees. For core employees, global-competitor organizations need reward systems very much like those in high-involvement organizations. These people are the high-involvement core of the organization and need to be treated as long-term employees whose financial well-being is tied to company success. They also are usually in the most critical positions, and thus it makes particular sense to tie their rewards to the success of the organization and to pay them at a level above the market for individuals with their skills.

The very fact that core employees are treated differently from the rest of the workforce highlights one of the major differences between what is appropriate in a global-competitor organization and what is appropriate in a high-involvement organization. Global-competitor organizations need to and should differentiate among employees when it comes to reward system practices. They need to have core employees who get stock while others don't and who get more training and development support than others do.

Yes, different treatment may create different classes of citizens, but it is necessary given the business model that global-competitor organizations operate with. This is not to say that global-competitor organizations should automatically rule out corporate-wide stock plans, profit sharing, and other collective reward-for-performance systems. These practices may fit some global-competitor organizations, but they are much less obviously the right practices to adopt in global-competitor organizations than they are in high-involvement organizations.

The relatively short tenure of some employees and the difficulty of getting them involved in the overall business performance of the organization leads to a second major difference between global-competitor and high-involvement organizations. Because global-competitor organizations find it harder to establish a line of sight between organizational performance and individual performance, it makes sense to have more individual incentives and short-term bonus plans in these organizations. This is particularly true when it comes to contract workers and employees who are not in the core.

Bonuses can be powerful drivers of motivation in the short term, and this is exactly what is needed for contract employees, temporary employees, and other employees who are not on board for the long term. All too often organizations look at non–core employees and assume it's not even worth putting them on a pay-for-performance system because they are not long-term employees. This is a dangerous conclusion.

Since non–core employees are not highly involved in their organizations, they are unlikely to be motivated to make the organization successful or to advance their careers in the organization.

Thus a well-designed financial incentive system may be the only viable way to motivate them to perform well. Particularly since a well-designed incentive plan requires a clear statement of goals and objectives, it can be a much-needed way of managing the performance of contract and temporary employees, who often do not have an understanding of an organization's business strategy.

Competency-based pay systems that reward individuals for growing and developing their skills often don't represent as good a fit for a global-competitor organization as they do for a high-involvement organization. Since global-competitor organizations tend to be more in a buy mode when it comes to human capital, they need to take a different approach to rewarding skills and competencies.

Traditional pay systems based on job evaluations and job descriptions don't fit global-competitor organizations. They fail to recognize the special value that some individuals bring to organizations. What does fit is an approach to pay that focuses on the market value of the skills and competencies that individuals have. The key, of course, is not to just base pay on any competencies individuals happen to have; it should be based on those that are critical to their role in the organization.

To have the best individuals, global-competitor organizations need to at least match the market for individuals they recruit. In many cases, they may need to pay a premium over the market to be sure that they are seen as a very attractive place to work by those individuals who have difference-making skills.

What Is Needed

Having an effective performance management approach in organizations is clearly not simple. It requires a number of pieces to come together to create a system that directs and motivates individuals, teams, and ultimately, organizations to perform effectively. The key elements of the system need to fit together and be supported by an information system and a reward system that informs and rewards performance. The following are the key features that need to be built into performance management systems of HC-centric organizations:

- Senior management commitment to the importance of performance management

- Goals that are cascaded down the organization and are based on business strategy
- Timely assessment of performance against the goals
- Measures of the skills individuals have
- Pay based on the market value of the skills individuals have
- Separate discussions of pay and development needs
- Ongoing feedback to individuals about how they are performing
- Rewards tied to the performance measures
- The appropriate mix of rewards for individual performance, group performance, and organizational performance

CHAPTER SIX

INFORMATION AND DECISION MAKING

Front and center: That is where information about talent and organizational capabilities should be in an HC-centric organization. The right kind of human capital information is critical when it comes to decisions about strategic planning, organization design, and change management. But how can an organization determine what information it needs, and then get it to the right individuals?

Most companies track the human capital basics: how many employees they have, what their benefit and wage costs are, and the demographic characteristics of the workforce (age, diversity, and so on). And some collect attitude survey data on engagement, motivation, and satisfaction. But when it comes to issues of talent development, talent utilization, organizational capabilities, and core competencies, the information systems in most companies are underdeveloped.

Savvy and engaged HR executives know this. Consider Table 1, which is based on data from HR executives in a hundred large corporations. It presents the results of a survey that looks at the effectiveness of corporate human capital information systems.[1] The effectiveness ratings are consistently low. The lowest is perhaps the most important: systems that connect human capital practices to organizational performance. Only 9.1 percent say their systems are effective at providing data about this critical link.

All the answers to the questions about strategy are low, but one stands out: assessing and improving the human capital strategy of the company. This is one area where there is no excuse for not having effective systems.

TABLE 1. HUMAN CAPITAL INFORMATION SYSTEM EFFECTIVENESS.

How effective are the information, measurement, and analysis systems of your organization when it comes to:	Effective or Very Effective (%)
Connecting human capital practices to organizational performance	9.1
Making decisions and recommendations that reflect your company's competitive situation	30.3
Assessing the feasibility of new business strategies	20.2
Supporting organizational change efforts	40.5
Assessing and improving the human capital strategy of the company	27.6
Contributing to decisions about business strategy and human capital management	27.2
Identifying where talent has the greatest potential for strategic impact	24.2

CFOs agree. When asked how satisfied they are that the human resource information systems in their organizations allow them to assess their human capital and make decisions with human capital in mind, most CFOs in a recent survey were not satisfied.[2] Nearly half of the CFOs surveyed (47 percent) did say that the information available to them allowed them to track turnover, but that is hardly a major accomplishment, and even this number is low for such an important human capital measure. Their satisfaction level dropped dramatically—to 15 percent or less—when the issues involve "systematic workforce planning," "measuring employee skill levels," "return on human capital investment," and "measuring leadership capabilities."

So how can this situation be improved? What is needed are sophisticated human capital information systems that include metrics, analytics, and tools for finding, assessing, assigning, and managing talent. In HC-centric organizations, human capital information should be at least as available and complete as is information about financial capital, equipment, and operations.[3]

In this chapter I tackle the topic of human capital information from an overall perspective, discussing the available tools, technologies, and approaches that can be used to build an effective information system for HC-centric organizations. I then consider how decisions should be made using this and other information.

WHAT SHOULD A HUMAN CAPITAL INFORMATION SYSTEM LOOK LIKE?

Consider the very well-developed financial information systems that most companies have in place. The reason why these systems are well developed is obvious; for decades companies have considered financial capital their key asset and source of competitive advantage. In addition, companies are required to report to shareholders and the government on the condition and use of their financial assets.

Most companies also have well-developed information systems that report on their physical assets including their machinery, equipment, and natural resources. Good manufacturing companies, for example, know a lot about their equipment. They have extensive equipment maintenance records, production records, and depreciation records. They calculate the return on their equipment purchases and develop other metrics, which guide their movement and use of assets. In short, they take their physical assets seriously and try to optimize their utilization. But they don't just stop there; they also include in their reports to shareholders and regulatory groups how the assets are performing.

In many respects what is needed for human capital is exactly the same kind of attention that is paid to the physical and financial assets of a company. This is true whether a company is a high-involvement or a global-competitor organization. Admittedly some of the procedures that apply to physical and financial capital are not directly applicable to human capital, but the vigor and analytic focus with which information is pursued is applicable. Without it, human capital management cannot be a source of competitive advantage.

INFORMATION ABOUT INDIVIDUALS

The starting point for any human capital information system should be information about individual employees. It is needed for business strategists to make the connection between the specific characteristics that employees bring to the organization and the successful development and execution of the company's strategy. At minimum, companies need to be able to answer these two questions: What business skills and relevant competencies does each individual employee have? And to what degree are those skills and competencies used in their current work assignments?

To create a complete system, companies also need to gather data from individuals about their motivation and about their attitudes toward work, career, and the organization. Specifically, they need data that reflect the degree to which individuals are motivated to perform their jobs, whether they plan to continue to work for the organization, and how well they understand the organization's business plan and organizational model.

Business understanding is particularly important because it is a key determinant of whether individuals can self-manage and provide the kind of competitive advantage that HC-centric organizations need. HC-centric organizations can only have a competitive advantage if they have well-trained, motivated individuals who understand the business model and are capable of executing it.

Because high-involvement organizations are designed to involve employees in business decisions, they need to put a particularly strong emphasis on the degree to which individuals understand the business, get information about the business, and feel that they can influence it. From a metrics point of view, this means that high importance should be placed on measures that focus on whether individuals understand the business and whether they feel they can influence decisions.

American Standard

American Standard is a large corporation operating in a variety
of businesses. It has more than sixty thousand employees in
twenty-eight countries. Because of its size and diversity, American
Standard can calculate the relationship between human capital metrics and business unit performance. Recognizing this,
Larry Costello, American Standard's senior vice president of
HR, hired McBassi & Company to do an attitude survey that
assessed the organization's competencies and capabilities, and to
relate the results of that survey to organizational performance.
The performance outcomes that McBassi studied included
sales, employee turnover and retention, safety, and customer
satisfaction.

The results of this study showed a direct relationship between
managers' performance in a number of areas and the financial
and safety performance of their business units. For example,
plants where managers scored in the top half on an index of talent management practices had an average safety incident rate
that was 14 percent better than those in the bottom half. This
analysis provided a powerful incentive for the corporation to document the most effective practices it was able to identify and then
introduce them throughout the organization.

In another analysis, McBassi found that district sales offices
that scored better in developing managerial talent produced
higher financial results. Managers in an office with a below-
average development score produced $1 million less revenue
than their counterparts with an above-average score. Again,
this result provided a strong indication of where change efforts
should be focused in order to improve sales.

Ultimately, this research allowed American Standard to
develop a "decision science" for its human capital management.
The analytic information that American Standard now has (and
the understanding of how to monitor and update that information) is guiding the investment of its HR budget based on where
additional investments of time and money are likely to pay off.

As of this writing, American Standard has not made the full
results of its survey public, but it clearly contains the kind of
information that investment analysts would find useful. It has the
potential to provide analysts with indicators of the organizational

competencies and capabilities that are directly related to the performance of the organization. By tracking these indicators over time, American Standard can point to improvements that it has made in its internal management processes and the effect that these improvements have had on the bottom line.

Adequate data on individuals are likely to be available only if, in addition to having an effective performance management system, an organization conducts regular (and well-developed) attitude surveys that monitor how individuals feel about their work and their organization. An annual survey should be a key piece of this data capture, and regular short "pulse" surveys should be used to provide important insights on employee attitudes about current events, business initiatives, short-term operational effectiveness, and changes in the organization.

When Web-based pulse surveys are used, employees, senior managers, and key individuals throughout the organization can be given immediate information about what other employees think. Pulse surveys can be particularly helpful at a time of change and turmoil, as they can provide a real-time guide to change. One powerful approach is to do a partial sample of the organization every few weeks; another is to do all employees in the organization and feed the data back to work groups, teams, and business units so that managers and employees can understand how their particular part of the organization is functioning.

Short pulse surveys should be complemented by longer annual surveys that measure motivation, satisfaction, and commitment, or what is increasingly called *engagement*. The results of these surveys should include a comparison to other companies' results and the results of past surveys. Needless to say, an HC-centric organization is unlikely to be successful if its results are not better than those of most other organizations.

Consumer-oriented firms should consider comparing the quality of their human capital information to the quality of their customer information. Good marketing-oriented firms have well-developed metrics and analytics capabilities with respect to their customer bases. As a result, they know a lot about the characteristics of their customers. They understand their customers' wants and needs, and they are constantly striving to improve their predictions of customer reactions to new products and new services. At the very least, HC-centric organizations should have the same capability when it comes to their talent.

Some corporations have established key performance indicators (KPIs) when it comes to human capital. These often get reported as part of a dashboard or balanced scorecard on the condition of the organization and its human capital.[4] For example, Cisco Systems considers building talent a priority and includes on its dashboard measures that show how many people change jobs and the reasons why they move. This KPI allows Cisco executives to quickly identify divisions that are developing talent and those that are not. Since talent management is a major objective, Cisco follows up by rewarding those managers and business units that contribute to corporate talent development.

Typical human capital KPIs include turnover, revenue and profit per employee, success in recruiting, diversity, health and safety, voluntary resignations, and absenteeism. Having these measures is important and worthwhile but not sufficient when it comes to the information that needs to be available in an HC-centric organization. Other metrics must be developed that are related to the business plan and the degree to which individuals are key contributors to the success of the business strategy. With this in mind, the following are examples of the kind of human capital management metrics that organizations should consider collecting:

- Hiring of individuals with key skills as compared to plan
- Retention of key skills and targeted employees
- Condition of talent inventory
- Percentage of individual development plans implemented
- Success rate of individual development plans
- Employer brand in the minds of job applicants and employees
- Employee satisfaction
- Employee motivation
- Employee commitment
- Age distributions by positions and skills

- Employee understanding of the business strategy
- On-time and effective performance reviews
- Bench strength for key positions and skills

These are sample metrics; not all are appropriate for every organization, nor do they represent all the metrics that any particular firm should collect. They do represent the kind of metrics that, when combined with measures of organizational effectiveness, are needed to assess whether an organization can gain a competitive advantage as a result of its ability to organize and manage its talent.

THE NEXT LEVEL: INFORMATION ABOUT ORGANIZATIONAL EFFECTIVENESS

To have a competitive advantage, it is not enough to assemble a group of great individuals; the individuals must function together in ways that deliver outstanding organizational performance. That is why HC-centric companies also need to monitor and assess their organizational capabilities and core competencies. Organizations need to know what the skills and competencies of their talent add up to. Do they lead to better customer service? Higher-quality products? More innovation? Faster product development?

An old saying is worth repeating here: what gets measured gets attention (that is, gets done). HC-centric organizations are designed to gain a competitive edge by their ability to have their human capital perform in ways that differentiate them. To make this more than a hope, they need to measure the performance areas that differentiate them and understand how the management of talent can make outstanding levels of performance possible.

Talent must be organized, led, trained and developed in ways that lead to the development of the right core competencies and organizational capabilities. HC-centric organizations' capabilities and competencies are their means of creating value. Measuring them is as important as counting inventory and keeping track of cash.

To do an adequate job of measuring competencies and capabilities, organizations need to identify what the most important competencies and capabilities are for each of their key products, services, and business units, then they need to focus on how they can be measured.

At least an annual assessment is needed of how well an organization is doing in developing its competencies and capabilities. Their development needs to be looked at relative to the skills and competencies of individuals and of course to the relationship they have to the financial performance of the business.

The relationship to business success is critical because it helps develop an understanding of what leads to business success. Understanding this is critical to the development of future strategies, the management processes in an organization, and investment decisions concerning organization and human capital development.

Executives in HC-centric organizations need to think hard about which competencies and capabilities are important enough to warrant measurement at the business unit and organization level. The organization's strategic intent should drive this decision. Kaplan and Norton's *Strategy Maps* approach provides one disciplined way to decide which capabilities to measure.[5] A completed "strategy map" can show how key competencies and capabilities lead to the implementation and success of a strategy.

The important point is that an HC-centric organization must measure and constantly monitor its make-or-break competencies and capabilities. Measurement is necessary from the point of view of both strategy development and process improvement. As research on quality has shown, it is very difficult to improve a process without good metrics on how the process is operating and how it performs. Unlike financial analysis, which often shows only that you need to change, analysis of capabilities shows *what* you need to change, and it can be an indicator of performance long before the financial numbers warn you that something needs attention.

Providing metrics data can be a powerful source of motivation to improve capabilities, particularly when the metrics are used for goal setting in performance management systems and are tied to rewards. In addition, without measurement it is difficult to alter anything when an important change in the environment calls for improved levels of performance. Thus good measurement of capabilities is important both from an operating performance perspective and from a change management perspective.

In a *Harvard Business Review* article, Dave Ulrich and Norm Smallwood offer a good example of how an organization can use measures of organizational capabilities.[6] Ulrich and Smallwood asked InterContinental Hotel executives to assess their company on both the actual state and the desired state of their capabilities. The results showed that for the firm to execute its current strategy, it needed a great improvement in collaboration and speed. In the areas of shared mind-set and accountability, however, the company was already at a satisfactory level. This analysis provided important momentum toward change. Once the results were broadly shared within the organization, InterContinental's staff began improving their collaboration and speed.

The adoption of the balanced scorecard approach to measuring and reporting organization performance usually increases an organization's focus on competencies and capabilities. Although the implementation of this approach varies enormously from company to company, it always includes some nonfinancial metrics: customers' perspectives, key internal processes, and the learning and growth activities of the organization.[7] The details of what is measured under these three nonfinancial areas should vary significantly from organization to organization, as they need to reflect a company's particular identity and strategic intent. However, the scorecards of HC-centric organizations should always include metrics of the organization's competencies and capabilities. In combination with the customer perspective and financial performance measures, these metrics provide a comprehensive look at how the organization is able to perform and how well it is performing.

ANALYTICS

It is impossible to determine the kinds of human capital measures that need to be collected and how they should be interpreted without using analytic models. Data aren't useful unless they can inform strategic and operational decision making.[8] Doing this requires answering two questions: What are the important determinants of each human capital metric? and What are the consequences of the metric being at different levels? Only if these two questions are answered can human capital data be fully and effectively used.

Admittedly, even without a thorough analysis, it may be easy to get agreement that on most measures it is better to have positive results than to have negative results. For example, most organizations want to have low turnover and low absenteeism. They also want to have workers who are highly motivated to do a good job. Many other behaviors can be measured and made part of an organization's information system. The challenge is to identify the ones among them that are particularly critical from an organizational performance point of view and to determine what the optimal level for each metric is.

What makes metrics critical is not just that they measure performance in a meaningful way but that they themselves can be influenced by things that the organization can control and change. Also important is the cost-effectiveness of making changes to improve performance in a particular area.

Turnover is a behavior that most organizations are concerned about, and one that is frequently measured. Without question, it often is costly, and in many cases reductions in it can in fact improve organizational performance. But reducing it may not be worth the cost in all cases.

For example, reducing turnover may not be cost-effective if the job is very low-skilled and the supply of replacement labor is plentiful. This can also be true if the job is a particularly non-critical one in terms of its impact on revenues and costs. On the other hand, in an HR-centric organization often even a small decrease in turnover can result both in cost savings and revenue increases (for example, in the case of skilled salespeople and technical workers).

Effective analytic efforts can identify what causes various measures to change, what the consequences are of their changing, and how cost-effective it is to improve the behavior that is measured. This is the information that is needed to make judgments about how an organization can and should improve its performance.

All too often organizations fail to do the kind of analysis of their measures that tells them how they should act. In Chapter Four, one key to an effective analytic strategy was mentioned: identifying pivotal skills and jobs. Analysis of what the key skills are suggests where in an organization to intervene to improve organizational performance. Specifically analytics can suggest how much improving certain skills can impact performance.

Of course a key consideration here is the cost and feasibility of improving the skills of individuals in the targeted area and how much that will improve organizational performance. It may be desirable, but is it cost-effective? This is precisely the kind of question that analytic models can answer for organizations.

Baseball provides an interesting example of the evolution of metrics. Earlier I discussed the Oakland A's Billy Beane and his approach to talent management, as chronicled in the book *Moneyball*. His analysis pointed to on-base percentage as a key indicator of an individual's worth to the team. Missing from this analysis, however, is the financial impact of winning and the cost of players' salaries.

The Cleveland Indians are among the teams that employ a model that goes significantly beyond the *Moneyball* example.[9] It focuses on WARP or "Wins Above Replacement Player" in order to determine the wisdom of hiring specific free agents. It starts with an analysis that shows how many more wins a team would achieve by having a player with a certain performance level. By taking the number of wins and translating it into revenue, this formula makes it possible to compute the dollar value of a player. The next step is to look at what it will cost to hire a player and to decide whether it is worth it from the point of view of revenue enhancement. This of course is the key issue in today's free agent baseball talent market.

One of the more interesting issues this analysis raises is whether a team should try to optimize the number of wins it achieves in a season. Reaching a decision about this requires an analysis of how wins affect the revenue of the team. This is not a simple analysis because revenue comes from multiple sources— media rights, attendance, parking, merchandise, and concessions. There also is the value of the franchise, which may be influenced by its talent and win-loss record. It may be that extra wins do not bring in extra revenue. As a result, the organization's most profitable strategy may well be to have lower-paid employees because it will not greatly reduce revenue but will reduce costs (the Chicago Cubs may be an example here).

Many kinds of analyses must be done to provide decision makers with the information they need for informed decision making about organizational improvement efforts. Most of them are very similar to the kind of analysis that often goes on when an organization is buying a new piece of equipment or acquiring additional capital. Alternatives are explored with respect to cost and their impact on performance.

The final choice of a piece of equipment or a source of capital is based on this analysis. The same kind of analysis is appropriate when it comes to making decisions about human capital, whether it involves raising the compensation of a particular group of employees, changing the design of jobs, providing training, or outsourcing part of the organization's work. Careful analysis needs to be done that includes valid and comprehensive data about what the current situation is and what the likely results of the change to a new policy or practice are.

In addition to informing and improving decisions about changes, analytics should be used to decide which KPI measures are the most appropriate focus of the organization. As noted earlier, many possible human capital and organizational performance measures can be monitored. Collecting data on all of them and monitoring all of them clearly runs the danger of creating an enormous overload in most organizations. What is needed is a thoughtful evaluation of the available measures and the identification of those that have a particularly critical impact on organizational performance.

IMPACT OF PUBLIC REPORTING

Public companies spend a great deal of money and time preparing the financial statements they issue to their shareholders. In HC-centric organizations, the issues involving the reporting of performance go beyond whether they share accurate financial results with their investors and employees. They need to address important issues concerning something not usually reported to investors: the condition of their talent, core competencies, and organizational capabilities.

Organizations are not required to report on the condition of their talent or their capabilities, and most do not report either internally or externally on anything but financial accounting metrics. In many cases, this is because they simply don't have the measures; in other cases, it is because they have chosen not to. Yet measures of talent and organizational capabilities are often precisely the kind of leading performance indicators that investors, customers, and employees of an HC-centric organization want and need in order to make decisions.

All too often the only thing about an organization's talent in annual reports is photos of the senior executives and perhaps a group photo of happy, smiling employees. A study by Haig Nalbantian and Rich Guzzo has documented just how little information there actually is in corporate annual reports about human capital.[10] About 90 percent of the annual reports studied contained some mention of the company's workforce, but most of them included little or no discussion of how human capital management fits into the company's business strategy. They also failed to include measurements of the quality, cost, and nature of the company's human capital management programs.

Only 14 percent of the companies actually provided at least one hard indicator of workforce behavior. The most common number was the turnover rate. Some also provided limited data from an employee attitude survey. Obviously, one hard data measure is a very low standard for companies reporting on their human capital management, yet few companies meet even that.

Fully understanding a company's human capital management programs and practices requires multiple measures that are consistently reported over a period of years. Virtually no company reports annually on the same indicators. Instead, they tend to pick an indicator or two that support a point they want to make about how they've improved their talent management. Typically lacking is any kind of standard against which to assess the number and any historical trend with respect to the particular measure.

These days organizations are increasingly issuing sustainability annual reports. These reports are a possible place to report on how working for an organization affects people. Most of these reports, however, focus almost completely on the environment, virtually ignoring the workforce. For example, the 2006 Weyerhaeuser report does discuss human capital issues, but it only presents data on accident rates and diversity in management positions, nothing else. It also fails to show how these data have changed over time.

At the present time public reporting of data other than financial accounting is not required in any country. This may well change as more and more of the value of corporations consists of intangibles and can only be understood by looking at nonfinancial measures. Right now, however, investors have to rely on statements by management and their perceptions of how well a company is able to execute its business plans when they assess its intangibles. This often results in inaccurate judgments and therefore in the quite erroneous market valuations for some organizations.

A movement toward some type of uniform reporting practices with respect to areas like customer relationships, organizational capabilities, and the condition of the organization's human capital could provide much-needed data to investors, as well as to potential employees. It also could stimulate a much greater focus inside organizations on these areas and how they are related to financial results.

One effort to add human capital metrics to an organization's public reporting was tried by the R. G. Barry company in the 1970s.[11] Its annual report included information on the dollar value of its human capital. Although this was an interesting and brave move on the company's part, it did not catch on and ultimately it was discontinued. Part of the problem with this approach is that the company used financial metrics and concepts to report on the condition of individuals. This led to various problems including how employees felt when they were told that they were being depreciated and that their value was dropping.

I believe a better approach to public reporting on human capital is to report some of the metrics that many organizations already collect, such as turnover rates, employee attitude scores, and the cost numbers associated with human capital management (for example, training and development, turnover). Reporting these kinds of data would at least give investors an idea of what's happening with the human capital of an organization. It also might provide an incentive for organizations to do a better job in human capital management because their activities in these areas would become transparent to the investor community.

Graphic Controls Reports to Its Shareholders

In 1975, the senior management team of Graphic Controls, led by CEO William Clarkson, decided to begin measuring the "quality of work life" in the corporation. Data were collected on satisfaction, turnover, and absenteeism, and the findings were shared with all employees. The company's leaders found the assessment process useful and decided to conduct an annual assessment of the quality of work life in the corporation. They then made an unusual and pioneering decision: to include the data from these assessments of work life at Graphic Controls in their annual reports to Graphic Controls shareholders.

In 1977, they made good on the commitment to provide their shareholders with human capital information by issuing an annual report that included independently collected and analyzed data on work life at Graphic Controls. It covered several years of data, so that changes could be assessed. While I was at the Institute for Social Research of the University of Michigan, Phil Mirvis and I gathered the data and wrote the report.[12] It included data on accidents, wages, minority employment, promotions, job satisfaction, absenteeism, and turnover. The Graphic Controls report was a first. Prior to its issuance, no publicly traded U.S. corporation had included in its annual report independently collected and analyzed data on a broad range of critical human capital issues.

To assess the impact of providing human capital data, Graphic Controls included a reader survey in the annual report. This survey was completed by 142 people, of whom 47 percent were shareholders and 34 percent employees. Roughly 70 percent of the respondents indicated they were very interested in the human capital data, while 10 percent said they were not at all interested. Nearly two-thirds said the information on human capital was as important to them as was the financial data. Sixty percent responded that the report supplied them sufficient information on human capital, while nearly one-fourth said they would like more data. Overall, 85 percent indicated the data contributed to their understanding of the company and 81 percent found it to be an important resource in evaluating the condition of the company.

(Continued)

Finally, more than two-thirds said they favored other corporations' issuing such reports. Analysts, employees, and shareholders all indicated a great interest in human capital data and favored the issuance of a public assessment of a corporation's human capital.

Graphic Controls was committed to providing human capital data in each of its future reports; however, in late 1997, it was acquired by Times-Mirror Corporation, and as a result issued no more annual reports. Times-Mirror ended the practice of gathering and reporting human capital data.

HC-centric firms need to do more than just report to investors; they need to make an active effort to share their human capital metrics with their employees. Sharing performance results with all employees has a number of advantages, most notably helping employees understand the business better and as a result understand when and how they need to change.[13]

INFORMATION SHARING

Table 2 presents survey results concerned with how much Fortune 1000 corporations communicate information about their business results.[14] Every organization in the study is a public corporation and, by law, must provide financial information to shareholders. At a minimum, it seems that even low-cost operators would give their employees the same information they give their shareholders in their annual reports. So if anything is surprising about the degree to which Fortune 1000 organizations share financial information with their employees, it is that the number of organizations that share company financial results with all employees is so low (73 percent).

The results could be shared simply by distributing the annual report to all employees. The obvious conclusion is that in a significant number of companies, many employees are not treated as important stakeholders in or contributors to the company's performance, something that certainly is not consistent with being an HC-centric organization.

TABLE 2. PERCENTAGE OF EMPLOYEES RECEIVING INFORMATION (2005).

Information Sharing Practice	None or Almost None (0–20%)	Some (21–40%)	About Half (41–60%)	Most (61–80%)	All or Almost All (81–100%)
Corporate operating results	5	8	4	11	73
Unit operating results	2	13	11	25	49
New technologies	11	28	12	25	25
Business plans and goals	3	12	10	18	56
Competitors' performance	18	27	15	21	18

Although important in helping employees view the business as a whole, information about the overall performance of a large company may, for practical purposes, be of limited use to many employees. The corporate operating results are a considerable distance from their job activities and may not relate directly to what they do. Information on their unit's operating results is likely to be much more meaningful to most employees.

As the table shows, a total of 74 percent of the companies share data on the performance of their work unit with more than 60 percent of their employees. However, more than one-quarter of all companies do not regularly share unit operating results with most employees. This, of course, is just the kind of information most employees need to receive if they are to be involved in and care about the business of their organization.

The data on information sharing about new technologies show a low level of sharing. Only 50 percent of the corporations say they provide most of their employees with information about new technologies that may affect them. Without information about new technologies, employees cannot participate in the planning activities involved in the start-up of new technology, nor can they influence decisions about its adoption and acquisition. Lack of information concerning new technologies also prevents employees from knowing what skills and knowledge they need to develop in order to use a new technology and manage their careers.

Seventy-four percent of companies provide most employees with information on the plans and goals of the business. This is obviously a key information area with respect to employees' participating in problem-solving groups, self-managing work teams, and strategy or planning groups.

It is clear from the data in Table 2 that the typical employee gets limited information about competitors' business performance. Only 39 percent of the organizations provide data on competitors' performance to most or all employees. This is an important point because it means that most employees cannot make informed judgments about whether their business is winning or losing in the market, an unacceptable condition in any HC-centric organization but particularly disturbing in the case of a high-involvement organization.

It goes without saying that the kinds of information in Table 2 need to be shared with most, if not all, employees in HC-centric organizations. This is particularly true of high-involvement organizations. Without this information it is impossible for employees to participate in many of the workplace decisions that are part of influencing an organization's strategy and operations.

It is particularly important that all employees in high-involvement organizations know about the performance of their business unit and their products. Often in large organizations it is difficult for individuals to understand how they can influence the results of a total organization, so giving them results about their part of the organization is important. It allows managers to establish meaningful goals for individuals and their part of the organization and it allows them to talk about the business and its strategy in a meaningful way. It also provides a transparency that allows everyone to understand how their part of the organization is operating and to make the kinds of improvements and changes that are necessary to improve business unit performance.

KNOWLEDGE DEVELOPMENT

Employee involvement research shows that in order to have effective involvement in decisions, an organization needs to develop the skills and knowledge of its employees.[15] In other words, it's not enough to simply move decisions down the organization—the information needed to make decisions as well as the knowledge to make them needs to be moved to the location where the decisions are being made. Failure to do this is a prescription for major problems. It provides someone with a decision-making power but not with the tools to make decisions effectively.

Table 3 also draws on the survey of Fortune 1000 companies.[16] It presents results that cover the type of training individuals need to be effective in a high-involvement organization that uses group decision making and shares financial data with its employees.

Overall the results suggest that most organizations do not do what they need to do to give their employees the skills they need to be involved in business decisions. Most train less than 50 percent of their employees in group decision making and understanding the

Table 3.   Percentage of Employees Receiving Training in Interpersonal
and Group Skills in the Past Three Years (2005).

	None or Almost None (0–20%)	Some (21–40%)	About Half (41–60%)	Most (61–80%)	All or Almost All (81–100%)
Group decision-making and problem solving skills	40	34	11	12	3
Leadership skills	21	49	18	7	5
Team-building skills	26	41	18	9	7
Skills in understanding business	38	37	13	5	7

business. The failure to train most employees in understanding the business is particularly disappointing.

Understanding the business is the fundamental building block of high-involvement organizations. Without this understanding employees not only are unlikely to be able to participate in many kinds of decision making, they are also unlikely to be able to self-manage, operate in teams, and be motivated by business results. Although also a negative for global-competitor organizations, this kind of training is not as major a concern for them. They do not expect individuals to be generally involved in business decisions and for individuals to be strongly committed to the organization.

INFORMATION AND KNOWLEDGE MEET DECISION MAKING

One of the major features of any organization is where and how decisions are made. It is inseparable from the issue of what kind of information is gathered, how it is communicated, and the knowledge individuals have. In the traditional hierarchal organization, the most important decisions are supposed to be made at the very highest levels of the organization. The reason for this is obvious: that is where it is assumed the information is located and where the greatest decision-making and analytic expertise rest.

For certain kinds of decisions, particularly major strategic decisions, few would argue with the position that the final decisions are best made at the very top of the organization. This is true whether the organization is a traditional hierarchical one or an HC-centric organization that has adopted the principles of employee involvement.

However, my research on high-involvement organizations strongly suggests that using decision processes that involve people throughout an organization can have a significant positive impact on organizational performance.[17] Thus, in high-involvement HC-centric organizations, it is critical that individuals throughout the organization have their say when major decisions are made. This is critical, because they often have a great deal of valid and useful information that can improve the decision, and their participation leads to their accepting the ultimate decision.

In global-competitor organizations, it is also important to gather information from knowledgeable individuals, but the effort can be more targeted because participation in decision making in this management approach often doesn't include strategy decisions. It is more likely to involve strategy implementation with respect to operations, customer service, and work method improvements.

Where operational decisions are made needs to be heavily influenced by an organization's design. Regardless of whether the organization takes a high-involvement approach or a global-competitor approach, decisions need to be made so they are close to the point where relevant information is generated and action needs to be taken. For example, in a business unit most of the major business decisions and change decisions need to be made at some level in that business unit, not at the corporate level. The specific level of hierarchy where each decision should be made in the business unit needs to reflect the reality of who understands and has a line of sight with respect to the business, which in turn is determined by how much information is shared by an organization.

One more point on the difference between high-involvement and global-competitor organizations. Given the long-term employment relationships characteristic of high-involvement organizations, the opportunity exists for managers in them to get individuals involved in a wide range of participative decision-making activities.

Often creating self-managing work teams and strategic task forces takes a considerable amount of time and a special set of skills on the part of employees. In a high-involvement organization, skill development and the building of teams is a logical and prudent investment. However, this type of investment may not be logical in a global-competitor organization because of the potentially transitory nature of the employment relationship.

In global-competitor organizations, it may only make sense to have extensive employee involvement in decisions that can be made in relatively short periods of time and implemented quickly. One exception to this, of course, is for employees who are the core members of a global-competitor organization. Because their commitment to the organization is expected to be long term they are good candidates to be involved in strategy development decisions and decisions concerning the evolution of the business model of the organization.

WHAT IS NEEDED

The following information and decision practices should be present in all HC-centric organizations:

- Sophisticated human capital information systems that focus on the condition of the organization's talent
- Analytic models that assess the impact of human capital management practices
- Measures of the condition of an organization's core competencies and capabilities
- An effective communication program for sharing business results and information with all employees
- Public reporting of the condition of an organization's human capital
- Decision processes that involve individuals in key decisions with respect to human capital management and future directions of the business

Overall, what has been learned about decision processes and HC-centric organizations is captured in the following points:

- Major strategic change decisions need to be made at the top level of organizations based on input from metrics that reflect the organization's performance capabilities and financial performance.
- Decisions about improving ongoing operations and existing processes are often best made at the level of the organization where these processes are centered and managed. In particular, input from employees can improve decision quality.
- It is critical to create an alignment between decision processes, information processes, and organization structure.

- Making information about organization performance and strategies available to all employees is an important way to improve decision quality and decision acceptance.
- Organizations that involve employees effectively in decision making perform better; as a result, they have a competitive advantage.
- High-involvement organizations need a strong and comprehensive emphasis on sharing financial information with employees. They need to give them the skills and knowledge to understand, and ultimately to influence, business strategy and business operations.

CHAPTER SEVEN

REINVENTING HR

You would think that in most organizations, the HR department would be a key player: gathering and disseminating information about talent, helping to develop and implement strategy, and developing practices and systems that motivate individual employees to ever-higher levels of performance. The reality, however, is that this is not the case in most organizations.

Often the HR department is essentially an administrative function, handling payroll, benefits processing, and formal training programs.[1] Even HR departments that conduct regular employee attitude surveys and report and interpret results of talent assessments most often have limited or intermittent connections to the development and implementation of their organization's strategy.

An enormous opportunity exists for the leaders of HR functions in all organizations, but especially in HC-centric organizations, to enhance the role of their departments. The need exists for a function that makes it its business to develop and integrate all the elements of organizing and managing talent into a coordinated approach that fits the business strategy. I believe that HR departments that do not meet this need face a growing threat of elimination or at best impotence.

HC-centric organizations have no choice: someone must take on the responsibility for determining how talent is organized and managed. Three approaches are possible:

- The existing HR function can transform itself and become the go-to unit for human capital issues.
- The company's leaders can replace the existing HR staff with individuals who are up to the challenge and make the new HR department the go-to unit.

- The administrative tasks of the HR department can be outsourced or with the help of information technology done by a much-reduced HR department. Senior executives not in HR can enlarge their roles to include doing what it takes to make talent a competitive advantage.

In some HC-critical organizations, HR is not and never has been a major player when it comes to talent management and organizational effectiveness. For example, in universities, professional service firms, and law firms, when it comes to key human capital issues, the line managers simply do not have HR involved beyond basic administrative activities. The line managers themselves recruit, select, train, develop, and organize the professional staff of these organizations. The same thing is also true of sports teams, where player personnel management is usually the province of a line manager, not an HR manager. Most of the important staffing decisions are made by the general manager and president. A separate administrative function worries about HR administration.

An approach that gives the responsibility for human capital to line management has some real strengths. However, it has a major weakness that prevents it from being the best choice for most large organizations. First of all, it can make unreasonable demands on the operating managers' time. And it usually fails to incorporate into decisions the kind of fact-based and research-based human capital knowledge that can be brought to decisions involving human capital when an effective human resource management function exists.

What I believe is needed in most organizations is an HR function that combines administration with expertise in human capital management and organizational effectiveness. This chapter first explores in more depth the current state of HR in most companies, and then turns to how HR can and should operate in HC-centric organizations.

THE CURRENT STATE OF HR

HR has historically not been considered one of the most important departments in organizations. Many of the reasons for this still exist today, as a result most HR functions are less important and less well staffed than most finance departments, information services departments, and marketing departments. It's worth examining the current state of HR departments before we consider their future. It needs to be acknowledged and understood before we consider how they should perform in an HC-centric organization.

ADMINISTRATIVE DEMANDS

The administrative side of HR has been, and continues to be, an increasingly complex and time-intensive activity. As a result, it is easy for HR to become overly focused on executing it. In many organizations, the execution of basic HR administration has diverted HR from addressing issues concerned with talent development, organization design, and organizational effectiveness. When somebody doesn't get a paycheck or is having trouble with medical coverage, it is hard for HR to say, "We'll get to that later; we're currently working on a new competency model for the organization."

But before falling into the trap of describing HR as a victim, I need to note that it often is a willing participant in its relegation to an administrative role. HR managers tend to be comfortable dealing with administrative activities. Often these issues are relatively straightforward and involve solvable problems that provide a sense of accomplishment and positive feedback. As such, they become a power source, or at least a survival source, for the HR function and its staff. Administrative issues provide HR with a tangible reason for existence and an area of competence that no one else in the organization has. Thus the HR function often justifies its existence by pointing out the important contributions it makes with respect to HR administration.

Many HR departments used to get some of their power from arguing that they were uniquely positioned and skilled when it came to handling unions and labor law issues. The efforts of HR helped keep union organizing drives at bay, and helped keep companies out of legal difficulties with respect to employment law. Today, union organizing is not a major issue in most organizations, but organizations still can and do face a growing number of potential employment law issues. Thus HR still has the option—and perhaps uses it all too often—of arguing that its most important role is keeping the organization out of legal problems.

Unfortunately, acting as a watchdog often leads to HR being considered a hindrance to effective talent management rather than an aid. In one company that I know of, the CEO refers to the HR function as the BPU—the "business prevention unit"—because, according to him, all his HR function does is tell him why he can't do things and what he can't do; it rarely contributes ideas about how things can be done better within the law and regulations, much less in order to gain a competitive advantage.

HR STAFFING

One reason why HR often is not a key player is the quality of the staffing in HR. All too often, high-potential, business-savvy individuals do not want to join the HR function because it is mired in administrivia and compliance. They see joining the HR function as a career dead end, and all too often it has turned out to be one.

HR used to be known as personnel administration. It switched to HR in the 1980s in an effort to improve its image and expand the type of issues it focused on. Clearly some change has happened, but HR is still not a player in the way finance and marketing are.[2] Among the indicators of this is that HR often looks like a silo from a career development point of view. The best individuals progress up the hierarchy within HR but rarely end up as the CEO or for that matter running a business unit. They simply don't get the kind of exposure and training that is needed to understand a business and to develop and implement business strategies. Thus, although they may move up the hierarchy in HR, they rarely move to a general management position, much less a CEO job.

CORPORATE BOARDS

HR can and should provide expertise to corporate boards in a number of areas. Research by my Center for Effective Organizations shows that the primary support activity of the HR function is in the area of executive compensation.[3] In second place is executive succession. These are clearly areas where HR should provide support to boards, whether organizations are HC-centric or not.

Disappointingly low on the list of support areas are issues involving strategy and talent management on an organization-wide basis. For example, information about the condition and capability of the workforce, change consulting, and strategic readiness are at the bottom of the list of activities that boards use the HR function for. In an HC-centric organization, these are the very areas where boards should focus their attention and receive help from HR.

Why don't boards use HR for more activities related to organizational effectiveness? One possible explanation is that they don't think of HR as a source of information and expertise concerning organizational effectiveness. A second explanation is that they do not trust the HR function to provide good data and advice in these areas. A third, less likely, explanation is that they simply don't regard information and advice about talent, change, and strategic readiness as useful in their decision making. Whatever the reason, this condition should not exist in an HC-centric organization.

As discussed further in Chapter Eight, boards should ask for and get information on strategic readiness, the condition and capability of the workforce, and change management from somewhere. If it is not from the HR function, then, as discussed later in this chapter, maybe it should come from a new function that provides an integrated look at the capabilities, strategic readiness, and effectiveness of the organization.

WHAT HR SHOULD DO

For the last several decades, writings on what HR should be doing have emphasized HR becoming more and more of a "business partner."[4] I may be in the minority here, but I've become increasingly unhappy with that term; for me it "protests too much." (You don't see the people in finance calling themselves "business partners," do you? No. They *are* business partners—so they don't have to say it.)

When HR executives claim the title "business partner" they invite the rest of the organization to identify and highlight all that they *don't* do. Better to say, simply, that HR should be adding more value to the organization, and go from there. Then the question becomes where and how can HR add value? At this point, few in the HR community would argue that HR should mainly be concerned with the administrative side of its role. There is general recognition that HR should become more of a player when it comes to business strategy and organizational effectiveness. But data collected by me and by others strongly suggest that this sort of change is extremely difficult to pull off.

In 1995, HR executives reported that their function spent about 77 percent of its time on administration and providing services; in 2004, they reported spending exactly the same amount of time.[5] Interestingly enough, in both 2004 and 1995, when asked how much time they spent five years ago in this area, they reported a much higher number. In other words, they reported that they had decreased the percentage of their time spent on HR administration, but the historical data do not support their contention. This clearly suggests that HR executives are in denial when it comes to the amount of progress they are making in moving away from being an administrative center to being a strategic player.

It does not mean, however, that HR must be forever mired in administration. A piece of the problem, I suspect, is that HR executives have attempted to add additional responsibilities and activities onto their basic set of administrative responsibilities without allowing themselves time to step back and consider the whole. This is understandable: enrollment periods cycle around; payrolls must be processed; there can be little if any time to look at the big picture. But doing administration well is not the way to establish credibility as a strategic resource in an HC-centric organization. It is a necessary precondition, but that is all it is.

What is needed is for HR leaders in HC-centric organizations to redefine the core purpose of their function and then use that new definition to inform decision making going forward. I think that in the new definition HR should have three major responsibilities:

- *HR administration:* Providing high-quality, low-cost HR services to all employees of the organization.

- *Business support:* Helping the managers and leaders of the organization become more effective and make better human capital management decisions.
- *Strategy development and implementation:* Aligning human capital management, organization development, and organization design with the organization's business model.

These "product lines" build upon one another. If HR doesn't have the first down cold, then it cannot deliver on the second. If it cannot deliver on the first and second effectively, it will not have the credibility or information to be heard on the third. It's worth looking in more detail at what's involved in delivering each of these three product lines and how they can be delivered effectively.

HR ADMINISTRATION

Providing a high-quality, low-cost HR administrative service is not optional. It is fundamental to the expectations of the organization and therefore to the credibility of the HR function. Failure to provide good service can lead to the HR organization being discounted in other areas and thereby undermining its ability to be an effective strategic and business player. Simply stated, HR administration has to be done in a cost-effective, timely, high-quality way. In the past, this has not always been easy to accomplish because HR administration involves a lot of detail and complexity that make it labor-intensive and slow. But there is good news!

Information technology and the development of a new industry can provide a way to get HR administration done at a lower cost and more effectively.[6] Web-based applications can now do virtually all HR administrative activities. What is more, most of them lend themselves to self-service. Employees can visit a Web site and sign up for benefits, change their address, enroll in training programs, and set their goals and objectives for the year. Managers can give out bonuses and raises, transfer employees, and find internal talent to fill positions with a visit to their company's intranet. In short, a great deal of what used to be done on a slow, paper-intensive basis by employees and by the HR administrative staff can now be done faster, quicker, and more effectively with Web-based software applications.

Eli Lilly

Effective succession management systems are critical to producing the right talent. In many companies, these systems are secretive, managed by a few individuals at the top of the organization. In the paternalistic era of structure-centric organizations, that approach was acceptable, but it doesn't work well for a company that emphasizes human capital. Succession planning in an HC-centric organization should be public, and employees need to have a say in their own development. To have a say, they need an organization that both gives them information and provides them with the resources they need to develop themselves.

One organization that has created a Web-based HC-centric talent development system is Eli Lilly, the global pharmaceutical company. At Lilly, all employees are responsible for updating their own personal information and development plans. The information provided by employees is vetted by their supervisors, but the primary responsibility for providing the information rests with the employees. Not surprisingly, this has increased the accuracy of the previously secret system because employees usually know more about themselves than anyone else. At Lilly, individuals are not ranked in terms of their potential, but they are slotted into broad categories by senior managers who assess whether they have additional potential and just how high they might be able to progress.

To facilitate the development process, Lilly makes a Web-based tool available to all employees on their desktops. A click on the career icon takes employees to a portal with their personal information and the job opportunities that are available. Managers, for their part, can use the intranet to search for new employees and can also get information on issues like the number of candidates available for different positions and the number of candidates with particular skill sets. Thus managers can assess pipelines in particular talent areas, the ratio of potentials to incumbents, and the gender and ethnicity of various talent pools.

Lilly tracks several succession management metrics including the overall quality of talent in its managerial pipeline and the number of positions with multiple "ready now" candidates in the organization. For senior positions, the system shows three potential successors. Targets are set for talent pools and when areas or jobs fall below the target, it is the responsibility of management to develop the needed human capital to bring the metric score above the goal for that particular position. Lilly creates a quarterly scorecard that tracks pipeline data as well as diversity and turnover rates. The executive team reviews this scorecard each quarter and takes action where needed.

Those transactions that cannot be easily put into a self-serve mode can be assigned to a call center that provides advice and helps employees with their decision making. A well-developed combination of a Web-based self-service system and a call center can handle most of the HR administrative activities that in the past have occupied the time of a large portion of the HR staff. In addition, it can provide some of the data needed to build an HR information system that supports effective performance management and talent management systems. It also can provide the raw data for metrics concerning the condition and capabilities of the workforce.

It is a no-brainer. Organizations need to invest in developing Web-based HR administrative systems. This is true whether they are HC-centric or structure-centric. HC-centric organizations have the most to gain because of their reliance on human capital and their need to attract, retain, develop, and organize it effectively, but it makes sense for structure-centric organizations as well. It simply is the best way to get HR administration done.

Once an organization decides to use Web-based systems for HR administration, the key decision becomes whether or not to outsource those systems' operation as well as the operation of the call center. Until recently, a number of organizations offered outsourcing expertise in benefits administration, recruitment, training, and other targeted HR processes—but none would take on all of a company's HR administrative activities. To say that times have changed would be an understatement. Many well-known large firms now are competing for business in the HR business process outsourcing space (HR BPO). These firms run self-service

Web-based HR administration programs for multiple companies and they operate call centers.

Accenture, IBM, Fidelity, and Hewitt Associates are among the major firms that have entered this business and gained a substantial market share. At this point, the outsourcing of multiple HR processes to a single vendor is a well-established practice and has gained a number of major customers. Unilever, Bank of America, IBM, Prudential, PepsiCo, Sun Microsystems, and BP are just a few examples of the major corporations who have entered into long-term, multiple-hundred-million-dollar contracts for HR BPO.

Research suggests that the major reason organizations have signed HR BPO contracts is cost savings.[7] Organizations also expect to achieve quality and speed improvements. The results suggest that they usually do accomplish all three goals. Outsourcing firms have something that even large companies such as IBM cannot equal: scale. HR outsourcing is a software-intensive business and the development of new software and the updating of software is expensive. Thus, even though an organization may have several hundred thousand employees, it can't spread its software development costs over the size of population that the major outsourcing firms have. Each of these firms is (or soon will be) providing HR administration for millions of employees.

In addition to scale, outsourcing firms are rapidly developing experience and knowledge about how to run call centers and how to provide HR services. Since they deal with multiple companies and have a chance to observe multiple processes, they can develop more knowledge than exists in a single firm. Simply stated, it is their core competency, while in their customer firms, it is an administrative backwater. Thus they often are able to offer process improvements to companies as well as cost, quality, and speed savings.

As you can undoubtedly detect, I am very favorable toward the HR BPO approach. For most companies I believe this is the right way to handle HR administration. It essentially gets HR out of doing a set of administrative activities that often are no-win activities for internal staff groups. If execution is flawless, staff groups are rarely praised, but if it is poor, blame is plentiful and the reputation damage is serious.

Outsourcing certainly doesn't solve all the problems with HR administration, but it solves more than even the best internal delivery approaches can—and, perhaps most important—it gets HR out of day-to-day administration. In other words, it has the potential to free HR up to do other things. However, it doesn't guarantee that HR will do those things or that it will do them well. All it does is give HR the opportunity. To take advantage of the opportunity, HR needs to make other important changes.

BUSINESS SUPPORT

In HC-centric organizations, the ultimate business support role for the HR function is improving the performance of the organization by improving managerial behavior and the quality of decision making about talent management and organizational design. Members of the HR function cannot and should not manage and lead people throughout the organization. (Chapter Nine examines the role of managers and leaders in HC-centric organizations.) What HR can and should do is improve the leadership and managerial performance of individuals throughout the organization.

In addition to the obvious business skills that managers need to be effective in running a business, they need to be effective at talent management. They need to coach, train, develop, select, and appraise the performance of the individuals they work with and manage. Not surprisingly, many managers lack the skills to do this effectively. Often they have not been trained in talent management and simply don't know what good practice is in a lot of areas. Their education is in a technical field or in economics; if they have an MBA, most likely they have taken only one course in organizational behavior. Often they have had little experience working either in a peer role with individuals or in a situation where they have subordinates.

One thing an HR organization can do to improve the performance of managers is to provide systems and training that help with performance management, goal setting, the assessment of individuals, and the structuring of jobs. These are critical areas in an HC-centric organization and areas where an effective HR department can add value by improving managerial performance. It can coach managers and help them focus on the impact of their behavior, provide them with feedback, and help them with talent management issues. It can base help on research-based knowledge, not just intuition or "accepted best practice."

At this point, there is a tremendous amount of good research on what makes managers effective, how they should deal with people, how to create effective teams, how to set motivating goals, and so forth.[8] Evidence-based management is possible when it comes to things such as how a company should select new employees, what interview techniques are valid, how to manage change, what approaches to leadership are effective, and when a company should use teams. Most managers are not aware of the research findings on these and many other topics.[9] Thus the HR function can add tremendous value by being an expert resource when it comes to the application of existing knowledge.

IBM Reinvents HR

IBM is one of the few companies that excelled in the old days as a structure-centric organization and has also managed to transform itself into an HC-centric company. Credit for this transformation from hierarchy to global competitor goes in part to IBM's HR department.

Up until the 1990s, IBM's practices in the area of compensation, selection, training and development, benefits, and job security all supported its structure-centric approach to management. IBM was seen as a leading employer, and it had a very clear and attractive brand for someone who wanted to work in a high-tech company with a somewhat bureaucratic and paternalistic approach to management.

Then, in 1993, Lou Gerstner became CEO. Recognizing that IBM faced a long period of decline if it did not reinvent itself, Gerstner decided to emphasize the company's services and software products. He also decided to adopt a global-competitor approach to management.

Needless to say this change required major changes in the HR systems of IBM. Most of the changes the company has made in this area are predictable and involved the HR function aligning its practices with the other elements of an organization that is designed to be a global competitor. For example, IBM changed its benefits by eliminating its traditional defined benefit retirement program. Job security and lifetime employment became a thing of the past. And management development programs were retooled to focus more on performance.

But in some areas, IBM and its HR function have moved well beyond the predictable. IBM has experimented with new approaches to strategy formulation and selection with its Web-based WorldJam sessions. And HR has outsourced a significant part of its transactional work.

The HR function has also taken a particularly innovative step with regard to funding training. Unlike many global competitors that simply say to individuals, "It is up to you to meet your needs for training and development; you are on your own when it comes to directing *and* funding your career," IBM offers a company-sponsored alternative. It has created a specialized savings account for training and education, modeled on 401(k) retirement accounts. Workers can put up to $1,000 a year into their learning accounts and IBM will contribute fifty cents for every dollar put in by the employee.

Consistent with the idea of individuals' being responsible for their own development, employees can decide how and when to spend their money. While they're making the decision, the money is held in an interest-bearing account and is portable when and if they decide to leave IBM.

The IBM program is truly innovative. It helps to make clear that the employment contract for employees at IBM is one where they are in charge of their career. It is a long way from the traditional "organization man" contract that IBM was famous for when it was a structure-centric organization. It sends the message that IBM is a place where people can enhance their skills and become more competitive in the labor market. The hope is that it will create a climate that allows IBM to have an edge in attracting and retaining the right talent.

In the past, few HR managers have brought research-based information into an organization and provided it in a timely manner to managers. I suspect this is partly because they have been spending most of their time dealing with administrative issues, but it also may be because they have not had the needed expertise. As a result, in many organizations managers have relied on their own theories of how best to do such things as select new employees and set goals, despite the fact that research results establish what should be done. In organization after organization that I have studied, this is tolerated, even though these same organizations do not allow their managers to decide how they are going to do accounting or inventory management.

Outsourcing administrative tasks can help HR have the time to offer evidence-based business support, but it is not enough. Consider: In one case where I studied the outsourcing of administrative activities, the HR staff, post-outsourcing, simply continued to do the administrative work they had always done, only they did it via the intranet.[10] The managers who had always relied on HR to complete and process forms continued on as they had always done. They were, in fact, relieved that they didn't have to go into more of a self-service mode and deal with new software and the third-party provider; they were happy to have the HR managers do it for them.

The result was that the HR function did not significantly change its role once HR BPO was instituted. Instead, what continued was a kind of co-dependency between the HR managers and the line managers. The co-dependency was not based on HR making business managers better; it was based on HR managers' helping business managers with the administrative side of their jobs.

Senior management quickly realized what was happening and within six months decided to eliminate most of the HR staff because it was now unnecessary and simply doing what could fairly be described as "make work." However, they didn't completely give up on having an HR function. They waited a while—at least until the managers became self-sufficient—and then restaffed the HR organization with managers who could be effective in a business support role.

STRATEGY DEVELOPMENT AND IMPLEMENTATION

A study I did with Susan Mohrman and John Boudreau found that senior HR executives in only 39 percent of the Fortune 1000 companies studied felt that their HR function was a full partner in developing their company's business strategy.[11] Executives were particularly likely to feel it was if they worked in an organization that tried to gain competitive advantage through knowledge and information utilization. Thus, research evidence supports the argument that when an organization looks to human capital assets as a source of competitive advantage, it is more likely to give HR a major role in strategy.

In the same study, we asked line managers to report whether their HR executives were a full partner in business strategy formulation and implementation. They answered that this was true in only 24 percent of the cases—a significant drop from the 39 percent reported by HR executives. Whether the correct number is 24 percent or 39 percent is not the critical issue here, however. The critical issue is that in at least 60 percent, and most likely closer to 75 percent of companies, HR is not a full partner in the formulation and implementation of strategy. This seems like a very high percentage given how many corporations today are in businesses where having the right talent and the right organization design is a make-or-break issue. It certainly raises the question of why HR isn't involved in so many companies. One reason may be lack of data.

When it comes to discussions about strategy, the heads of finance and marketing come to the table with data. If HR leaders don't come to the table with the kind of data, numbers, and analysis discussed in Chapter Six, they are not going to have a major say in strategy formulation and implementation.

Most HR organizations do not currently have the metrics and analytic capabilities needed to be a strategic partner. Table 4 reinforces this point. It shows the results from a survey of large

TABLE 4. USE OF METRICS.

Does your organization currently. . . .	Yes (%)
Collect metrics that measure the business impact of HR programs and processes?	30.3
Use dashboards or scorecards to evaluate HR's performance?	39.4
Have metrics and analytics that reflect the effects of HR programs on the workforce (such as competence, motivation, attitudes, behaviors, and so on)?	29.3
Have the capability to conduct cost-benefit analyses of HR programs?	28.3
Measure the financial efficiency of HR operations (for example, cost-per-hire, time-to-fill, training costs)?	47.5
Collect metrics that measure the cost of providing HR services?	30.3

U.S. firms.[12] Less than half of them have metrics and analytics that can be used to assess and improve their HR operations and programs. Given this, it is hardly surprising that HR organizations often have less influence in organizations than marketing, finance, and production do.

Because of their different designs, high-involvement and global-competitor organizations may need to focus on different metrics and may find some differences in what metrics predict performance. For example, high-involvement organizations may want to focus more on organizational commitment and the causes of turnover. But both kinds of HC-centric organizations need human capital and organizational effectiveness data, and they need managers who understand how to interpret and use the data.

When it comes to strategy formulation and implementation, data speak loudly! HC-centric organizations simply cannot have HR functions that cannot speak as loudly as marketing, finance, and the other functions. When an organization's competitive advantage depends on its talent performing at a superior level, it needs facts about what works and what doesn't. High-involvement and global competitor organizations are similar in this respect—they both need good data about what leads to superior levels of performance, and about the current status of the key determinants of performance.

If the HR function can bring to the table the right data, the right individuals, and a record of successful HR administration, its leaders should be able to do more than just have a seat at the table when it comes to strategy; they should be able to set the table. They should be able to raise critical strategy issues from an informed perspective that is built on data.

In HC-centric organizations nothing is more basic to the formulation of business strategy and to its implementation than talent and organizational effectiveness. Knowledge about talent is critical to determining what type of competencies and capabilities can be developed as well understanding what an organization currently can do in terms of strategy execution. This is true whether an organization has a high-involvement approach or a global-competitor approach to management. In both, strategy needs to be based on what type of human capital an organization has and can obtain, as well as how it can be organized to provide specific competencies and capabilities.

Staffing HR

How the HR function is staffed is a critical determinant of whether it can deliver on the three product lines that were examined in the preceding section. As noted, all too often HR is not seen as a function that attracts fast-track, high-potential talent, nor is it seen as a necessary stop on the way to senior management positions. As a result, it tends to end up being staffed with individuals who are not top-tier talent.

In some cases the people placed in HR do not even have any HR training; they are thought to be "good with people." This occurs because organizations fail to recognize the importance of HR and the reality that it should be an evidence-based function staffed by trained professionals. Typically a company does not put people into finance, for example, unless they have some background and training in it, or are seen as fast-track general manager candidates.

Staffing HR with less than the best talent, failing to respect HR, and depending on HR for no more than administrative ministering is a vicious cycle that must be broken in an HC-centric organization. What is needed is for an organization's top managers to break the cycle by instituting for HR the same staffing standards that exist for finance, marketing, and IT. In some cases, the standard should even be higher. Particularly in a high-involvement organization, HR is likely to be a pivotal job and may need a staffing level slightly above that of the other staff groups. If talent is the key competitive advantage of an organization, then the best talent in the organization ought to be responsible for its attraction, development, retention, and organization.

Adequately staffing the HR function overall can best be accomplished by establishing two, or perhaps three, career tracks. The first track is that of a subject-matter expert. Individuals on the corporate staff who are responsible for key areas such as talent management and compensation ought to have deep knowledge in those areas, as well as an excellent general knowledge of HR. In most cases, the career of a subject-matter expert will be in the HR function; typically these individuals should hold advanced degrees in HR and be certified by a professional association in their particular area of expertise. (For example, for compensation the association is WorldatWork.)

In large corporations, at least some of the HR staff should have the kind of deep subject matter knowledge that is typically present in leading consulting firms. HC-centric organizations, in other words, should have in their HR departments the kind of talent management expertise for which many companies today turn to third-party consultants. They don't need to be self-sufficient when it comes to HR expertise, but they do need to be knowledgeable buyers and consumers.

Expertise can be and should be bought from the outside, but overreliance on consulting firms and external talent is dangerous. Without deep internal expertise it is hard to know what products and services are state of the art. In addition, when internal expertise is lacking, it's difficult to change outside service providers if it is determined they aren't offering the best service. Their departure often means the loss of corporate memory and a great deal of difficulty in maintaining existing systems. Internal expertise is critical to making external experts less critical and allowing an organization to move on if a poor relationship develops with a consultant or service provider.

Exhibit 6 presents a fictitious help-wanted ad for an HR executive who will be responsible for senior management development. It nicely captures the type of individuals HC-centric organizations should have in their HR function. A high level of talent is required

---

EXHIBIT 6. HELP WANTED.

Need an HR executive who will think like a brand manager for the top 200 executive group.
Qualifications:

- Driver of change
- Business acumen
- Excellent judgment about people
- Courageous, able to stand up to line managers
- Persuasive, but good listener
- Trusted by senior line executives
- Enabler of tough decisions
- Outstanding subject matter expertise

---

in these positions if HR is to provide the best compensation systems, training and development systems, and so forth.

In addition to subject-matter depth experts, HR functions need generalists who can fill the business support role. This role ought to be staffed by individuals who at some point in their career have had business experience outside HR and may have it in the future. It is particularly helpful if they have had the chance to manage a business unit or at least an operations area. Individuals fulfilling this role should be seen as candidates for senior management positions outside the HR function.

One useful principle for career development in HC-centric organizations is to say that everyone who aspires to a top-level management job in the organization needs to have spent some time in HR, preferably in a generalist or business support role. In some countries (Japan, for example), HR is seen as sufficiently important that serious candidates for senior management positions are expected to spend part of their careers there. This is not the case in the United States, but it should be in HC-centric organizations.

The senior HR executives in most U.S. corporations (over 70 percent) have spent most or all of their careers in HR.[13] The exception usually is someone who has rotated into HR from the line organization. Such a move often makes a statement concerning the importance of HR in the organization: putting a high-performance executive who is a potential CEO or general manager candidate into HR as an important step in their preparation for promotion makes a very positive statement. By contrast, when—as happens in some cases—a company puts a surplus or failed manager who needs a last job before retirement into an HR leadership slot, it makes a very negative statement.

The only two legitimate reasons for rotating somebody into HR should be to improve or strengthen the function and to prepare the individual for a general management position. Both of these make enormous sense in an HC-centric organization (although, in a mature HC-centric organization, transferring somebody in to improve the talent in the function should be unnecessary).

As HR becomes more and more a key organizational function, it should be a talent magnet and an ideal development stop for someone on the way to being a CEO. Today, virtually no CEOs of major U.S. corporations have spent any significant amount of time in an HR or organizational effectiveness unit (one exception is Anne Mulcahy, the CEO of Xerox). This hardly makes sense when talent management is such a high priority and such an important activity.

ORGANIZATIONAL DESIGN AND HUMAN RESOURCES

To establish a strong relationship between the HR function and the rest of the organization, many HR functions have adopted a type of customer-focused or front-back organization structure.[14] HR generalists are assigned to serve a particular function or business unit; often, their offices are on location with the division or function they serve. With this type of approach, the corporate-level HR office provides expertise and services the generalists, often through "centers of excellence" that provide support and expertise in training, labor relations, compensation, recruiting, and other HR areas. In addition, if the administrative work is not outsourced, the corporate HR office houses the service centers and call centers or alternatively manages the outsourcing contracts.

This front-back approach usually does help to create a closer relationship between HR and the business than is present when HR is a corporate function made up of different silos or functions (compensation, training, and so on). It is not clear, however, that this design makes HR more of a strategic resource when it comes to the formulation and the implementation of business strategy. For HR to contribute to strategy, more needs to happen. The right centers of excellence need to be created at the corporate center, and they need to be staffed with individuals who can address issues involving talent, organization design and business strategy.

CENTERS OF EXCELLENCE

It is very important to have a center of excellence that deals with the kind of development, collection, and analysis of metrics mentioned in Chapter Six. This center needs an analytic capability so that the effectiveness of policies and procedures can be assessed and the importance of different metrics determined.

Let me give an example of the kind of analytic work that is useful for a corporate center of excellence to do. In an organization with a strategy based on providing exceptional customer service, the HR analytics and metrics function should focus on predictors and causes of customer service satisfaction.

The analytic group should gather data about customer satisfaction, determine how satisfaction is related to qualities of the staff providing the service, and look for predictors of salesperson effectiveness. Research should also be done on the effects of work design, turnover, and training on the effectiveness of salesperson behavior and, of course, on what employee attitudes correlate with and predict customer satisfaction.

Where possible, comparative customer satisfaction data should be gotten. This is needed so that the organization can determine whether it in fact provides superior customer service as its customers see it. The analytic group should look at the costs of generating the employee behaviors that affect customer satisfaction. Finally, it should make cost-benefit analyses of changes that will affect customer satisfaction and determine the financial impact of increases in customer satisfaction.

Developing the right analytics and metrics is just the first step in having HR truly influence and drive strategy. The results of the analytic work done by the center of excellence need to be translated into business plans that include change programs, strategy alterations, and organization designs. Making this transfer usually involves developing a compelling case that will influence senior executives to make changes.

Sometimes the HR function can develop a compelling case by itself, but often developing one requires an integrative effort that includes expertise in strategy, finance and information systems. Indeed, it often requires a joint effort between the information systems part of an organization, the finance function, the HR function's centers of excellence, and the business strategy function to come up with a coherent and integrated business plan. The need for an integrated plan is obvious. HR by itself often has the expertise to bring only one set of issues to the strategy table. There is a real danger that this one set will not be powerful enough to compel change, and that it will not be well developed and integrated with the other issues an organization faces.

ORGANIZATIONAL EFFECTIVENESS

A better alternative to having separate HR and strategy functions may be to make a more innovative structural change: create an organizational effectiveness function. This corporate staff function would combine business strategy and planning, financial analysis, human capital management, organization development, and organization design. It would be headed by a chief organizational effectiveness officer (COEO), who would have responsibility for strategy formulation, implementation, and talent management.

Having an organizational effectiveness function is a good fit for HC-centric organizations because it integrates expertise in business strategy and talent management. It is unlike the typical organization design of most large organizations because it recognizes and creates a function charged with managing the connections among the points on the star. All too often, these are not considered because no one, except perhaps the CEO, is responsible for the fit among the different points on the star, despite the fact that fit issues are a critical determinant—or perhaps *the* critical determinant—of organizational effectiveness.

My colleague John Boudreau often makes the point that accounting is in the transactions business, while finance is concerned with management decision making when it comes to money.[15] Sales and marketing have a similar relationship: sales is transactions, and marketing is strategy.

What I am proposing is that for human capital, HR should be the administrative and transactional piece while the organizational effectiveness unit should be the strategy and design piece. In this design, there would be an HR function responsible for transactional HR and for working with managers on business support issues. It would report to the COEO as would business strategy, talent management, organization development, and organization design.

WHAT IS NEEDED

Without question, a tremendous opportunity exists for the human resource function to add value in all HC-centric organizations. However, to realize this potential, the HR function and the individuals in it need to change significantly. HR executives need new skills and knowledge, and of course HR needs to be able to execute human resource management and administration activities effectively. Doing the basics well is a platform the HR function needs if it is to build its role as a strategic player. But simply doing the basics well is not enough.

HR needs to be staffed with individuals who understand the business and have evidence-based knowledge of what constitutes good human capital management. It needs to develop metrics that reflect the condition of the human capital of an organization and the ability of an organization to execute a variety of strategies. It needs analytic work to show how specific organization designs and human capital management policies, practices, and structures affect the financial performance of the organization.

Unless HR has individuals who can think strategically and understand the business as well as organizational effectiveness data, it will always be a secondary player in strategy implementation and formulation. HC-centric organizations need data and knowledge about human capital and organizational effectiveness. The HR function should be in a position to meet this need.

As a general rule, the way HR needs to operate in a high-involvement organization is not significantly different from how it should operate in a global-competitor organization. Both types of organization require essentially the same kind of support from the HR function, and both require a highly competent and effective HR organization.

The major differences in what high-involvement and global-competitor organizations require concern the skills business leaders need to develop and some of the metrics and analytics that should be provided by the HR function. For example, high-involvement organizations need more participative leaders and managers and also more metrics that focus on how much employees are involved and committed to the organization. On the other hand, global-competitor organizations need a strong emphasis on the skills individuals have, external labor market conditions, and the availability of key talent.

The following are the key ways that HR needs to operate in all HC-centric organizations:

- HR should handle the transaction or administrative side of its responsibilities effectively. HR must provide outstanding business support when it comes to human capital management and organizational effectiveness.

- HR should have an active role in both the establishment and the implementation of business strategy.
- HR should provide key data and services to the corporate board.
- HR should support its business strategy recommendations with the appropriate metrics and analytics.
- The HR organization should be staffed with individuals who have deep expertise in HR functions and individuals who understand the relationship between HR and business effectiveness.
- Working in HR should be a mandatory key career stop for senior executives and general managers.
- The talent in HR should equal or exceed that in the other parts of the organization.

CHAPTER EIGHT

GOVERNING CORPORATIONS

Corporate boards are changing. The accounting scandals of the last decade have increased the pressure on corporate boards to behave ethically and provide accurate financial data to shareholders. Large shareholders are demanding that boards hold management accountable for corporate performance. Without question, corporate boards have become more effective and independent of management.[1] But to date, most of the changes in how boards operate have been driven by the need to comply with Sarbanes-Oxley regulations and stock market listing requirements. Little change has occurred in how boards contribute to organizational effectiveness. This needs to change.

Boards of directors certainly can and should make an important contribution to organizational effectiveness in HC-centric organizations. In addition to their usual oversight activities, boards should examine the human capital management practices as well as the status of the talent in their organizations. Board attention can have an enormously powerful and positive impact on a company's efforts to manage its talent effectively. It also can provide boards with information they need in order to make important decisions.

Remember: In an HC-centric organization, it is impossible to separate talent from business strategy. The availability of talent needs to drive strategy, and the organizing and management of talent needs to be driven by strategy. At a time when more and more of the assets of corporations fall into the intangible category, boards that wish to maximize their ability to contribute to shareholder value and provide effective corporate oversight must focus on the key intangible in HC-centric organizations: talent.

Investors are paying more attention to human capital issues, according to a survey of 191 CFOs of large companies.[2] Forty-nine percent report that investors are beginning to ask about human capital issues to at least a moderate extent. But only 23 percent of the CFOs say that their boards are highly involved in human capital issues, though they expect this involvement to increase.

Boards need to know at least as much about the condition and utilization of the organization's talent as they do about the condition and utilization of its financial and physical assets. They need to use this information when they make strategy decisions, do evaluations of senior managers, and make decisions about organization design, change, and effectiveness.

WHAT A BOARD NEEDS

Recent research on corporate boards identifies five conditions boards need in order to deal with organizational effectiveness issues. They are power, knowledge, motivation, information, and opportunity.[3] The following sections discuss each of these five conditions with human capital issues in mind.

POWER

In the past, many corporate boards had relatively little power to act independently of the CEO. Often, the members were appointed by the CEO, and a number of the directors (often more than half) were also executives in the firm and thus reported to the CEO. The result was that boards often depended on the CEO for their power, and in many cases, were so beholden to the CEO that they could only get done what the CEO wanted them to do. This is still the case with some companies, where the CEO is the board chair and has a strong say in who is appointed to the board.

What's more, where members of the board are CEOs of other firms, the board may hesitate to delve too deeply into how an organization is run. There is a "gentleman's agreement" among CEOs that when all is said and done, the CEO should be making the key decisions with respect to how the organization is run, not the board.

But there is a great deal of evidence that over the last decade, boards are gaining significant power in the United States and in the United Kingdom. Thanks to regulatory changes, the boards of most major U.S. and U.K. corporations are now dominated by outsiders who feel increasingly powerful. Indeed, they are more and more frequently firing CEOs, and as a result the rate of turnover among CEOs and senior corporate executives has increased.

Do boards have as much power as they need to be effective in dealing with human capital issues? In most cases, I think they do. They have a meaningful say in who gets to be CEO, and, if they want to, they can influence many of the talent management practices of corporations. As a result, it is reasonable to say that if a board is not doing a good job of dealing with human capital issues, it is unlikely to be because it lacks the power to influence major decisions.

If most boards want to get something done in the human capital management area, it is likely that they can get it done. For example, they can, if they want, have a major say in their company's management succession planning. This includes not just changing policies, but actually influencing who gets jobs, at least the senior management jobs, and of course who ultimately becomes CEO.

Probably the hardest thing for boards to influence is the overall management approach of the organization. Most boards are not in a position to mandate or require that an organization be managed as a high-involvement or global-competitor organization. But, they still can strongly influence how a company is managed by determining who gets the senior management positions and who gets to be CEO.

They can also indirectly influence how the company is managed by asking questions about the management approach used by individuals who are in the top management team and who are candidates for the CEO job. And they can ask for measures of the corporation's management approach (for example, attitude surveys) in an effort to determine if the right management and leadership style is being enacted.

Overall, at this point, most boards have the power they need to ensure that the organization is taking the right approach to organizational effectiveness and talent management. Whether they know how to use their power is another matter.

KNOWLEDGE

Knowledge about talent management and organizational effectiveness is an obvious foundation that boards need in order to make high-quality talent management decisions. Essentially, boards have two major sources they can draw upon for knowledge. The first is their members, and the second is nonmembers who are invited to make presentations or consult to the board and its committees. The latter group typically includes executives from the firm as well as outside consultants who are hired to provide a particular kind of expertise.

In many respects, the most available and potentially most influential source of expertise is board members. But do boards have members with expertise in human capital management? Unfortunately, in most cases they do not.

The chief human resource officers (CHROs) of corporations are almost never on their corporate board. Prior to the movement to having more independent board members, a few CHROs were on their corporate boards. For example, UPS and TRW had their respective CHROs on their boards. But most companies simply didn't invite their CHROs to be on their boards, even when insiders sat on boards. And now that boards are increasingly dominated by outside or independent directors, it is almost a certainty that if CHROs are going to be on a board at all, it will not be the board of their company.

But what about the outside board members? Do many of them have a deep expertise in human capital management? The answer for major corporations is no. Occasionally, corporations have an academic or a consultant who has some expertise in HR on their board, but this is very rare, as is having another company's CHRO on their board.

Who, then, are the independent directors populating U.S. boards? Overwhelmingly, they are either current CEOs or retired CEOs. If they are not CEOs, they most often are industry experts or finance specialists.

When asked about the importance of different types of functional experience when recruiting directors, board members give a low rating to the importance of holding a senior human capital management job.[4] Information technology, law, marketing, operations, audit, and finance are all rated more highly. When it comes to boards having directors with functional experience, HR comes in last.

Interestingly when I have interviewed board members to ask who they rely on for HR expertise, they cite the CEOs on their board. There is no doubt that many CEOs have some understanding of the human capital issues that corporations face, but they rarely have the kind of in-depth expertise that a professional in HR could bring to a board.

Effective talent management requires a great deal of expertise in organizational systems and a great deal of understanding of motivation, abilities, traits, and behavior. Skilled managers often have a good understanding of people and some organizational systems, but they rarely have the kind of expertise that a knowledgeable HR executive can bring to bear on the major talent management and organization design decisions that organizations need to make.

There is an interesting contrast between where boards look for financial expertise and where they look for human capital management expertise. Boards almost always have one or more members with an extensive background in finance. But the same does not hold for human capital. Why?

My observation is that a variety of things cause this difference, including doubt about the existence of an important body of expertise that can be brought to bear to improve human capital management. I have often heard executives say, "Everybody is an expert in people management!" Not surprisingly, my view is a little different from theirs.

It is true that many people have experience in dealing with human capital issues, but that does not mean they are experts in dealing with human capital management in complex HC-centric organizations. Quite the contrary is true–they often have learned the wrong things.

Human capital decisions need to be based on research evidence, facts, data, and informed judgment. They are critical to the success of high-involvement and global-competitor organizations, and should be based on the best knowledge, information, and judgment that is available. Because of this, boards need to have one—and in most cases two—members with an in-depth knowledge of human capital management.

Given the importance of human capital management and the absence of HR expertise on corporate boards, it might be expected that most of the time, boards would have someone working in the HR function or an outside HR expert present when they meet and when their committees meet. I know of no research that documents the presence of outside HR experts when it comes to board meetings and committee meetings, but I have gathered data on whether the CHRO is likely to attend board meetings.[5] In only 19 percent of the Fortune 1000 corporations is the head of HR always present for board meetings. This is a dramatic contrast to the frequency with which the CFO is always present: 91 percent of the time!

Clearly, by who is present at the board meetings, boards are indicating that they place more importance on financial assets than on human capital assets. It is interesting to contrast this with what Jack Welch, former CEO of General Electric, has said: "If your CFO is more important than your CHRO, you're nuts!" The conclusion one has to reach based on this is that most boards are "nuts" because they do, in fact, have their CFO present but not their head of HR.

One way to increase the amount of expertise that boards have in talent management and business strategy is to provide them with some training. Boards increasingly do engage in educational activities. The recent increase in training activity is mainly due to the requirement that boards of New York Stock Exchange–listed companies do at least some training every year.

No research currently shows what kind of training is typically done by boards. My guess is that boards rarely receive training that focuses on strategic talent management issues. Because of the recent emphasis on financial reporting and auditing, a good guess is that much of the training has to do with regulatory and financial accounting issues.

Training in talent management is important to do, but it is unrealistic to expect any board training program to develop a depth expertise in board members who have little or no background in talent management. Board members spend relatively few hours on their board activities—around two hundred a year, according to my research—and only a small fraction of this can reasonably be expected to involve education of any sort.

In any case, it is unrealistic to expect a board training program to turn board members into talent management experts. As was pointed out earlier, there is an enormous amount of knowledge about talent management. The time management issues in large organizations are complex and warrant the kind of careful data gathering, analysis, and informed decision making that can only be done by, or with the help of, experts. Thus, although it is important to provide board members with some training in talent management, it is unreasonable to expect them to develop a deep level of expertise. What they need to become is good consumers of talent management information.

It is unclear how much boards use HR consultants. They do use them to work on executive compensation issues and to do board and executive searches, but no evidence indicates that they use them to help with most talent management and organizational effectiveness issues. In any case, it is doubtful that even the skillful use of consultants can make up for the lack of someone with deep HR expertise being regularly present at board meetings.

What grade can we give boards when it comes to their expertise in the talent management area? Based on the available evidence, the most reasonable grade would be an F. They neither have HR experts on the board nor avail themselves fully of the internal HR expertise in their corporations. Further, they make only limited use of consultants.

Perhaps the best way to summarize the situation on board knowledge is to say that their limited expertise may be what is needed in a structure-centric organization. However, it is seriously inadequate in HC-centric organizations, where talent management and organizational effectiveness are the primary sources of competitive advantage.

The best way to bring boards into the HC-centric world, with respect to knowledge, is to change the actual composition of the board. Advisers and experts can help bring additional expertise to technical matters of talent management, but they are not an adequate substitute for having one or more individuals on the board that truly have deep expertise in talent management.

Deep expertise is an absolute necessity in organizations that are HC-centric, and certainly should be a priority, even in most structure-centric organizations. Structure-centric organizations have their own set of talent management issues, such as employee satisfaction, motivation, and turnover, that need to be addressed and require a high level of expertise. They also have a critical need for expertise in management development and senior executive succession planning.

MOTIVATION AND PERFORMANCE MANAGEMENT

There are multiple reasons why board members should be highly motivated to perform their jobs. However, I believe that there may be a motivation problem when it comes to board members paying the proper attention to talent management issues.

Being on the board of a poorly performing corporation clearly has a significant downside. When companies perform poorly, board members are often singled out for "public hangings." And, of course, boards face potential financial liability if they fail to do sufficient due diligence when it comes to illegal activities on the part of the corporation. Finally, there is the issue of board member compensation, which is more and more based upon the value of the company's stock. This creates a weak but real connection between their compensation and the performance of the board.

But are board members motivated to focus on the human capital aspects of organizational effectiveness and performance? As already mentioned, information on this important determinant of an organization's performance is rarely reported to shareholders. Thus board members may not be as motivated to focus on it as on financial performance. Talent management is also an area where board decisions may not have an immediate effect on corporate performance, unlike decisions regarding a merger, an acquisition, or the introduction of a new product. This delay may act as a deterrent to focusing on talent management issues.

Even stock ownership by board members can work in a subtle way against boards' being motivated to focus on talent management issues. Since the talent of an organization is an intangible, it tends not to affect the stock price of a company as directly and immediately as financial results do (a possible exception here being changes at the senior executive level). The line of sight from financial and operational results to stock price is much more direct than the one from talent issues to stock price. Thus boards are likely to pay more attention to financial and operational results than to the things that cause them (such as talent management).

Improvements in talent management and organization design often don't affect results for several years, and by that time the board members involved may have already exercised their stock options or, for that matter, moved on to a different board or career. As a result of this, it's not surprising that boards spend more time talking about financial results and operations than they do about talent and other intangible assets.

Let me be clear: I am *not* suggesting that companies abandon the idea of stock grants or stock options because they are counterproductive to a talent focus on the board. But I do have one suggestion: All stock plans that cover board members should be long-term plans. One of the last things board members should be doing is myopically focusing on the short-term stock price of their company. Such a focus is particularly likely to cause board members to ignore key organizational activities that have a lag impact on the financial results of the company.

Corporate boards need to do more than just focus on how their organizations manage talent. They need to be talent managers. Boards need to evaluate the performance of the CEO and other senior executives, and they need to evaluate their performance as a board and that of their members.[6]

Why evaluate board members? Because members of the board are a critical part of talent in any large organization. Thus they need to be evaluated and rewarded just like other members of the organization. And they need to be active in evaluating others on the board, and in some cases executives in the organization. A valid ongoing evaluation process should be the basis for decisions about continuing board membership. When it is the basis, it can have a motivational impact that stock-based rewards programs lack.

In terms of evaluating members of the organization, the board's most important responsibility is to evaluate the CEO. Today, virtually every Fortune 1000 company has a formal evaluation process for the CEO. Board members rate the performance of their boards in this area very highly.[7] Well over 80 percent of board members say that they do a very effective job. This may be a bit optimistic, since boards have few agreed-upon standards upon which to evaluate what an effective evaluation of a CEO looks like, but it is encouraging. It would be more encouraging if the board members had expertise in talent management.

At the very least, an assessment of a CEO should include gathering data from multiple sources as well as being based on clear-cut, pre-set objectives. It should also, of course, include a thorough written evaluation at the end of the performance period and good feedback to the CEO. Surprisingly enough, according to my research, in only 40 percent of the cases is the CEO actually given a written report by the board. Boards score much higher in the survey when it comes to setting objectives and giving developmental feedback to the CEO.

Boards do not score as well when it comes to evaluating their performance as a team and the individual members of the board. Today, virtually every board does have a formal board evaluation process, but these processes are rated as effective by only 75 percent of board members. A majority, sure, but the figure should be higher for this important activity.

Like the evaluation of the CEO, a board evaluation (one that evaluates the board as a group) should consist of data gathered from multiple sources, pre-set objectives, and a formal annual review of the data. I don't know of any research at this point that has looked at what actually takes place in the evaluations boards do of themselves. However, based on my conversations with board members and my observations, I doubt that in most cases the evaluation is as effective as board members think it is. All too often, it seems to be lacking in pre-set objectives and fails to gather data from large shareholders and investment analysts. It also often does not gather data even from the members of the board about how effectively they see the board performing.

Finally, we need to return to the issue of whether and how well individual board members are evaluated. Until recently evaluation rarely occurred, but with the increased accountability pressure on boards, my research shows that about 80 percent of boards have some type of evaluation system that looks at individual directors.[8]

In most cases, the evaluation of board members is a rather informal review that does not gather data from other board members, nor does it provide a written report to the board member. Often it involves a meeting with the chair of the board in which a general discussion is held of how the individual feels the board is performing and what they are contributing. The board chair may offer some advice or input about how the board member could contribute more, but there is rarely a formal evaluation of board members.

One of the main reasons why individual board members are not evaluated formally is reluctance on the part of the board chair to do it. I clearly remember interviewing one board chair who said it would be insulting to actually evaluate the members of his board. He went on to add that they were nice enough to be on the board and, as a result, should not be subject to evaluation. This attitude, of course, is vastly out of step with the importance of board performance and the heavy responsibility that board members carry. It also ignores the fact that board members are often paid hundreds of thousands of dollars for the favor that they are doing.

Particularly in HC-centric organizations, boards need to do a rigorous evaluation of individual board members. They need to demonstrate the importance of talent to the organization by showing that they believe that board performance depends on the skills and contributions of individuals. One of the best ways to show this is to assess and develop the performance of the individuals on the board. Boards should not tolerate sub-par performance among board members, and they should do everything they can to encourage members to develop their skills and knowledge in ways that will make the board more effective.

The performance assessments of individual board members probably should not affect their compensation level in most situations. It is a contract job and rewarding individuals on their performance can be administratively difficult. But as mentioned earlier, it certainly should affect their membership on the board. All too often, boards tolerate individuals who are not good performers because they don't have a reasonable evaluation process and are uncomfortable asking individuals to leave the board as a result of poorly documented performance problems.

Board members are generally aware that the individual evaluation process of most boards is not highly effective. For example, less than 40 percent rate it as either effective or very effective. This is a notable contrast to the evaluation of CEO performance, which, as mentioned earlier, is rated as effective or very effective by over 80 percent of board members in the same study. Clearly this gap needs to be closed in order for boards to manage their own talent effectively.

Board members should not lead the evaluation of senior executives, but it is quite reasonable for them to be active providers of data to the CEO or to whomever is actually managing the evaluation process. Whether they are active or not in evaluating senior management is not the key issue; it is whether they see the results of the evaluation and actively discuss them with the CEO.

Yes, this may appear to be micromanaging, but in HC-centric organizations, it is a necessary and important activity. Only by doing this are members of the board able to assess the key talent in the organization. It is needed so they can reach their own conclusions about the adequacy of succession plans, the quality of backups for key positions, and a host of other human capital questions that boards should be concerned about when the key asset of their organization is talent.

INFORMATION

Perhaps the single most important change organizations can make to focus their boards more on talent management and organizational effectiveness is in the information area. As noted, companies rarely report to the public on the condition of their talent, core competencies, and capabilities. Indeed, they often do not even have good metrics that assess talent and organizational effectiveness issues. Given this, it seems almost inevitable that boards will give less attention to talent management than to financial capital management.

The solution to the problem of underattention is obvious: corporations need to develop and report to the board metrics that accurately report on their ability to perform and on the condition of their talent. Also, they need to develop and report to the board analytics that show which talent management metrics drive corporate performance. This information will allow boards to make good decisions about where to spend their time, what metrics they should monitor, and where they should call for change.

Adding comprehensive talent management data is a major change in the information that boards receive, and doing it requires a great deal of development work. But it must be done; without talent management information and analytics, it is dangerous for boards to make decisions about talent. Boards need metrics and analytics with respect to talent and organizational effectiveness in order to make informed decisions about strategy, as well as about financial and talent allocation and utilization.

The Center for Effective Organizations (CEO) has been doing an annual survey of corporate board members for the last decade. The survey consistently asks questions about the information that board members have about the condition of the organization.[9] When asked whether the board receives sufficient information to carry out its responsibilities, the answers have consistently been, "Yes, to a very great extent." Similarly, when asked if the CEO keeps the board informed about significant matters affecting the company, the answer is yes (average of 4.4 on a 5-point scale).

But when asked about talent management and organizational effectiveness issues, the board members respond quite differently. They are much less positive when asked, "Does the board monitor the company's culture through surveys and other data gathering activities?" and "Does the board have independent information channels that provide useful information about company operations and management practices?" Perhaps of even greater concern is the answer to the question about whether the board tracks measures of the company's talent. Here the proportion of favorable answers is much lower than when the issue involves financial information. In 2006, only 32 percent said they track measures of human capital to a great extent.[10]

The survey also asks about the involvement of the board with respect to the development of key executives. The results here indicate very little involvement on the part of the board.

Overall, the results of the CEO survey strongly suggest that board members get more information about the financial and operational performance of their company than they do about the condition of its talent and capabilities. The lack of good information about the condition of an organization's capabilities and talent is clearly a major problem in an HC-centric organization. These intangibles are a key capital of HC-centric organizations and for boards to correctly evaluate the performance of senior management and understand the performance of the company, they need information on just these issues.

Herman Miller, a world leader in delivering innovative office design solutions, is one company that has staffed its board with experts in the key organizational capabilities it needs in order to implement its strategy. Its strategy calls for it to be a leader in design and innovation. In addition to having an expert in talent management on the board, it has an expert in design and innovation. According to the board chair, Michael Volkema, this gives the board the in-depth expertise it needs to be sure that Herman Miller has world-class design and innovation capabilities.

With the possible exception of information about the top few executives, boards do not need fine-grained information about individuals. What they do need is information about the talent management activities of the company and the condition of the talent in the company.

For example, it is critical that boards receive audits of the organization's talent. These audits should be focused on the critical positions in the organization and the talent that the organization has available to fill them. They should look not only at who is in the jobs but what backups those individuals have and what the labor market is like should outside recruiting be needed.

In some cases, it is desirable for boards to bring in outside auditors to do talent assessment work. All too often, CEOs and others in organizations cannot be counted on to give valid data about the talent available in the organization. They may overstate it to make themselves look good when it comes to talent management, or perhaps they may try to hide individuals who are so highly talented that they represent a threat to them and their position in the organization. The latter is particularly likely to happen in organizations where the CEO is insecure or performing poorly.

In most cases, the board needs the same type of information whether management takes a high-involvement approach or a global-competitor one. In both cases, they need data on how well the organization is living up to its employment contract, what its employer brand is, and, of course, what its supply of critical talent is.

Boards of both global-competitor and high-involvement organizations need data on the attitudes of the workforce. In addition to getting data from general surveys on organizational effectiveness, they need to see data from pulse surveys that are taken regularly. These data can give the board an idea of how the organization is reacting to internal changes and current business conditions, and how effectively management is leading the company.

In the case of global competitors, the focus on talent needs to include more data on the availability of key talent outside the company, and it needs to focus on the effectiveness of the recruiting efforts of the company. Global competitors rely more on buying talent, so talent market information needs to be more prominent in the reports given to their boards.

In high-involvement organizations, boards need more information on talent development activities. Board members need to know how effective the organization is at creating the right skills for the organization's capabilities and core competencies. They also need to focus on turnover, with a major focus of the kind and quality of talent that is leaving. Where possible, reports should include where key talent is going and why it is leaving.

Board members definitely should have access to balanced scorecard data that includes measures of the condition of talent. As mentioned in Chapter Six, it should include retention numbers, attitude numbers, and recruiting success. Where possible it should include data that allow comparisons to other companies, just as is often done in the case of quality and customer satisfaction. The data available to boards should also include information on the organizational competencies and capabilities that the board and senior executives have identified as being needed to implement the organization's strategic plan.

Herman Miller provides its board with extensive information on the condition of its critical talent. Twice a year, the board gets information on the company's talent and succession planning activities. In the case of key performance areas (for example, design), it looks at the top four levels of the organization; in others, it looks at the top two levels. The data alert the board members to possible talent shortages and to whether they need to look outside in order to add new organizational capabilities and competencies.

In addition to the quantitative data that board members can get from dashboards and scorecards, it is important that they get experiential data on what it is like to work for their company. They also need experiential data on how employees deal with customers and each other. The most obvious way for board members to gather this kind of data is to become customers. This is particularly useful in a service business and is increasingly becoming a requirement for board membership.

Board members should be "mystery shoppers" for their organizations. Yes, there is a risk here of board members getting a nonrepresentative sample of what things are like in the company, but it is a risk worth taking and can be diminished by asking board members to be frequent shoppers, not just occasional shoppers.

In addition to being "mystery shoppers," board members can learn a great deal about the organization by conducting, or observing, focus groups in the organization. Often the videotape of a focus group is a good way to get board members familiar with what it is like to work in their organization.

Site visits are another helpful vehicle in acquainting board members with the human capital and management issues the company faces. Boards increasingly are requiring that board members do site visits during the year. It is very important that the site visit do more than just examine the physical assets of the company. Board members should have a chance to interact with employees, and if possible to observe work in process.

A board should also ask for and receive data on how the company's human capital management practices and employment contracts are seen by potential employees. In other words, they need to get market research data on the organization's employer brand.

Finally, it is worth repeating that when it comes to making talent management decisions, boards are not the only ones that need information and do not receive it. Most organizations simply do not collect and have readily available the kind of information that managers, executives, *and* boards need in order to make adequate decisions about talent management.

OPPORTUNITY

Board members are almost always very busy individuals. The board meeting agenda is typically crammed with must-do items; as a result, getting board members to focus on anything other than the financial results that need to be reported to the public and such key business decisions as mergers, acquisitions, new products, and major capital investments can be difficult. Nevertheless, the boards of HC-centric organizations must have the opportunity to review the talent issues in the organization.

Increasingly, boards are holding strategic retreats during which they devote one or more days to an overall look at the business and its strategy. This is an excellent time to take a serious look at the talent and organizational effectiveness issues that boards should address.

Boards can use their time at retreats to review candidates for senior management jobs, as well as to review talent availability in the organization and in the marketplace. In addition, it is an excellent opportunity to focus on the condition of the organization's competencies and capabilities because this discussion should go hand in hand with strategy reviews and formulations.

In addition to considering talent and organizational effectiveness issues at their strategy off-sites, boards need to pay attention to talent issues during their regular meetings. These issues should be on the agenda of every board meeting, just as financial data are on the agenda at every board meeting. Failing to put talent management on the agenda sends exactly the wrong signal to management (and board members, for that matter) as to the relative importance of human capital versus financial capital. It also perpetuates the all too common phenomenon of board members' not understanding, discussing, or even seeing data about the organization's talent.

Boards are increasing the number of committees they have and the amount of time they meet. The many reasons for this include the difficulty of getting entire boards together and the need to focus in depth on such critical issues as corporate governance and, of course, financial reporting. My research on boards shows that as a result, boards are relying more and more on committees to get their work done.

If boards had a committee on talent and organizational effectiveness, the trend toward committees doing more board work could result in a greater focus on talent management. But this hasn't happened—most boards simply do not have such a committee. Some boards do have committees on human resources, but they typically focus on CEO and executive compensation and perhaps succession planning at the executive level, not on the overall talent strategy and effectiveness of the organization. The failure to have a meaningful and active committee on talent is one more indication of the relatively low priority that boards give to it.

What is needed is a human capital committee that addresses succession planning for senior management positions and the evaluation of the CEO and the top management team. It also needs to monitor the development, placement, and recruitment of talent for the organization. In addition, the human capital committee should deal with issues concerning organizational capabilities and core competencies. The committee's responsibilities should include looking at the condition of the organization's competencies and capabilities, whether they fit the business strategy, and how adequately they are supported by the talent in the organization—in short, whether the organization is doing a good job of managing them.

What the committee should not do is get involved in the micromanagement of individual careers and monitoring the performance of individuals outside the top management group. Admittedly, there is a fine line between the committee being involved in micromanagement and being a strategic arm of the board. Clearly, it needs to be the latter, and to do that it needs the kind of information about the condition of the organization's talent that is discussed in Chapters Six and Seven.

Finally, the board committee on human capital management needs to be chaired by a board member who understands how talent management systems work—how to assess the talent of an organization and how to tie human capital management to business models and strategic plans. This may also be an area where the board needs to hire consulting expertise.

The human capital management committee needs to work with the senior human resource executives in the company, so that it gets the right information and is informed about the organization's human capital strategy. It also needs to ask them for data, talk to employees, have a secure confidential Web site that employees can use to contact it, and generally have access to the organization so it can gather data and understand how talent is being managed.

EXECUTIVE COMPENSATION IS CRITICAL

I want to stress that boards have a special responsibility for executive compensation in HC-centric organizations; when it comes to leadership in HC-centric organizations (see Chapter Nine), it is extremely important that executive compensation pass a credibility test.

Boards that approve indefensible compensation packages for senior executives do a great deal of damage to the commitment of the workforce and to the credibility of themselves and senior management. This may not be a critical problem in a structure-centric organization, but in an HC-centric organization— particularly a high-involvement one—it can be a major problem. It makes it difficult for the CEO to lead from a platform of credibility and integrity. It also can motivate senior executives to behave in ways that have dysfunctional consequences for the rest of the workforce. (For example, they may engage in unneeded layoffs and cut back on training and development to provide a short-term boost in corporate profit and the stock price.)

Boards must be assured that the organization's critical resource, its talent, regards the leadership of the organization as being in the boat with them. Without an alignment between their interests and those of senior management, employees are not likely to be responsive to the leadership efforts of senior management or be committed to the success of the organization.

What kinds of compensation packages lead to alignment between the talent of the organization and senior executives? This is not a difficult question to answer. Profit sharing plans, stock option plans, and stock purchase plans that cover everyone, or almost everyone, in the organization are vehicles for creating this alignment. Research shows that when everyone in an organization has an ownership interest, talent throughout the organization is more committed and involved in the organization.[11]

Does the difference in total compensation between those at the very top of the organization and those further down make a difference in how individuals feel about their organization? The answer is yes, research suggests that when the senior executives make hundreds of times more than the rest of the workforce, it has a negative effect on employees and separates the leaders from others in the organization. This is not to say that everyone in the organization should be paid the same, or nearly the same. Most employees know and accept the reality that some positions have a higher market value than others and that this sometimes necessitates large differences in pay.

The key is to avoid being an outlier that pays executives above market. It is also worth giving serious consideration to being a low payer relative to the market. CEOs like John Mackey at Whole Foods have credibility in their organizations in part because they have a relatively low compensation level relative to other CEOs.

BOARDS FOR DIFFERENT TYPES OF HC-CENTRIC ORGANIZATIONS

What boards need to do in high-involvement organizations is not dramatically different from what they need to do in global-competitor organizations. In both HC-centric management approaches, essentially the same things need to be attended to: talent, organizational capabilities, core competencies, and the development and implementation of business strategy.

The differences are largely in the kind of metrics that need to be attended to and some of the practices that the board needs to monitor. In the case of metrics, for example, boards need to pay more attention to culture and attitude measures, as well as leadership style measures, in a high-involvement organization than in a global-competitor organization. In the case of compensation, the board of a high-involvement organization should be more concerned about the alignment between executive compensation and the compensation of individuals elsewhere in the organization.

Finally, in looking at strategy, boards in high-involvement organizations need to focus on the issue of whether the appropriate talent exists or can be developed to implement the strategy, and if not, to determine if the organization can avoid layoffs and reductions when it sets out to implement the strategy. In the case of global-competitor organizations the key issues are much more ones of whether the strategy requires talent that actually is available in the market and whether the necessary individuals can be recruited so the strategy can be implemented.

What Boards Should Do

The following are what boards need to do in all HC-centric organizations:

- Boards need enough power to have a significant influence on the way talent is managed. Specifically they need to ensure that the right approach to talent management is adopted and that it is well integrated with strategy.
- Boards in HC-centric organizations need extensive knowledge of the principles governing behavior in organizations as well as a good understanding of talent management systems and business strategy.
- Board members should be rewarded based on the long-term effectiveness of their organization. Boards need to evaluate their own effectiveness as well as the effectiveness of the CEO, the members of senior management, and the individual members of the board.
- Boards need to make time available at their regular meetings to discuss talent management and the conditions of an organization's capabilities and competencies. They also need to look at how this corresponds to the effectiveness of the organization.
- Boards need to have a committee on organizational effectiveness and talent management.
- Boards need to have access to a number of metrics concerning the talent of the organization, particularly those that have to do with talent availability, utilization, and performance.
- Board members need to be sure that the executive compensation packages that they approve support the management approach of the organization and reward developing and managing human capital as well as organizational performance.
- Boards need to focus on management talent. They need to constantly ask about leadership development activities, meet with high-potential leaders, and assess the management talent.

CHAPTER NINE

LEADING

All too often the effectiveness of an organization's leaders is the default explanation for many of the good and bad things that happen in—and to—organizations. We have a strong need to explain why things happen, and a strong tendency to assign a causal basis to the behavior of top executives. They typically get the credit when a company is successful—and the blame when a company stumbles or fails.[1]

Without question, senior executive leadership is very important to the effectiveness of all organizations. The quality of an organization's CEO, and the quality of those who hold senior executive positions, clearly affects financial performance and the motivation and satisfaction of its talent.

But senior leadership is only one of the major determinants of organizational effectiveness. Many studies, in fact, show that the *key* determinant of most employee behavior is not the leadership of the CEO or the senior executives but the behavior of the employee's immediate supervisor or supervisors.[2] These are the individuals who provide much of the day-to-day motivation and sense of direction to most of the employees in organizations. These are the people who possess—and pass along—technical and organizational knowledge when it comes to strategy implementation, change management, and work processes. They are also the ones who set the culture for employees; their behaviors shape the culture in a much more immediate and tangible way than the behavior of the senior executives.

Because too much power is ascribed to how the very top executives lead, all too often organizations focus too little on the way in which individuals in management positions throughout the organization behave, and on the impact of their behavior. In organizations that aspire to be HC-centric, this focus needs to change. As Mark Hurd, the CEO of Hewlett-Packard (HP), has argued, in HC-centric organizations, leadership should be a "team sport" that is played by everyone.[3]

Leadership opportunities are always present throughout organizations. Any employee can create a leadership moment by encouraging someone, being a role model, explaining a corporate policy or business decision, and, yes, by expressing disapproval of what someone does or doesn't do.

Effective leadership at all levels is particularly critical to the success of HC-centric organizations for two reasons. First, it is what substitutes for the bureaucratic controls and structures that are absent in HC-centric organizations. Second, it provides the kind of motivation and culture that will make talent a competitive advantage.

LEADERS, MANAGERS, OR BOTH?

Much of the writing on leadership makes a distinction between managers and leaders. Although there is no consensus definition as to what separates a leader from a manager, the distinction generally rests on doing the basic blocking and tackling of organizing (assigning tasks, monitoring the work of others), versus providing a sense of meaning, direction, motivation, and inspiration.

When behavior is more oriented toward providing feedback to individuals on their performance, setting standards, and maintaining a well-organized workflow, an individual is generally considered to be managing. On the other hand, when behavior is focused more on providing employees with a sense of mission and inspiration—when it involves helping employees find and understand their niche within the company—an individual is considered to be leading.[4] The difference between leaders and managers is often characterized by the saying: "Managers do things right; leaders do the right things."

In HC-centric organizations—particularly high-involvement organizations—people can provide a competitive advantage only if they are both well led and well managed. Thus, individuals should be in management positions in HC-centric organizations only if they have both good managerial skills and good leadership skills. HC-centric organizations, then, should not focus on developing senior executives, or for that matter managers at any level, who are just good leaders or just good managers; they should develop individuals throughout the organization who are good managers and good leaders.

Fortunately, nothing about being a good manager prevents somebody from being a good leader, and nothing about being a good leader prevents somebody from being a good manager.[5] Indeed, the behaviors that go along with being a good manager and being a good leader are typically quite complementary. Finally, it is important to note that individuals don't have to be managers in order to be leaders. Individuals who are not in managerial jobs can and often do act as leaders in HC-centric organizations.

What Managers Need to Do

Managers throughout an HC-centric organization—from the senior-most executive to those supervising the lowest-paid employees—need to do a number of critical things. (For simplicity's sake, I'll use the term *managers* going forward to refer to all individuals who have supervisory responsibility and not as a term to distinguish leaders from managers.) These things can be done effectively only if an organization has built the kind of systems discussed in earlier chapters. Simply stated, managerial effectiveness depends in part on organizations' having the right structure, the right information and decision processes, an effective HR function, good talent management systems, and a board that understands and focuses on the right talent management and organizational effectiveness issues.

Look to the Future

Effective managers learn from the past by debriefing the successes and failures that have occurred, but their major focus needs to be on the future. An important part of this focus on the future is setting expectations, and providing an inspirational view of how the performance of people can provide winning business performance.

How does this get done? A piece of the answer lies with understanding the competitive environment and how it is changing. Many competitive advantages can quickly become outdated as other organizations copy them. Thus managers need to constantly monitor the external environment to see what the next source of competitive advantage is likely to be and prepare their organization for it. The ability to do this effectively is, in fact, just the kind of sustainable competitive advantage that HC-centric organizations need.

Managers also need to show employees how to get from theory to practice. Implementing a source of competitive advantage such as becoming more customer-focused or more innovative is rarely a simple task. Far from simply being a matter of buying new software or a new piece of capital equipment, developing organizational capabilities usually requires change in all the points on the star. New pay systems are needed that reward the right behavior. Budgets need to be changed to provide resources to support developmental activities. And of course, training is needed to provide the necessary skills.

I could go on and list other changes, but I think I have made my point. Shifting competencies and capabilities can't happen in a vacuum. That's why I reiterate that an organization needs the right systems, structures, and processes if managers are to be effective. Even if individual managers are very effective leaders in their own right, they cannot develop new organizational capabilities if the organization isn't designed to support their development.

Manage Attention

Warren Bennis and other leadership researchers have noted that it is often difficult for managers to focus the attention of the organization on the really critical issues that determine its success.[6] This is because the constant demands of the day-to-day details of doing business divert managers and employees alike from paying attention to critical issues.

Effective managers deal with the day-to-day, but they are also constantly asking about and focusing on their short list of things that truly determine the effectiveness of an HC-centric organization. They stay on message and return to this short list again and again; doing so is a behavior that is built into their schedules and recognized in performance reviews.

Included on the short list of every manager should always be: What kind of talent development is going on? What are the key causes of organizational performance and how well are employees attending to them? How is the company doing vis-à-vis its customer service and quality goals (or whatever it is that its strategy says are the key sources of competitive advantage)? Are the systems in place to track the key performance areas? If not, what needs to change?

MANAGE PERFORMANCE

As is discussed in Chapter Five, performance management systems are most effective when they are owned by senior management and used as tools by managers at all organizational levels. These systems will not work if they reside in HR and are performed because HR says they are important.

Effective execution certainly begins with having a well-designed system that employees understand, but it takes more than a good design to be effective; it takes managers who have good interpersonal and communication skills. Often managers are uncomfortable with some of the interpersonal aspects of the appraisal process and they may well need training in how to do goal setting, give feedback, and administer rewards.

That said, there is no substitute for having a manager who can set effective goals, communicate why the goals are important, and communicate how they relate to the overall direction of the business. Managers must also be clear about how goal accomplishment and goal achievement are related to rewards and ultimately to the career progression of the individual.

As stressed in Chapter Five, having an effective performance management system is particularly important and at times challenging in HC-centric organizations. The agendas of HC-centric organizations often change, so managers need to revise and update the goals of their direct reports on an ongoing basis.

Since their direct reports may have more knowledge than they do about how to do a task and what types and levels of performance are possible, managers need to be highly skilled at engaging in a dialogue about what are appropriate goals. They often need to establish goals and set direction in situations where cooperation is needed among a large number of individuals whose areas of experience and expertise differ from one another's as well as from theirs.

One implication of the importance of a manager's ability to do effective performance management is that managers need to be appraised, trained, and rewarded based on their ability to execute performance management activities. If they aren't, it speaks volumes about how unimportant this managerial activity is.

In addition to having a well-designed performance management process, organizations need to provide managers with the right performance metrics. Effective performance management requires information. Such obvious results as productivity and sales are not enough; it also requires information on the reaction of employees to the leadership behaviors of individuals, customer reactions to service delivery, and of course data on how effective managers are in developing talent.

Finally, effective performance management requires reward systems that allow managers to reward the right behaviors and provide individuals with rewards for appropriate skill and knowledge development. This of course is particularly important in a knowledge-intensive organization, but it is important in any HC-centric organization. Given that human capital is the critical source of competitive advantage in HC-centric organizations, the reward system must be able to respond to changes in the value of human capital.

Manage Talent

Effective talent management is critical in an HC-centric organization. Talent management can be executed effectively only if an effective performance management system is in place. Managers need information on the condition of human capital in the organization and of course a clear understanding of the business strategy and the skills, competencies, and capabilities needed to support it.

At the top of the organization, executives need to be clear in defining what metrics are the best measures of the condition of the talent in the organization and also be decisive in establishing what core competencies and organizational capabilities are needed for the business to be successful. They then need to articulate how this relates to the business objectives and how individual managers will be held accountable for developing talent.

Critical to the effectiveness of HC-centric organizations is the willingness of individual managers to develop the people reporting to them and to put aside their self-interest when it comes to providing development experiences for talent. This of course is particularly true in a high-involvement organization because it has a build rather than a buy model with respect to talent.

Unfortunately, as noted earlier, many organizations do not have a viable decision science approach to talent management. They usually do have considerable expertise in allocating financial assets and standard models for doing it. What they don't have but need to develop are similar models for allocating human capital.

As mentioned in Chapter Four, talent management models need to involve the importance of jobs and the kind of skills individuals need to develop and the availability of talent. Analytics are needed that show the financial impact of different types of talent decisions. For example, they need to show what the financial impact is of the length of time an individual stays in a particular job and what the costs are of developing an individual to reach a certain level of proficiency. This kind of information is critical for any evidence-based talent development and allocation model that truly addresses the decision science of talent management.[7]

In addition to developing systems that support effective talent management decision making, organizations need to develop their managers' knowledge of talent management. All too often managers do not have adequate knowledge of the key behavioral principles that drive employee behavior in organizations. Table 5 presents data from a survey that asked both HR executives and other executives to assess the degree to which business leaders understand and use sound principles when making talent management decisions.[8] It turns out that managers generally rate business leaders higher than HR managers rate them, but both rate them very low on most points.

TABLE 5. BEHAVIORAL PRINCIPLES.

To what extent are these statements true about your organization?	HR Sample (% Great or Very Great Extent)	Manager Sample (% Great or Very Great Extent)
Business leaders understand and use sound principles when making decisions about:		
Motivation	33.3	42.9
Development and learning	26.2	36.8
Labor markets	28.6	37.7
Culture	32.4	50.0
Organization design	31.3	46.8
Business strategy	62.6	64.9
Business leaders' decisions that depend upon or affect human capital (layoffs, rewards, and so on) are as rigorous, logical, and strategically relevant as their decisions about resources such as money, technology, and customers.	42.3	55.9

Only 55.9 percent of the managers say that business leaders' decisions that affect human capital are as rigorous and logical as those that affect other key organizational resources. When HR executives rate business leaders, the number is significantly lower (42.3 percent). Clearly poor decision making about talent is not acceptable.

Managers in HC-centric organizations need to understand and use the same rigor in making decisions about human capital as they do in making decisions about other types of capital. Indeed, the argument can be made that they need to be more rigorous and have better judgment when it comes to human capital management because it is the key competitive advantage of HC-centric organizations.

It is interesting to note in Table 5 that the ratings are much higher for decisions affecting business strategy. In many respects this is not surprising since managers have more training and often spend more time making business strategy decisions than they do making human capital decisions. But again, it is not acceptable to have individuals in management positions who are more skilled in business strategy decision making than in talent decision making.

Managers in HC-centric organizations need to have high levels of expertise in such human capital management issues as motivation, talent development, performance management, and organization design. If they don't have the expertise and the ability to make good talent decisions, they shouldn't be in a management job.

Making good talent management decisions is important in both high-involvement and global-competitor organizations. What needs to differ between them is the decisions they focus on. The global-competitor approach involves looking outside for talent and considering whether it is better to build or buy a particular type of talent. The high-involvement approach is focused on internal development and decisions about the careers of an organization's existing talent.

CONFRONT PERFORMANCE PROBLEMS

One of the hardest things for many managers to do is confront individuals who are not performing well or are doing inappropriate things. Time after time I have seen a manager faced with a subordinate who has performance problems fail to confront the individual, or, almost as bad, wait for a scheduled performance review before raising the issue. When asked why, they point out that they expect employees to figure out that sort of thing for themselves or that it is not worth the trouble—the employee is just not capable of changing.

In short, the manager, instead of confronting the issue, chooses to "work around it." Sometimes working around performance problems includes giving the employee only easy assignments and giving the more complicated work to others, sometimes it simply involves giving the employee less work to do and sometimes it means ignoring it until a case can be made for firing the employee.

Creating a Truth-Telling Culture at DaVita

DaVita Corporation, a California-based provider of dialysis services, is in a talent-critical business. High-quality customer service is a central piece of its offering, so improving performance is always a concern. To that end, DaVita CEO Kent Thiry has worked hard to create a truth-telling culture that ensures managers throughout the company will hear both the good news and the bad news—and be able to respond effectively.

For example, Thiry has created a program called Reality 101. He has every manager spend a week working in a dialysis center seeing firsthand what is involved in making one of the company's centers work effectively. This program has helped DaVita managers understand the business and greatly increase their ability to relate to the kind of issues that are raised when employees provide feedback.

Employee communication is built into the way DaVita operates. The company schedules about twenty small town hall meetings a year to learn from employees how things can be improved in all areas of the organization. These meetings, chaired by vice presidents, gather at least seven employees per session. During the meetings, employees can ask any questions they choose; they can also offer feedback on any issue. The sessions add value on several fronts: they give senior management information on what is and isn't working, and they give employees unstructured access to members of the company's senior management team.

According to Thiry, DaVita employees should think of themselves as members of a village, with a shared responsibility and a shared vision of reality. He helps them achieve this common perspective by providing key data. DaVita puts a heavy emphasis on collecting data on a range of issues, including operations, quality of care, employee satisfaction, and customer satisfaction for each of its dialysis centers. These data inform managers and help them respond effectively to change.

Thiry also believes that executives who seek frank feedback must follow through even when it reveals their own managerial shortcomings. This is difficult to do; it's easier to focus on solving

(Continued)

other people's problems. But Thiry believes it's another key to sustaining the culture he has tried to create.

His view is similar to that of Bill George, former CEO of Medtronic. Both argue that CEOs and other managers must take a realistic look at their own behavior. When they get negative feedback they need to own up to their performance shortcomings and make an effort to eliminate them. At one point, Thiry himself got a bad grade from his thirteen senior executives for giving too much negative feedback. He owned up to it and has made a conscientious effort to change his behavior.

Effective managers in HC-centric organizations address performance and other problems by creating "moments of truth"—not by working around them. This is particularly critical in HC-centric organizations because they rely on human capital for their competitive advantage. If its managers can't manage human capital in a way that optimizes its performance, an organization has no hope of achieving a competitive advantage. It cannot optimize the performance of its workforce without having well-managed moments of truth that involve accurate and compelling feedback. Performance truth telling is one of the most powerful managerial behaviors that exists.

Moments of truth don't come easily in organizations. They happen only if strong leaders at the very top model the right behaviors and encourage managers throughout the organization to engage in moments of truth. Managers usually need to be trained in executing a moment of truth. It is not an easy discussion to initiate or execute. Without training, many managers fall into the trap of simply attacking an employee who is performing poorly or who criticizes them. This usually results in the employee withdrawing or becoming defensive.

The key is to turn the discussion of a performance problem into an analytic session that tries to identify the causes of the problem and the kind of corrective action that can be taken. Once this has been accomplished, the next step is to have follow-up discussions to ensure that the corrective steps have been taken and performance has improved. Effective moments of truth lead to the kind of ongoing performance feedback mentioned in Chapter Five, which is so critical to the success of any performance management system.

Challenges Facing Executives

One of the biggest challenges facing executives in an HC-centric organization is the distance—real and implied—between the corner office and the bulk of employees. Senior executives often travel a great deal; their compensation packages encourage and facilitate a lifestyle that includes a variety of special perquisites and amenities. Private jets, private offices, country club memberships, executive dining rooms, the list can go on and on.

None of the perquisites that executives typically receive are by themselves necessarily bad or inappropriate, but in combination they can create a major separation between executives and the people who work for them. In essence they can undermine the opportunity for executives to experience their organizations and the external world as others experience them. Executives can end up having little contact with most employees, and as a result, communication and understanding are limited. In an HC-centric organization, this is a fatal flaw.

Reward Differences

Large differences in rewards between the top and bottom of an organization can undermine the credibility of executives when they try to lead by talking about what "we" have to do to make this organization successful. It also can happen when they try to provide an inspirational message about their commitment to the organization and how others can contribute to it. This is particularly true when they ask individuals to make a sacrifice in difficult times or to give exceptional service to win over customers. As one Home Depot employee put it, commenting on the high pay of CEO Robert Nardelli, "All of us felt that the raises we should have gotten were going into Nardelli's pocket."

Consider the distribution of stock ownership. It is one thing for CEOs to talk about how "we are all in this together" when everyone owns stock in the company. It is another for them to talk about it when they have a large number of stock options and stand to gain millions of dollars if the stock does well while others have little or no ownership in the company.

Financial ownership and psychological ownership go hand in hand. Managers who are good leaders recognize this and provide themselves with a credible platform when they talk about what people need to do for the organization to be successful. The bottom line is that senior executives in HC-centric organizations need to work actively to minimize the gap between them and their employees.

I believe it is particularly important for the CEOs of high-involvement organizations to remain close to their employees when it comes to rewards and perquisites. High-involvement organizations depend very much on the sense of a common fate for everyone in the organization and everyone being committed to a common goal. As noted, when senior executives profit disproportionately or in ways that are not available to the rest of the organization, it makes it particularly difficult for them to be seen as walking the talk of a high-involvement organization.

Customer service organizations, it is worth noting, are a special case when it comes to having a minimal reward distance between senior levels and the rest of the organization. Best Buy, Starbucks, and Whole Foods all have CEOs who recognize this and have kept their salaries relatively close to those of most employees, and as a result, have employees who respect the CEO and the company. As a result of their feelings toward senior management, employees are less likely to feel like second-class citizens and communicate this in their service behavior. They are also more likely to follow the lead of their CEO.

Global-competitor organizations require a different approach to rewards for executives than do high-involvement organizations. Since these organizations are often talent meritocracies that must attract senior management talent, having relatively high rewards for senior managers may in fact be functional. Good rewards at the top can be critical in attracting and retaining the kind of very competent senior management that global-competitor organizations need.

Imperial CEOs

There has been a growing tendency for CEOs to adopt a model of leadership I'll call the "imperial" model. They make decisions and develop strategies with little input and discussion. Their decisions are above criticism and challenge. They adopt lifestyles that make them celebrities and their companies become vehicles that make them "rock stars." They are supported by technology that is designed to keep them in touch 24/7. But in reality, most imperial CEOs are dangerously out of touch with the people they lead, particularly when it comes to the issue of strategy implementation and development.[9]

Strategies and business plans in HC-centric organizations are likely to be successfully developed and implemented only if the individuals who have to implement them know that they are listened to and have a say. Even if a brilliant CEO or senior executive can craft a successful strategy without input, the issue of how it is going to be implemented remains. Without individuals throughout the organization having a say in what is in a strategy and agreeing it is the right strategy, it's highly unlikely they will want to and be able to implement it.

In an HC-centric organization the gap between leader and led should never be large. It is simply too important for leaders to gather information from others and receive feedback about their performance. Leaders need to be approachable. They need to be told when they do something wrong or have made a mistake and they need to be able to hear it. Only if they are understood by the critical capital in the organization, which is the talent that works there, will they be able to create a high-performance organization.

In addition, managers need to demonstrate visibly that they value employees. When cost-cutting is a priority, they should explore alternatives before cutting staff. When it is necessary, they should be sure it is executed in a way that fits their employer brand. When leadership training is done, they should take part. When it is time for talent reviews, they should lead the process.

Jeff Immelt, GE's CEO, stated what CEOs need to do in GE's 2005 annual report: "Developing and motivating people is the most important part of my job. I spend one-third of my time on people. We invest $1 billion annually in training to make them better. . . . I spend most of my time on the top 600 leaders in the company. This is how you create a culture. These people all get selected and paid by me."

Some recent firings of CEOs suggest that corporate boards are recognizing that imperial CEOs may not be the best CEOs. In 2005, CEO Carly Fiorina was fired by the board of Hewlett-Packard. Hank Greenberg, who has been described as the prototype "imperial CEO," was forced out at American International Group after three decades.[10] Perhaps the most visible case was the firing of Bob Nardelli by Home Depot following his dreadful decision to have his board of directors *not* attend Home Depot's annual meeting!

When Frank Blake became the new CEO of Home Depot he recognized the importance of moving away from the imperial leadership style of his predecessor. In addition to taking a much lower salary, he discontinued the catered executive luncheon that the company's top management team had enjoyed under Bob Nardelli and "suggested" that the members of senior management eat in the cafeteria with the other employees. This act sent a clear message to the employees that he intended to be a different kind of leader.

EFFECTIVE COMMUNICATIONS

Perhaps the most common mistake that top executives make in all types of organizations is not recognizing the importance of communicating directly and effectively with employees. One CEO who does recognize the importance of this is Jim McNerney, the CEO of Boeing. Boeing has a global workforce of 160,000 employees, so communicating with everyone is not a simple task. When asked recently if he was going to spend more time with customers and stock analysts, he replied that it is more important for him to spend time with Boeing's employees than to spend it on increasing his profile and his visibility in the press. According to him, employees "have got to know that working with them is more important to me than public forums where I'm making big speeches."

David Newman, chairman of Jet Blue Airways, takes an interesting approach to getting to know his employees and also demonstrating consistency between what he advocates employees do and what he does. According to Newman, "I fly at least one flight a week. I serve the customers snacks. They call me 'snack boy' on the flight. I pick up the trash, and when the plane lands I help clean the airplane. I go out on the ramp and I throw bags. I make people feel proud to work for a company where a CEO isn't being driven around in limousines and flying in private jets."[11]

Clearly what Newman does is not appropriate for every CEO, but in customer-service-oriented, HC-centric organizations it is a dramatic way to get to know employees and what they do, and to communicate to them that what they do is important to the leadership of the organization. He is not alone in his approach to leadership. Key executives at Southwest Airlines have done the same thing for decades, while DaVita expects its managers to do frontline customer service jobs as a part of their development.

I could go on giving examples, but I don't think I need to. There are thousands of things managers can do to improve communication between the levels in an organization. Managers need to find what works for them and do it!

Developing Managers

I am often asked why so few people are able to combine the managerial and leadership skills required to be an effective manager. Clearly this question has no simple answer. Despite the hundreds of thousands of articles and books that have been written on leadership, the reality is that many individuals don't have what it takes to be a successful manager in an HC-centric organization. In fact it may partly be because so many articles and books are written on leadership that many managers don't know what it takes!

Many of the articles and books on leadership ignore or give only brief consideration to managerial skills. Further, when all is said and done there is hardly a dramatic consensus in the leadership literature on what it takes to be a successful leader. The books vary greatly in the types of leadership styles they recommend and claim are successful. They range all the way from presenting highly simplistic views of what constitutes effective leadership (for example, *The One Minute Manager*) to very dense academic tomes that review the massive empirical research on leadership.

Today many managers have gone to business school, but this does not necessarily mean they have leadership and managerial knowledge and skills. All too often they learn more about finance and economics than about human behavior. Thus most organizations must create their own ways to find the managers they need. In a global-competitor organization one way is to buy talent from the few academy companies (such as GE and PepsiCo) with a surplus of talent. In a high-involvement organization, it almost always means making a serious commitment to developing effective leaders.

The research literature on leadership development is quite clear in showing that experience is the best developer.[12] Development experiences need to involve a challenging task as well as conceptual information on how to be an effective leader and what the leadership expectations of the organization are.

Every HC-centric organization ought to have a clear, well-developed set of leadership competencies that it expects every manager to master. These ought to be more than just the general phrases like "be a good listener" and "educate people about the business." They ought to drill down to another level of specificity so that it's clear what behaviors are part of being a good listener and what parts of the business model should be taught and how it should be taught.

Organizations also need to regularly assess whether managers have the requisite competencies. This can best be done by gathering survey data from observers of their behaviors and by testing their content knowledge of leadership behaviors. It is not easy to develop individuals who can lead an HC-centric organization, but it is a necessity. Without effective leadership throughout, an HC-centric organization is destined to be ineffective.

LEADERS DEVELOPING LEADERS

One outstanding way for senior executives to show their commitment to leadership development is to actively participate in leadership development programs. Depending on their skill sets they can be active teachers or simply show their support by attending sessions. A number of highly visible CEOs in fact are excellent role models of how senior executives should behave in this respect.[13]

When Roger Enrico was the CEO of PepsiCo, he regularly taught sessions on leadership with his direct reports. Similarly Bob

Eckert of Mattel has sponsored numerous leadership development programs at Mattel and has taught and participated in them. When asked why he participates in Mattel management development programs, Eckert doesn't hesitate. He says it is because he learns from the programs and it gives him a chance to see the company managers in action. He adds it also shows his support for talent development.

Enrico and Eckert exemplify what effective leaders of HC-centric organizations need to be. It is not the hero or imperial leader who can single-handedly take an organization by its neck, shake it, and send it in the right direction. It is a leader who can turn leadership into a team sport and who can develop a company of leaders.

Leadership Development at Procter & Gamble

Procter & Gamble (P&G) has businesses in 160 countries and sells thousands of products. Despite being over a hundred years old, the company has been able to change and adapt to changing consumer preferences, globalization, and technological change. How has it been able to do this? CEO A. G. Lafley is convinced that *the* key reason for the success of P&G is the quality of its managers.

Lafley takes leadership development very seriously; in fact, he estimates that he spends about a third to half of his time on leadership development. His concern is reflected in the behavior of his senior managers. Dick Antoine, for example, the senior vice president for human resources, regularly reviews the individuals in the top four or five management levels in P&G to identify high-potential employees and keep track of future senior executives. He also shares his observation of candidates for senior positions with members of the P&G board so that they too can have a role in determining the company's future leaders. Directors, for their part, are expected to go into the field and meet potential senior executives while these candidates are doing their current jobs.

P&G also has an IT-based talent development system that contains names of more than three thousand managers. This

(Continued)

system, which includes details of their employment histories, backgrounds, and performance histories, is another key to the company's ability to identify future leaders.

Leaders throughout the company are given a great deal of information about the training opportunities available to them and are expected to have 360-degree performance reviews on a regular basis. The performance management system is designed to evaluate individuals both on how well they've accomplished their results and how they have accomplished them. Getting good results is not good enough; they must be accomplished in the right way.

Like other great CEO teachers, Lafley believes in looking for "teaching moments" to improve the skills of his management team. When he sees an opportunity to discuss a leadership act by one of his executives, he uses it to draw lessons about effective leadership and how individuals should be led at P&G.

At P&G, leadership is not an "HR issue"; it is a senior management focus. As a result, leadership development permeates the culture. It is not a once-a-year activity. Individuals are continually being evaluated and mentored in terms of their leadership skills. This process begins when people are hired, and continues throughout their careers at P&G.

In a business world that is turbulent, constantly fluctuating, and intensely competitive, what is needed is an organizational ability to adapt and constantly learn. This in turn requires having leaders at all levels who can lead change. A very important part of the leadership activities of managers at all levels should be searching for better and newer ways to do business, new approaches to organizing, and for changes in the environment that should alter the business strategy.

Where possible, the search for better alternatives ought to involve experimentation, use of metrics to validate the effectiveness of new procedures, and sharing learnings with others. Admittedly this type of mind-set and behavior needs to start with leadership by the CEO, but at its very core is the principle that leaders everywhere in the organization need to ensure that learning, experimentation, and attention are focused on what is happening in the external environment.

Jeffrey Pfeffer and Robert Sutton, in *The Knowing-Doing Gap,* make a statement that captures my feeling about how managers should think about their jobs.[14] According to Pfeffer and Sutton, the major job of managers is architecting organizational systems that establish the conditions for others to succeed. In other words, good managers are a combination of coaches and builders that enable performance by others. They help define success as well as identify relationships and processes that will lead to it. This applies at every level of the organization. In a shared leadership organization the expectation is that leaders at all levels are thinking about and creating systems and situations where teams, individual contributors, and entire business units are able to be successful.

CREATING SHARED LEADERSHIP

It is one thing to identify what a shared leadership organization looks like; it is another to actually create one. In my experience, the senior management of an organization can create a virtuous spiral of shared leadership when they provide the proper support. Before identifying the specific factors involved, I'd like to briefly describe what I mean by "virtuous spiral of leadership."

Earlier I mentioned the idea of organizations' getting into a virtuous spiral of improved performance. This same concept is applicable to leadership. Once people start seeing they can practice leadership and be rewarded for it, more and more want to be part of the action. As more do take on leadership roles, the organization's performance improves, as does the level of leadership and the desire of more and more individuals to take on leadership roles. The organization develops a clear leadership brand, and as a result, attracts the right kind of applicants.[15] This in turn helps populate the organization with effective leaders.

Goldman Sachs is a good example of a company that has developed a virtuous leadership spiral. At Goldman Sachs, everyone, no matter how junior, is expected to lead. As Henry Paulson, its former CEO, puts it, "We're global and multicultural like other professional service firms. We also have huge capital commitments and risks to manage. It takes many, many leaders. Goldman Sachs is leaders working with leaders."[16]

There is one key to establishing a virtuous leadership spiral: commitment on the part of senior management to developing it. Senior management support is clearly the building block on which the whole concept of shared leadership needs to rest. Senior management support is critical because the people at the top need to be teachers as well as advocates of shared leadership. Nothing will kill a shared leadership culture faster than a senior management group that dismisses leadership efforts by individuals below them and fails to support the development of leadership skills throughout the organization.

What does it mean for senior management to support leadership development throughout the organization? A wide variety of things. They need to be sure that the recruitment, selection, and retention processes of the organization put an emphasis on identifying individuals who are comfortable taking leadership roles.

Senior management also needs to put a major emphasis on leadership training not just for people at the very top of the organizations but throughout the ranks. Admittedly, some different management behaviors are needed at different levels of the organization, but that doesn't mean individuals from all levels of an organization shouldn't be trained in how to influence others and how to provide leadership.

In addition to training in leadership, all members of the organization need training so that they understand the business and the business strategy. Time after time surveys of organizations show that many individuals do not understand the business of their organization and its strategy. Encouraging individuals who do not have this knowledge to help lead an organization is not just unwise—it's positively dangerous. There is a very high probability that they will lead the organization in the wrong direction and end up destroying the entire idea of shared leadership in their organization.

Finally, it's critical that senior executives recognize and reward leadership behavior wherever it occurs in their organization. They can reward it through formal rewards like pay raises, bonuses, and promotions, but they also need to reward it in informal ways. They need to give praise to the individuals who take on leadership roles and make a significant contribution to the development of the organization.

HOW GLOBAL-COMPETITOR AND HIGH-INVOLVEMENT LEADERS SHOULD DIFFER

It is very important in a high-involvement organization that leadership be shared throughout the organization and that anyone can be and is a leader when the situation and the skills of the individuals call for it. The flat structure and lateral approach to organizing used by them simply cannot succeed without individuals throughout the organization taking on leadership responsibilities. This is not to say that shared leadership is not important in a global-competitor organization; it clearly is. But global-competitor organizations, because of their more transient employee population, often don't need to or perhaps more accurately cannot afford to spread leadership responsibility quite as broadly as in a high-involvement organization.

High-involvement organizations can afford to spend more time on training and developing leaders because they can reasonably expect that their talent will be around long enough to pay back the investment. In global-competitor organizations it is wise to be more selective about investing in training and development for leaders because of the relatively transitory nature of the employment relationship.

Everyone in a high involvement organization should be able and prepared to take on a leadership role. Not everyone can have direct managerial responsibilities, except for self-management; however, everyone can engage in leadership moments by coaching others, acknowledging good performance, organizing work, and moving the organization in the direction of outstanding performance.

High-involvement leaders need to differ in one important way from global-competitor leaders. They need to be much more concerned with leading in a participative and involvement-oriented way. Leaders in high-involvement organizations need to be sure that individuals at all levels are given the kind of information and training that will allow them to be full participants in the business and as a result identify with its successes and failures. This is crucial to their willingness and ability to self-manage and to creating a culture where rules and administrative control structures are not needed to guide behavior.

In the case of global-competitor organizations a certain amount of participative leadership is appropriate, but it does not need to be a defining feature of the company's identity and leadership brand. Managers in global-competitor organizations do need to be particularly skilled at setting reasonable goals and doing effective performance management. The nature of the employment contract at global-competitor organizations makes it less likely that individuals will be highly committed to the organization and focused on what they can do to make the organization successful. They are much more likely to be concerned with the rewards they are likely to receive as individuals in the short term. Thus, performance contracts and rewards based on performance are an important part of their relationship to both the organization and their manager.

WHAT ALL MANAGERS SHOULD DO

I have set a very high bar for what managers should be like in HC-centric organizations. This raises the inevitable question of whether it is realistic to expect all managers to be good managers and leaders. To some extent this question needs to be answered on a situation-by-situation basis, but I think it is possible to identify some skills that all managers must have, regardless of whether they work in a high-involvement organization or a global competitor:

- *Expertise in performance management.* They need to be effective coaches and committed to making it possible for people to perform effectively. Nothing they do in their job is more important than this. They need to own performance management and employee development as their number one priority.
- *Expertise in talent management and organizational effectiveness.* They should make talent decisions with rigor equal to the decisions they make concerning financial resources and operations. In short, they need to have a decision science approach to the management of human capital.
- *Ability to look into the future.* They need to help the organization and its members develop a sense of what future challenges are and constantly encourage their organization to develop the kind of competencies and capabilities it needs to meet future challenges.

- *Ability to create truth telling and open communication with individuals throughout the organization.* They need to minimize the social distance and maximize the communication between themselves and those who work for them.
- *Ability to develop leaders.* They should know how to provide leadership development experiences and to educate individuals throughout the organization about what it takes to be an effective leader.
- Know how to *and "walk the talk."* Discrepancies between what managers say and what they do are all too obvious and very damaging in HC-centric organizations. Managers must know how to walk their talk.

CHAPTER TEN

MANAGING CHANGE

How do most of today's organizations stack up against the characteristics that are needed to be an effective HC-centric organization? Unfortunately, most fall far short. In every chapter, when I discussed what an HC-centric organization should do in an area and compared it to what most organizations do, I had to conclude that there is a large gap. Most organizations have none or only a few of the most important characteristics. Most look and act more like structure-centric organizations than like HC-centric organizations.

Why is this the case? Evidence abounds that the HC-centric approach is superior for managing organizations where human capital is critical. And more and more consulting, training, and publications are available to help leaders and managers who want their organizations to become HC-centric. So it's not for lack of knowledge about what to do or resources that can help get it done.

What is it then? Well, one major reason—in fact, probably the major reason—is that in many cases, the decision makers in today's corporations are unable or unwilling to take an HC-centric approach to management, or both. The reasons for this are understandable and easy to identify, but not necessarily easy to change. As a result, they represent very real barriers to the creation of HC-centric organizations.

WHY NOT?

In this chapter, I first explore the reasons why many leaders don't take an HC-centric approach. For leaders, I hope this examination will serve as a useful analysis of managerial decision making and persuade some of them that they should adopt an HC-centric approach. I say "some" because (as I noted in Chapter Two) not all should. Following this discussion, I move on to explore what is known about how to create HC-centric organizations.

INABILITY

A great deal of knowledge now exists about how HC-centric organizations should be managed, but many senior managers today are not familiar with it. They got their business education and started their management careers when this knowledge was not available, so any awareness they have of it is a result of either recent experiences or exposure to postgraduate management education.

Even today, talent management and organization design are not taught in many business schools. Business schools do a great job of teaching how to manage financial assets and how to market products, but by and large they do a very poor job of teaching business students how to manage human capital and design organizations in which people are the competitive advantage.[1]

Business schools are showing an increased interest in teaching "the soft skills"—but that usually means teaching interpersonal relations and conflict management. These are important skills, and very much needed in both structure-centric organizations and HC-centric organizations. But they are not the only or in most cases the key skills that managers need to manage an HC-centric organization effectively.

In addition to having soft skills, managers need to know a great deal about organization design, organizational effectiveness, employee motivation, talent management, and the other issues reviewed in this book. Unfortunately, in many cases, today's managers simply don't know what the research evidence shows with respect to the right way to design organizations and manage talent.[2]

UNWILLINGNESS

Many of today's senior managers *are* senior managers precisely because of their ability to operate effectively in traditional organizations. Furthermore, they have made a major commitment to becoming senior executives because they want the rewards that go along with being a senior executive.

Getting to the top of a structure-centric organization carries with it numerous financial and status rewards as well as a great deal of power. It requires high levels of intelligence, ambition, competitiveness, and in many cases good political skills. But it requires relatively little ability to work in groups, build teams, create a shared leadership model, develop others, and involve others in decision making.

In short, individuals who make it to the top levels of most corporations often have the wrong skills, the wrong motives, and the wrong values for managing in an HC-centric organization. Thus, to change their organization from structure-centric to HC-centric, executives have to learn new skills and give up some of the rewards that formed the basis for their desire to achieve the position.

Given this reality, it is not surprising that most managers who have reached senior-level positions in corporations are not inclined to lead a transformational change from structure-centric to HC-centric management. Indeed, the mere mention of this type of change is quite threatening and often leads them to strongly resist change—even though it might be good for the organization and ultimately for them.

Before going too far in the direction of making existing executives the villains, it is important to emphasize again that changing from a structure-centric to an HC-centric approach to management is not a trivial matter. Systemic organizational change is difficult. In recent years, such major U.S. corporations as Polaroid, Kodak, U.S. Steel, Ford, Westinghouse, Chrysler, American Motors, and General Motors have declined substantially or disappeared entirely because they couldn't or didn't try hard enough to change.

Recall the Star Model. Given that in order to change from structure-centric to HC-centric, all points on the star need to change as well as the behavior of leaders and the corporate board, it is a major transformation. Beyond just changing the strategy of the organization, it involves changing an organization's fundamental identity and approach to organizing and managing people. Thus, to make the change, the organization needs strong leadership of the change process, and in almost every case, a multi-year effort.

Further, nothing guarantees that a transformational change from structure-centric to HC-centric will be successful. It requires exceptional leadership skills. Thus, it is hardly the kind of change effort likely to be successfully led by managers who have worked their way up to the top of a traditional structure-centric organization.

One more obstacle: In many cases, today's large corporations have experienced years of success using a structure-centric approach. If things are still going pretty well, managers and employees alike may be naturally hesitant to make major changes of any kind.[3]

It is precisely because change is so difficult that an organization that successfully implements an HC-centric approach can enjoy a sustainable competitive advantage. Unlike many new products and new marketing programs, a new management approach is very difficult for competing organizations to copy and, as a result, can provide a sustainable competitive advantage.

It is only when a company encounters very difficult times, and in some cases has a near-death experience, that its leaders are willing to look seriously at whether they are managing in the right way and whether an HC-centric approach to management might give them a chance to survive. In the absence of this type of trauma and pressure to change, it is much easier—and often, in the short term, much more profitable—to simply continue to manage with one of the two structure-centric approaches to management.

To inject a note of urgency: by the time a company's leaders finally accept that change is appropriate, it is often simply too late to execute the kind of complex transformation needed to move from a structure-centric to an HC-centric approach to management. Indeed, because of the increasing rate of change in the environment, it is increasingly common to find that corporations have waited too long.

MOVING TOWARD AN HC-CENTRIC ORGANIZATION

When it comes to installing an HC-centric approach to management, it is unquestionably most easily and most effectively done as part of the creation of a new organization. Many of the organizations that have been cited throughout this book as prime examples of effective HC-centric organizations are ones that, from the beginning—or at least from early on, adopted an HC-centric management approach. Whole Foods, Costco, Starbucks, Nucor, W. L. Gore, Intel, SAIC, SAS, and Google are examples of organizations that have, from their early days, been committed to an HC-centric approach to management.

But some dramatic examples of successful transformation do exist. Harley-Davidson has gone from a poorly run, bureaucratic, structure-centric organization to a high-involvement organization. IBM has gone from a bureaucratic organization to a global-competitor organization. They show that transformations can be successful and should serve as inspirations.

With a mind-set that it can be done, let's consider the task of transforming an organization from structure-centric to HC-centric.

CHANGE MANAGEMENT

It is useful, at the outset of this discussion of change, to establish that turning a structure-centric organization into an HC-centric organization is not going to happen all at once. It is likely to require multiple change efforts before an organization fully implements the right HC-centric approach.

It is also useful to understand that it is far easier to state the conditions needed for successful change than it is to execute the change. This is true even for a relatively simple change in the type of products or services that an organization offers, and it is especially true when the change is transformational like the change from a structure-centric to an HC-centric management approach. Everything known about large-scale organizational change needs to be brought to bear if an organization is going to shift from structure-centric to HC-centric.

In that spirit, consider what the literature has to say about large-scale organizational change. Numerous books, articles, and studies address this topic—all of them essentially agreeing on the basic conditions that need to exist for organizational change to take place.[4] These include:

- Felt need for change
- Clear direction for change
- Effective leadership of the change

- A systemic change effort that alters multiple systems in an organization
- Stabilizing the changes once they are in place

It is hard to disagree that these conditions are needed. For an organization to change, its employees not only need to be motivated to change, they need to know what kind of change is needed. In addition, of course, it also needs the ability and resources to change, and this is where human capital issues come into play from a skills perspective.

When all is said and done, transformational change most commonly fails because individuals don't have the skills to operate in the new way or are not motivated to change. Thus, the challenge for anyone *leading* change is to manage both a skill and competency change in their organization and the development of a workforce that is committed to the change. (The same sorts of issues that create executives who are unable and/or unwilling to change also apply here, to the broader set of employees.)

The good news is that when it is a matter of moving from a structure-centric organization to an HC-centric organization, it is typically relatively easy to convince a significant portion of the workforce of the advantages associated with the new management approach. Most individuals do like to be involved in decisions that affect their workplace, enjoy being part of a community, and want to develop new skills and abilities; in other words, working in an HC-centric organization is very attractive to them.

The bad news is that when the implications of this new environment sink in, it can be very frightening. Many employees may not in fact possess the skills needed to work effectively in the new environment—particularly if they not only have to operate with a new approach to management but also have to perform new and more complex tasks. As a result, they may very well feel threatened by the change and therefore resist it, particularly if the organization is unwilling or unable to make a large investment in training and developing existing employees. Ultimately, to be successful, a major change almost always involves changes in the staffing of the organization.

Because of the difficulties in transforming structure-centric organizations to HC-centric organizations, some existing organizations compromise. They recognize that comprehensive installation of HC-centric management is critical to their success and that it is very difficult to change their existing practices and people. Rather than focusing on changing their existing operations, they opt for installing HC-centric management approaches when they open or create new divisions, plants, or operating units. This results in what has been called an "ambidextrous organization."[5]

The literature on organizational change and HC-centric management is full of case examples of large organizations starting "greenfield" manufacturing plants that operate successfully as HC-centric units even though they are part of a structure-centric organization.

Procter & Gamble is one company that earned a well-deserved reputation for starting outstanding high-involvement plants in the 1960s.[6] Today, it operates most of its manufacturing plants in an HC-centric manner—in part as a result of transforming some of its existing plants, but primarily because of the numerous new plants it has started since the 1960s that use the high-involvement approach.

But it is important to be realistic about the effectiveness of change efforts that use the greenfield approach. The record of organizations who have taken the greenfield approach is marked by many unsuccessful total organization transformations.

For example, in the auto industry, General Motors, in combination with Toyota, started a new manufacturing plant in California (called NUMMI) that was designed to be HC-centric. It has operated successfully for a number of years; today it is run by Toyota. Toyota learned a great deal from this plant and has obviously become a successful manufacturer in the United States. It continues to open very successful new plants in the United States that have many high-involvement practices. It is much less apparent that General Motors learned a great deal from this plant or from its effort at Saturn to create a high-involvement division.[7]

Saturn, over the years, has moved away from most of its HC-centric practices and its cooperative labor relations approach with the United Auto Workers. General Motors is trying to revive Saturn by offering new models, but there is no evidence that it is trying to sustain or revive the high-involvement management approach that was the hallmark of the original start-up. Also, little—or perhaps I should say no—evidence indicates that General Motors has significantly changed its corporate approach to management from a traditional bureaucratic one to an HC-centric approach. If anything, General Motors seems to be moving more toward being a low-cost operator rather than toward an HC-centric approach.

One of the early movers toward high-involvement plants was General Foods. It opened a Gaines dog food plant in Topeka, Kansas, that was widely regarded as the premiere example of high-involvement management. I was one of several researchers who had a chance to study the plant and to contribute to its design. The data I collected from it showed that it was very productive and that the workforce was highly committed to its success.[8]

Despite the success of the Topeka plant, the senior management of General Foods failed to move other plants toward a high-involvement approach to management. It ultimately told the plant manager who was the champion of the high-involvement approach that his career opportunities at General Foods were limited because of his management approach.

Why did this happen? I can only speculate, but based on my conversations with the senior management of General Foods, I think that they saw the Topeka plant as a radical experiment that they feared they would lose control over. It was also clear to me that they had no interest in leading and probably were not capable of learning how to lead a high-involvement company. As a result they were very threatened by what they saw happening in their Topeka plant!

In structure-centric organizations, what happens with the introduction of an organizational unit that is very different from the rest of the organization is predictable. As with any foreign object that enters an organism, antibodies start to work to destroy it. As a result, it is harder and harder for the new venture to justify its different practices and to maintain its HC-centric approach to management. The bottom line then is that HC-centric "experiments" within structure-centric companies are potentially useful but need to be part of a systemic organizational change effort, not stand-alone change efforts. If a new plant or change efforts in a small department are just experiments in a different way to manage, they are unlikely to change the way the rest of the organization is managed even if they are successful.

Overall, the best conclusion with respect to change efforts in small units is that, by themselves, they are unlikely to create large-scale organizational transformation. They provide an opportunity to learn and the potential exists for the learnings to be transferred to the rest of the organization, but this will not happen without strong senior management support for the transfer. Over most of its recent history, this support has existed in Procter & Gamble, but it has not existed in Ford, General Motors, and many of the other companies that have experimented with HC-centric management.

One final point about changing from a structure-centric approach to an HC-centric approach. It is important to have employee involvement in designing and implementing the change. This is less important in the case of movement to a global-competitor approach because participation is not at the core of what the global-competitor approach is about. It is, however, at the core of what the high-involvement approach is about and, thus, involving individuals in designing and implementing a change to high-involvement management is very valuable. It is a way to both acquaint people with the involvement process and begin to change the culture of the organization from a top-down one to a more involvement-oriented approach.

When it comes to deciding how change efforts should be managed, it is important to remember that efforts to move toward the high-involvement approach need to have an active role for the members of the organization. Members need to be on task forces that work on the design, to help plan the implementation, and of course, where appropriate, to be the ones who actually carry out the implementation.

FOUR TYPES OF CHANGE

Let's drill down further into how to transform a structure-centric organization into an HC-centric organization. Four types of change can be identified as changes from a structure-centric to an HC-centric organization. The first two involve changing a low-cost operator to an HC-centric organization. The other two involve changing from a bureaucratic organization to an HC-centric organization. The issues in all four types of change are similar, but some important differences warrant consideration.

Low-Cost Operator to High-Involvement Organization

The move from low-cost operator to high involvement is perhaps the most difficult transformation, in large part because the gap between what is and what needs to be is the largest.

On every dimension of what an organization is and how it is managed, the low-cost-operator approach is at one end and the high-involvement approach is at the other. This is true for the employment contract, for the management style, and for all of the points on the star. Thus making this change is extremely difficult.

Just to pick an example, think of the difficulty of changing Wal-Mart to be more like Starbucks or Costco. It is doubtful that more than a few of the current managers would be comfortable with making that change, or even capable of making it. Similarly, think of how the information systems, structure, pay system, and working conditions would have to change to make this change happen. Chapter Two presents a number of questions that can be used to determine which of the HC-centric approaches is the right one. Unless the answer to them consistently indicates the high-involvement approach is a good fit, it is foolish for a low-cost operator to move to it.

It is tempting to conclude that changing a low-cost operator into a high-involvement organization is simply not worth it. The cost is too high. But before reaching that conclusion, it is important to consider how much can be gained by the change.

One major positive in the change from low-cost operator to high-involvement organization is likely to be the reaction of the employees. It is a good bet that most of them would rather work for a high-involvement organization where they will be better paid and do more interesting work. However, even here, problems can arise.

Some employees may not want the extra responsibility that goes with being in a high-involvement organization. After all, that is not what they signed up for. Further, they are unlikely to have the needed skills. If they had them, would they have chosen to work for a low-cost operator? Maybe—if they had no choice—but it is unlikely.

As will be discussed next, the best option may be to change to a global competitor approach. Alternatively, even though it has its weaknesses, the ambidextrous approach is a possible option, particularly if there is an opportunity to open a number of new locations and businesses.

Low-Cost Operator to Global Competitor

Changing a low-cost operator into a global competitor is almost as difficult as changing a low-cost operator into a high-involvement organization. New management systems are needed, along with a totally different approach to talent evaluation and management. As a result, most managers and most employees will need to be replaced unless a large investment in talent development is made.

The low-cost-operator approach in its present form is a relatively new one, so experience with transforming low-cost operators into global competitors is limited. In the past, low-cost operators have been transformed into relatively bureaucratic, structure-centric organizations as a result of union organizing drives or in the hope of cutting down on turnover.

For example, in the fast food business, some organizations are moving to more of a bureaucratic approach and away from the low-cost-operator approach simply because the costs of turnover are so high for a low-cost operator. But the bottom line, when it comes to changing low-cost operators to global competitors, is very much the same as it is for the change to high-involvement, so try it only if a compelling case can be made.

Bureaucratic to Global Competitor

What about moving from the bureaucratic approach to a global-competitor approach? Although this is a difficult change, it may well be easier than the change from the low-cost-operator approach to either HC-centric approach. It too requires, if not the replacement, the reorientation of much of the workforce and major changes in virtually all of the systems of an organization. But bureaucratic organizations sometimes do have skilled, if not effectively utilized, talent and some committed employees.

One example of an organization that successfully made this change is IBM. It was accomplished as a result of a Herculean leadership effort by Lou Gerstner and years of changing the workforce and management practices of IBM.[9] Today, for example, over 50 percent of the employees of IBM have been with the organization less than five years. This is a dramatic contrast with the traditional lifetime employment situation that existed in the old IBM.

Xerox is another organization that is in the process of changing from a bureaucratic organization to a global competitor. Under the leadership of Anne Mulcahy, it appears to be making significant progress. It is clearly further along than Kodak, which is yet another American icon corporation that is in the process of trying to make this same change. The evidence from IBM, Xerox, and Kodak is that it can be done, but that it is difficult even with skilled leadership and a strong case for change.

Bureaucratic to High-Involvement

Changing from a bureaucratic to a high-involvement organization is possible, but it is more difficult than changing a bureaucratic organization to a global competitor. I have already mentioned two organizations that have successfully done it: Procter & Gamble and Harley-Davidson. They represent two different ways of making it happen. In the case of Procter & Gamble, as mentioned, it was a combination of greenfield start-up plants and strong leadership from the top that created its successful change. In the case of Harley-Davidson, strong leadership from the top coupled with a near-death experience called everybody's attention to the importance of making the change. This was followed by a successful greenfield high-involvement manufacturing plant start-up that involved two unions.

FROM STRUCTURE-CENTRIC TO HC-CENTRIC

What is the best conclusion about organizational transformation from structure-centric to HC-centric? Transformation is possible but very difficult. Some very visible organizations have changed from being structure-centric to being HC-centric, but more have failed to make the transformation. Those that have made the transformation generally have characteristics that organizational change research views as being required for success in the effort. They have effective leadership; they have a strong case for change; they realize change must be systemic and act on that realization; and they install congruent new management systems.

Figure 8 shows the four types of change that I have discussed. They are rank-ordered in terms of their difficulty (1 = easiest; 4 = most difficult). I have to admit that my ranking is not based

Figure 8. Difficulty of Change.

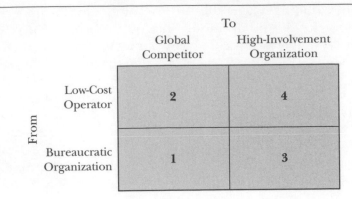

on any comprehensive research on the topic; unfortunately, none exists. I present the ranking as a thought starter rather than as a conclusion or final word on change.

Strategy and Flexibility in HC-Centric Organizations

Today's rapidly changing business environment doesn't just mean that many organizations should engage in a transformational change from being structure-centric to being HC-centric. It demands that organizations be able to change their business strategy and tactics on a much more frequent basis than in the past and in a highly effective way.

Slow change is a sure route to business failure. Being able to change quickly and effectively has become a basic requirement or organization capability in today's business environment. In response, not only are more and more organizations developing a change capability, increasingly new organizations are being created to take advantage of opportunities that existing organizations have trouble responding to. Thus a key factor in creating an HC-centric organization is ensuring it has the ability to change. Fortunately it is not difficult to do. HC-centric organizations have many of the features that are a part of organizations that are built to change.[10]

Difficult as it is for existing organizations to become more HC-centric, once they are established, HC-centric organizations are often easier to change than structure-centric organizations. They are quicker, more agile, and better able to respond to changing business conditions than are structure-centric organizations—whether they are bureaucratic or low-cost operators.

Why are HC-centric organizations better at changing in response to changes in their business environments? HC-centric organizations rely on people and people systems for competitive advantage. That is part of their identity. Often they don't have the heavy investment in capital equipment and technology that makes change difficult. What they have instead is a major investment in people systems and operating capabilities. It is an investment that, if properly made, can make their performance relatively easy to change when the environment calls for it.

Properly designed HC-centric organizations have many of the characteristics associated with organizational agility and the ability to change. What are these characteristics? The following are key features of organizations that are built to change:

- Rewards based on organizational performance
- Rewards for skill acquisition
- Broadly shared information about business performance
- High levels of contact with customers and the environment for all employees
- Flat, agile organization structures
- Absence of restrictive budgets and financial plans
- Lack of detailed job descriptions and work specifications
- Good information about talent and talent allocation
- A shared leadership approach to management
- Budget slack to allow experimentation and innovation
- An ongoing strategy process that continually defines and redefines corporate strategy
- A change-friendly identity

Not all of these are necessarily characteristics of HC-centric organizations, but most of them are design features covered in earlier chapters of the book. Thus HC-centric organizations should be relatively fast movers, particularly if they develop a change-friendly identity.

There may be some difference in the degree to which global-competitor organizations and high-involvement organizations are able to change. The staffing and skill competency model used by global-competitor organizations makes it somewhat easier for them to change and should allow them to respond more quickly to changes in the external environment. As mentioned earlier, their "travel light" approach to talent gives them the option to employ contract labor and to buy rather than build when critical new areas of expertise are needed.

The high-involvement approach argues for a somewhat more conservative approach to skill development; as a result, high-involvement organizations may be slower in responding to significant business strategy shifts. This may not be true, however, when it comes to smaller, more tactical moves with respect to business change. For example, if it is simply a matter of introducing a new product to an existing customer or altering the features of a product or service, it may be the high-involvement organization that is better at this type of change.

The high-involvement organization typically has the kind of internal relationships and flexibility that lead to excellent problem solving and change when the issue is tactical or operational. The opposite is likely to be true when it comes to a significant strategy shift. Where new skills and perhaps a new organization structure and new processes are needed, it's likely that the global-competitor approach will permit an organization to move more rapidly.

Regardless of whether a change is tactical or strategic, the bottom line is that an HC-centric organization should be better at change than a structure-centric organization. Focusing on human capital gives an organization more of the structures and systems it needs to cause people to change their behavior than a structure-centric organization can bring to bear.

What a structure-centric organization can do quickly is change its structure and some of its processes, but the history of change efforts that focus on structure shows a very negative track record. All too often, behavior and performance does not change; only the structure and the policies change. As a result, even the best organization designs and most needed change efforts fail miserably. The bottom line is that when it comes to strategic and tactical business change, there is every reason to believe that HC-centric organizations will outperform structure-centric organizations.

The Future Belongs to the HC-Centric Organization

There is every reason to believe that more and more organizations should and will adopt an HC-centric approach to organizing. It simply is a much better way to manage in an era populated by organizations that rely on human capital, intellectual property, and intangibles for their source of competitive advantage. Both the high-involvement approach and the global-competitor approach to management can provide a clear competitive advantage for many organizations.

Admittedly, it is difficult to transform structure-centric organizations into HC-centric organizations. As a result, the adoption of HC-centric approaches to management is likely to be relatively slow, at least among existing organizations. On the other hand, it is no more difficult to start up an organization with an HC-centric approach than one with a structure-centric approach—indeed, it may be easier.

Perhaps the major management limitation for a new organization starting out with an HC-centric approach is the knowledge of the individuals who start new businesses. They may only know how to start a structure-centric organization, because they have not had a management education that included information about organization design and HC-centric management. In addition, they are likely to have spent most of their lives working in and dealing with traditional bureaucratic organizations. This problem is likely to become less severe as more and more HC-centric organizations appear and become dominant players in the economy.

It is hard to ignore the success of a Google, a Whole Foods, a Starbucks, and the many other new HC-centric organizations that are performing extremely well in their respective businesses. Any thoughtful observer of their success quickly becomes aware that it is not based on their having the right product or good financing. It is clear that how they are managed differentiates them and provides them with a competitive advantage that is hard to match. They are the proof that an HC-centric approach to management can create a sustainable competitive advantage.

EPILOGUE

The history of modern management is largely one of managing tangible assets, not intangible ones. Many of the older organizations that exist today became successful because of their ability to manage tangible assets, most frequently natural resources and cash. Making the transition from excellence in managing tangible assets to excellence in managing intangible assets is an enormous challenge. In fact, it seems likely that many if not most organizations that need to make this transition to survive will never make it. Instead, they will fall prey to the creative destruction imperative that characterizes capitalist societies.

Creative destruction means that organizations that don't adapt to changes in their environment ultimately lose out because new organizations that better fit the current environment outperform them. New organizations often have a significant competitive advantage simply because they are created, conceptualized, and designed with the current environment in mind. The new companies take market share away from existing organizations and as a result, over time, organizations that are poor adapters ultimately disappear.

The creative destruction process is quite visible in a number of industries today, ranging from popular consumer goods such as automobiles and computers to retail businesses such as supermarkets and department stores. In these industries, organizations that manage in structure-centric ways are losing out to those that are doing a better job of organizing and managing their human capital. Toyota and Honda, for example, are growing, while Ford, Chrysler, and General Motors are closing factories. Costco is taking market share away from Sam's Club and Kmart. Nucor has become the largest steel company in the United States.

THE SOCIETAL PERSPECTIVE

From a societal perspective, the creative destruction of structure-centric organizations that fail to adopt an HC-centric management approach is not necessarily a bad thing. HC-centric organizations have the potential to improve the products and services that individuals buy. In addition, they provide a better quality of life for their employees. Work is more interesting, more flexible, and more rewarding when HC-centric organizations are able to develop the kind of virtuous spiral described in Chapter Two. In other words, this new form of organization has the opportunity to create a win for investors, consumers, employees, and communities.

Still, the HC-centric approach does not fit some businesses. Included in this category are companies that operate in industries where the work is inevitably low-skilled and low-value-added. Transactional retail establishments, agriculture, meat processing, and the manufacture of simple, labor-intensive products are prime examples. The work in these industries makes it very difficult to create an environment where individuals can add significant value, and therefore, where an HC-centric approach to management is likely to be successful.

But these jobs are increasingly rare in developed countries. They are being offshored or automated at a relatively rapid rate. In the United States, for example, forty years ago over 30 percent of the workforce was working in manufacturing jobs; today only 8 percent work in manufacturing jobs.[1] Part of this is due to off-shoring, but a considerable amount is due to a heavy investment in information and manufacturing technology. Much of this new technology simultaneously reduces the number of employees needed and creates jobs where employees can add much more value and should be managed with a human capital approach.

In short, yes, there are some work situations today, and there will be some in the foreseeable future for which HC-centric management is not a good fit. But there are many more where an HC-centric approach not only fits but is the key to survival. As true as this is today, it is likely to be more so in the future.

PACE OF CHANGE

I have no doubt that both HC-centric approaches—high-involvement and global competitor—are underutilized relative to what today's business environment calls for. Perhaps the number one reason why HC-centric management is not as widely practiced as it should be is the rate of change that has occurred in the business environment over the last several decades. An appropriate saying used to be, "Change is the only constant." A more appropriate saying for the last couple of decades is, "An increasing rate of change is the only constant."

Because of the way the business world has changed, more and more organizations today face the kind of environment that fits an HC-centric approach to management. In Chapter Two I outline the conditions that favor HC-centric management. To say the least, more and more organizations are finding themselves in environments with these characteristics. The pace of change has been so fast that it has been very difficult for companies to keep up.

Another reason that HC-centric approaches are underutilized is that many companies are biased toward a structure-centric approach because that approach has provided them with years of success. As a result, structure-centric processes and practices represent a comfort zone. Meanwhile, the individual and team freedom promised by a more HC-centric approach appears risky and the effort required to change daunting.

THE HIGH-INVOLVEMENT APPROACH—
A TOUGHER SELL?

No objective data conclusively show whether the global-competitor or high-involvement approach is most underutilized, but I am convinced that it's the latter. There are a number of reasons why this is the case. Perhaps the most important one is that the high-involvement approach represents the greatest deviation from the structure-centric approach. Particularly important is that the high-involvement approach requires more behavioral change on the part of the senior management of an organization.

In my experience, most senior managers simply feel more comfortable with the global-competitor model than they do with the high-involvement approach. The features that are particularly attractive are the global competitor's emphasis on individual performance and the accountability of individuals for their development and careers. Even though they may not act on it, the idea of individuals' having little job security also fits with many managers' ideas about what it takes to motivate people and to have an effective organization in today's rapidly changing business environment.

Finally, the global-competitor approach also looks like and often is a quicker fix for a troubled organization than the high-involvement approach. Quick fixes are increasingly important to many senior executives because of the pressure on them from institutional investors and buyout firms to produce ever better quarterly earnings.

The high-involvement approach requires the development of more self-management skills, teamwork, and a culture of understanding and knowing the business. On the other hand, the global-competitor approach promises a quick change in personnel and as a result the possibility of a rapid change in the organization's ability to perform. Thus, even though the high-involvement approach may promise greater long-term effectiveness, the fact that it requires more of an up-front investment, something that can be difficult to justify in today's business environment, often causes it to be a second choice.

IMPORTANCE OF SIZE

I do think that organizational size is a potential moderator of which HC-centric approach is likely to be most effective. In very large corporations, the global-competitor model is more often the best fit. Building the kind of relationships and culture that's required in a high-involvement organization is a challenge in any organization, but in organizations with more than ten thousand employees, it is difficult—particularly in the face of significant cultural differences based on the national origin of people and a multinational geography.

Certainly high-involvement practices can exist in a large organization, but the involvement of talent in the business often needs to be focused on parts of the organization. Large organizations also often face the challenge of coordinating the different parts of the organization when the delivery of a customer service or technology requires an integrated organizational approach to customers or products. This in turn can limit the autonomy that is possible in parts of the organization.

In medium to small organizations, individuals have a better line of sight to the overall operation of the organization and to its results. Face-to-face meetings are easier to hold; individuals can develop personal relationships with a higher percentage of the total organization; and leaders can personally touch and have a leadership relationship with a higher percentage of the workforce. Decades of research on organization size have also established that smaller organizations tend to create more satisfied employees who are committed to the success of their organizations.

It is possible that with the spread of modern information technology and the "connected generation" becoming a larger portion of the workforce, quite large global corporations will employ a new version of the high-involvement approach. For example, one may be utilized that is based on social networking and rapidly evolving relationships and structures.

FUTURE OF MANAGEMENT

If I had to bet on one approach becoming dominant in the next decade, I would pick the global competitor. This can be a positive for individuals, organizations, and societies if, and it is a big if, individuals, organizations, and societies can adjust.[2]

Individuals need to learn how to manage their careers as well as their finances, as it will be a self-management, high-risk world. They have to be willing and able to add new skills and change jobs.

Organizations have to become effective practitioners of the global-competitor approach when it comes to how they treat their most valuable asset, their talent. They also have to develop the capability to change rapidly in response to what is sure to be a business environment that is constantly and rapidly changing.

Last but not least, governments need to recognize and act on the reality that human capital is a nation's most valuable asset. They need to support their country's talent by managing education, research and development, and, of course, health care effectively.

It is one thing to say people are our most important asset; it is another to act on it. Those individuals, organizations, and countries that do the best job of acting on it will be the winners. Much of what needs to be done is clear; it is time to do it. The future of HC-centric management is now.

NOTES

Foreword

1. Steve Kerr took me through this exercise decades ago when I was a doctoral student, and the lesson has remained useful to my own classes.
2. F. Roethlisberger and W. Dickson, *Management and the Worker* (Cambridge, Mass.: Harvard University Press, 1939).
3. D. Ulrich and N. Smallwood, *Leadership Brand* (Boston: Harvard Business School Press, 2007).

Chapter One

1. Deloitte Touche Tomatsu and the *Economist* Intelligence Unit, *Aligned at the Top* (2007), p. 1.
2. PricewaterhouseCoopers. "9th Annual Global CEO Survey: Globalisation and Complexity; Inevitable Forces in a Changing Economy" (PricewaterhouseCoopers, 2006), p. 2.
3. B. Lev, *Intangibles: Management, Measurement, and Reporting* (Washington, D.C.: Brookings Institution Press, 2001).
4. D. Ulrich and W. Brockbank, *The HR Value Proposition* (Boston: Harvard Business School Press, 2005), p. 48.
5. J. O'Toole and E. Lawler, *The New American Workplace* (New York: Palgrave Macmillan, 2006); E. E. Lawler and J. O'Toole, (eds.), *America at Work: Choices and Challenges* (New York: Palgrave Macmillan, 2006).
6. E. E. Lawler and C. Worley, *Built to Change: How to Achieve Sustained Organizational Effectiveness* (San Francisco: Jossey-Bass, 2006).
7. E. Michaels, H. Handfield-Jones, and B. Axelrod, *The War for Talent* (Boston: Harvard Business School Press, 2001); C. A. Bartlett and S. Ghoshal, "Building Competitive Advantage Through People," *MIT Sloan Management Review 43,* no. 2 (2002): 36.

8. D. Finegold, "Is Education the Answer? Trends in the Supply and Demand for Skills in the U.S. Workforce," in Lawler and O'Toole, *America at Work: Choices and Challenges.*

9. G. Hamel, *The Future of Management* (Boston: Harvard Business School Press, 2007).

10. E. E. Lawler and C. G. Worley, *Built to Change: How to Achieve Sustained Organizational Effectiveness* (San Francisco: Jossey-Bass, 2006).

Chapter Two

1. T. Friedman, *The World Is Flat* (New York: Farrar, Straus & Giroux, 2006).

2. W. Cascio, "The High Cost of Low Wages," *Harvard Business Review 84,* no. 12 (2006): 23; W. Cascio, "Decency Means More Than 'Always Low Prices': A Comparison of Costco to Wal-Mart's Sam's Club," *Academy of Management Perspectives 20,* no. 3 (2006): 26–37; W. Cascio, "The Economic Impact of Employee Behaviors on Organizational Performance," *California Management Review 48,* no. 4 (2006): 41–59.

3. Based on J. O'Toole and E. Lawler, *The New American Workplace* (New York: Palgrave Macmillan, 2006), and on W. Cascio in E. E. Lawler and J. O'Toole, (eds.), *America at Work: Choices and Challenges* (New York: Palgrave Macmillan, 2006).

4. O'Toole and Lawler, *The New American Workplace.*

5. J. R. Hackman and G. Oldham, *Work Redesign* (Boston: Addison-Wesley, 1980); J. R. Hackman and E. Lawler, "Employee Reactions to Job Characteristics," *Journal of Applied Psychology 55* (1971): 259–286.

6. E. E. Lawler and C. Worley, *Built to Change: How to Achieve Sustained Organizational Effectiveness* (San Francisco: Jossey-Bass, 2006).

7. E. E. Lawler, S. A. Mohrman, and G. Benson, *Organizing for High Performance: Employee Involvement, TQM, Reengineering, and Knowledge Management in the Fortune 1000* (San Francisco: Jossey-Bass, 2001).

8. R. Teerlink and L. Ozley, *More Than a Motorcycle: The Leadership Journey at Harley-Davidson* (Boston: Harvard Business School Press, 2000).

9. L. V. Gerstner, *Who Says Elephants Can't Dance? Leading a Great Enterprise Through Dramatic Change* (New York: HarperCollins, 2002).

10. J. R. Galbraith, *Designing the Customer-Centric Organization: A Guide to Strategy, Structure, and Process* (San Francisco: Jossey-Bass, 2005).

Chapter Three

1. J. R. Galbraith, *Designing Organizations: An Executive Briefing on Strategy, Structure, and Process* (San Francisco: Jossey-Bass, 1995).
2. M. Porter, *Competitive Strategy* (New York: Free Press, 1980).
3. G. Bains and others, *Meaning Inc.: The Blueprint for Business Success in the 21st Century* (London: Profile Books, 2007).
4. C. K. Prahalad and G. Hamel, "The Core Competence of the Corporation," *Harvard Business Review 68,* no. 3 (1990): 79–91.
5. N. M. Tichy and W. G. Bennis, *Judgment* (New York: Portfolio, 2007).
6. J. R. Hackman and G. Oldham, *Work Redesign* (Boston: Addison-Wesley, 1980).
7. J. R. Galbraith, *Designing the Customer-Centric Organization: A Guide to Strategy, Structure, and Process* (San Francisco: Jossey-Bass, 2005).
8. B. E. Becker, M. A. Huselid, and D. Ulrich, *The HR Scorecard: Linking People, Strategy, and Performance* (Boston: Harvard Business School Press, 2001); J. W. Boudreau and P. M. Ramstad, *Beyond HR: The New Science of Human Capital* (Boston: Harvard Business School Press, 2007).
9. E. E. Lawler, *Rewarding Excellence: Pay Strategies for the New Economy* (San Francisco: Jossey-Bass, 2000).
10. Lawler, *Rewarding Excellence.*
11. J. Blasi, D. Kruse, and R. B. Freeman, "Shared Capitalism at Work: Impacts and Policy Options," in E. Lawler and J. O'Toole (eds.), *America at Work: Choices and Challenges* (New York: Palgrave Macmillan, 2006).
12. M. J. Hatch and M. Schultz, "The Dynamics of Organizational Identity," *Human Relations 55,* no. 8 (2002): 989–1018.

Chapter Four

1. J. Welch, *Winning* (New York: HarperCollins, 2006).
2. J. W. Boudreau and P. M. Ramstad, *Beyond HR: The New Science of Human Capital* (Boston: Harvard Business School Press, 2007).

3. M. Lewis, *Moneyball: The Art of Winning an Unfair Game* (New York: Norton, 2003).

4. J. P. Wanous, *Organizational Entry* (Reading, Mass.: Addison-Wesley, 1980).

5. G. Benson, D. Finegold, and S. A. Mohrman, "You Paid for the Skills, Now Keep Them: Tuition-Reimbursement and Voluntary Turnover,"*Academy of Management Journal 47,* no. 3 (2004): 315.

6. W. Cascio, *Costing Human Resources: The Financial Impact of Behavior in Organizations* (Cincinnati, Ohio: South-Western College Publishing, 2000).

7. E. E. Lawler and D. Finegold, "Individualizing the Organization: Past, Present, and Future,"*Organizational Dynamics 29,* no. 1 (2000): 1–15; D. M. Rousseau, *I-DEALS: Idiosyncratic Deals Employees Bargain for Themselves* (Armonk, N.Y.: Sharpe, 2005).

8. C. Benko and A. Weisberg, *Mass Career Customization* (Boston: Harvard Business School Press, 2007).

9. J. W. Boudreau and P. M. Ramstad, *Beyond HR: The New Science of Human Capital* (Boston: Harvard Business School Press, 2007).

10. Boudreau and Ramstad, *Beyond HR.*

11. F. L. Schmidt and J. E. Hunter, "The Validity and Utility of Selection Methods in Personnel Psychology: Practical and Theoretical Implications of 85 Years of Research Findings,"*Psychological Bulletin 124* (1998): 262–274; F. L. Schmidt and J. E. Hunter, "Select on Intelligence," in E. A. Locke (ed.), *The Blackwell Handbook of Principles of Organizational Behavior* (Oxford, England: Blackwell, 2000), 3–14.

12. M. W. McCall, *High Flyers: Developing the Next Generation of Leaders* (Boston: Harvard Business School Press, 1998); J. A. Conger and B. Benjamin, *Building Leaders: How Successful Companies Develop the Next Generation* (San Francisco: Jossey-Bass, 1999); R. M. Fulmer and J. A. Conger, *Growing Your Company's Leaders: How Great Organizations Use Succession Management to Sustain Competitive Advantage* (New York: AMACOM, 2004).

13. Center for Effective Organizations. *The Value of the PwC Professional Experience: What Employees Gain by Staying Longer at the Firm, and Why They Leave* (Los Angeles: University of Southern California, August 2004).

14. W. Cascio, *Costing Human Resources: The Financial Impact of Behavior in Organizations* (Cincinnati, Ohio: South-Western College Publishing, 2000).
15. E. E. Lawler, *Treat People Right!* (San Francisco: Jossey-Bass, 2003).
16. E. White, "Opportunity Knocks, and It Pays a Lot Better," *Wall Street Journal,* November 13, 2006, p. B3.

Chapter Five
1. E. E. Lawler, *Rewarding Excellence: Pay Strategies for the New Economy* (San Francisco: Jossey-Bass, 2000).
2. S. L. Rynes, B. Gerhart, and L. Parks, "Personnel Psychology: Performance Evaluation and Pay-for-Performance," *Annual Review of Psychology 56* (2005), 571–600.
3. G. P. Latham, *Work Motivation: History, Theory, Research and Practice* (Thousand Oaks, Calif.: Sage, 2006).
4. E. A. Locke and G. P. Latham, *A Theory of Goal-Setting and Performance* (Englewood Cliffs, N.J.: Prentice Hall, 1990).
5. J. R. Hackman and G. Oldham, *Work Redesign* (Boston: Addison-Wesley, 1980).
6. E. E. Lawler, "Reward Practices and Performance Management System Effectiveness," *Organizational Dynamics 32*, no. 4 (2003): 396–404; Lawler, *Rewarding Excellence.*
7. R. Simons and A. Davila, "Siebel Systems: Organizing for the Customer," Harvard Business School Case 9–103–014, 2002. Adapted by Chris Worley.
8. Locke and Latham, *A Theory of Goal-Setting and Performance.*
9. Lawler, *Rewarding Excellence.*
10. M. Lewis, *Moneyball: The Art of Winning an Unfair Game* (New York: Norton, 2003).
11. J. Welch, *Jack: Straight from the Gut* (New York: Warner Business Books, 2001); J. Welch, *Winning* (New York: HarperCollins, 2006).
12. Lawler, "Reward Practices and Performance Management System Effectiveness."
13. Lawler, *Rewarding Excellence.*
14. J. O'Toole and E. Lawler, *The New American Workplace* (New York: Palgrave Macmillan, 2006).

15. J. Blasi, D. Kruse, and R. B. Freeman, "Shared Capitalism at Work: Impacts and Policy Options," in E. Lawler and J. O'Toole (eds.), *America at Work: Choices and Challenges* (New York: Palgrave Macmillan, 2006).

Chapter Six

1. E. E. Lawler, J. W. Boudreau, and S. A. Mohrman, *Achieving Strategic Excellence: An Assessment of Human Resource Organizations* (Stanford, Calif.: Stanford University Press, 2006).

2. CFO Services and Mercer Human Resource Consulting, *Human Capital Management: The CFO's Perspective* (Boston: CFO Publishing, 2003).

3. J. W. Boudreau and P. M. Ramstad, *Beyond HR: The New Science of Human Capital* (Boston: Harvard Business School Press, 2007).

4. B. E. Becker, M. A. Huselid, and D. Ulrich, *The HR Scorecard: Linking People, Strategy, and Performance* (Boston: Harvard Business School Press, 2001); M. A. Huselid, B. E. Becker, and R. W. Beatty, *The Workforce Scorecard: Managing Human Capital to Execute Strategy* (Boston: Harvard Business School Press, 2005).

5. R. S. Kaplan and D. P. Norton, *Strategy Maps* (Boston: Harvard Business School Press, 2004).

6. D. Ulrich and N. Smallwood, "Capitalizing on Capabilities," *Harvard Business Review 82,* no. 6 (2004): 119.

7. R. S. Kaplan and D. P. Norton, *The Balanced Scorecard: Translating Strategy into Action* (Boston: Harvard Business School Press, 1996).

8. T. H. Davenport and J. G. Hearris, *Competing on Analytics: The New Science of Winning* (Boston: Harvard Business School Press, 2007).

9. V. Gennaro, *Diamond Dollars: The Economics of Winning in Baseball* (Hingham, Mass.: Maple Street Press, 2007).

10. H. R. Nalbantian, R. A. Guzzo, D. Kieffer, and J. Doherty, *Play to Your Strengths: Managing Your Internal Labor Markets for Lasting Competitive Advantage* (New York: McGraw-Hill, 2004); R. Guzzo and H. Nalbantian, "The Sound of Silence in Corporate Reporting," *Directors and Boards 30,* no. 2 (2006): 16.

11. E. G. Flamholtz, *Human Resource Accounting: Advances in Concepts, Methods and Applications* (Boston: Kluwer Academic, 1999).

12. E. E. Lawler and P. H. Mirvis, "How Graphic Controls Assesses the Human Side of the Corporation,"*Management Review 70*, no. 10 (1981): 54–63; and P. H. Mirvis and E. E. Lawler, "Systems Are Not Solutions: Issues in Creating Information Systems That Account for the Human Organization,"*Accounting, Organizations and Society 8* (1983): 175–190.

13. E. E. Lawler and C. Worley, *Built to Change: How to Achieve Sustained Organizational Effectiveness* (San Francisco: Jossey-Bass, 2006).

14. E. E. Lawler, S. A. Mohrman, and G. Benson, *Organizing for High Performance: Employee Involvement, TQM, Reengineering, and Knowledge Management in the Fortune 1000* (San Francisco: Jossey-Bass, 2001).

15. E. E. Lawler, *High-Involvement Management* (San Francisco: Jossey-Bass, 1986).

16. Lawler, Mohrman, and Benson, *Organizing for High Performance.*

17. Lawler, Mohrman, and Benson, *Organizing for High Performance.*

Chapter Seven

1. E. E. Lawler, J. W. Boudreau, and S. A. Mohrman, *Achieving Strategic Excellence: An Assessment of Human Resource Organizations* (Stanford, Calif.: Stanford University Press, 2006).

2. Lawler, Boudreau, and Mohrman, *Achieving Strategic Excellence;* J. W. Boudreau and P. M. Ramstad, *Beyond HR: The New Science of Human Capital* (Boston: Harvard Business School Press, 2007).

3. USC/Center for Effective Organizations and Heidrick & Struggles, *10th Annual Corporate Board Effectiveness Study, 2006–2007.*

4. D. Ulrich and W. Brockbank, *The HR Value Proposition* (Boston: Harvard Business School Press, 2005).

5. Lawler, Boudreau, and Mohrman, *Achieving Strategic Excellence.*

6. E. E. Lawler, D. Ulrich, J. Fitz-enz, J. Madden, and R. Maruca, *Human Resources Business Process Outsourcing* (San Francisco: Jossey-Bass, 2004).

7. Lawler, Ulrich, Fitz-enz, Madden, and Maruca, *Human Resources Business Process Outsourcing.*

8. J. Pfeffer and R. I. Sutton, *Hard Facts, Dangerous Half-Truths and Total Nonsense: Profiting from Evidence-Based Management* (Boston: Harvard Business School Press, 2006).

9. S. L. Rynes, A. E. Colbert, and K. C. Brown, "HR Professionals' Beliefs About Effective Human Resource Practices: Correspondence Between Research and Practice,"*Human Resource Management 41* (2002): 149–174.
10. Lawler, Ulrich, Fitz-enz, Madden, and Maruca, *Human Resources Business Process Outsourcing.*
11. Lawler, Boudreau, and Mohrman, *Achieving Strategic Excellence.*
12. Lawler, Boudreau, and Mohrman, *Achieving Strategic Excellence.*
13. Lawler, Boudreau, and Mohrman, *Achieving Strategic Excellence.*
14. J. R. Galbraith, *Designing the Customer-Centric Organization: A Guide to Strategy, Structure, and Process* (San Francisco: Jossey-Bass, 2005).
15. Boudreau and Ramstad, *Beyond HR.*

Chapter Eight

1. USC/Center for Effective Organizations and Heidrick & Struggles, *10th Annual Corporate Board Effectiveness Study, 2006–2007;* R. Charan, *Boards That Deliver: Advancing Corporate Governance from Compliance to Competitive Advantage* (San Francisco: Jossey-Bass, 2005); D. A. Nadler, B. A. Behan, and M. B. Nadler, *Building Better Boards: A Blueprint for Effective Governance* (San Francisco: Jossey-Bass, 2006); E. E. Lawler and D. Finegold, "The Changing Face of Corporate Boards,"*MIT Sloan Management Review 46,* no. 2 (2005): 67–70.
2. CFO Services and Mercer Human Resource Consulting. *Human Capital Management: The CFO's Perspective* (Boston: CFO Publishing, 2003).
3. J. A. Conger, E. E. Lawler, and D. L. Finegold, *Corporate Boards: New Strategies for Adding Value at the Top* (San Francisco: Jossey-Bass, 2001); E. E. Lawler, D. Finegold, G. Benson, and J. Conger, "Corporate Boards: Keys to Effectiveness,"*Organizational Dynamics 30,* no. 4 (2002): 310–324.
4. National Association of Corporate Directors, in collaboration with Oliver Wyman—Delta Organization & Leadership. *2007 NACD Public Company Governance Survey,* 2007.
5. E. E. Lawler and D. Finegold, "Who's in the Boardroom and Does It Matter: The Impact of Having Non-Director Executives Attend Board Meetings,"*Organizational Dynamics 35,* no. 1 (2006): 106.

6. J. A. Conger, D. Finegold, and E. E. Lawler, "Appraising Board-room Performance," *Harvard Business Review 76*, no. 1 (1998): 136–148.

7. USC/Center for Effective Organizations and Heidrick & Struggles, *10th Annual Corporate Board Effectiveness Study, 2006–2007.*

8. USC/Center for Effective Organizations and Heidrick & Struggles, *10th Annual Corporate Board Effectiveness Study, 2006–2007.*

9. USC/Center for Effective Organizations and Heidrick & Struggles, *10th Annual Corporate Board Effectiveness Study, 2006–2007;* J. A. Conger, E. E. Lawler, and D. L. Finegold, *Corporate Boards: New Strategies for Adding Value at the Top* (San Francisco: Jossey-Bass, 2001); E. E. Lawler, D. Finegold, G. Benson, and J. Conger, "Corporate Boards: Keys to Effectiveness," *Organizational Dynamics 30*, no. 4 (2002): 310–324.

10. USC/Center for Effective Organizations and Heidrick & Struggles, *10th Annual Corporate Board Effectiveness Study, 2006–2007.*

11. J. O'Toole and E. Lawler, *The New American Workplace* (New York: Palgrave Macmillan, 2006).

Chapter Nine

1. G. Greiner, T. Cummings, and A. Bhambri, "When New CEOs Succeed and Fail: 4-D Theory at Strategic Transformation," *Organizational Dynamics 32*, no. 3 (2002): 1–17; R. Khurana, *Searching for a Corporate Savior: The Irrational Quest for Charismatic CEOs* (Princeton, N.J.: Princeton University Press, 2002).

2. E. E. Lawler and C. Worley, *Built to Change: How to Achieve Sustained Organizational Effectiveness* (San Francisco: Jossey-Bass, 2006).

3. P. W. Tam, "Boss Talk: Hitting the Ground Running; New CEO of HP Immerses Himself in Studying Company; 'Management Is a Team Sport.'" *Wall Street Journal*, April 4, 2005, p. B1.

4. W. Bennis and B. Nanus, *Leaders: The Strategies for Taking Charge* (New York: HarperCollins, 1985); J. A. Conger and R. N. Kanungo, *Charismatic Leadership in Organizations* (Thousand Oaks, Calif.: Sage, 1998).

5. Lawler and Worley, *Built to Change.*

6. W. Bennis, *On Becoming a Leader* (Reading, Mass.: Addison-Wesley, 1989).

7. J. W. Boudreau and P. M. Ramstad, *Beyond HR: The New Science of Human Capital* (Boston: Harvard Business School Press, 2007).

8. E. E. Lawler, J. W. Boudreau, and S. A. Mohrman, *Achieving Strategic Excellence: An Assessment of Human Resource Organizations* (Stanford, Calif.: Stanford University Press, 2006).

9. A. Murray, *Revolt in the Boardroom: The New Rules of Power in Corporate America* (New York: HarperCollins, 2007).

10. Murray, *Revolt in the Boardroom.*

11. Sheridan Prasso, ed. "Piloting JetBlue and eBay," Business-Week, March 17, 2003:16.

12. M. W. McCall and G. P. Hollenbeck, *Developing Global Executives: The Lessons of International Experience* (Boston: Harvard Business School Press, 2002); J. A. Conger, *Learning to Lead: The Art of Transforming Managers into Leaders* (San Francisco: Jossey-Bass, 1992).

13. N. M. Tichy, *The Cycle of Leadership: How Great Leaders Teach Their Companies to Win* (New York: HarperCollins, 2004).

14. J. Pfeffer and R. I. Sutton, *The Knowing-Doing Gap: How Smart Companies Turn Knowledge into Action* (Boston: Harvard Business School Press, 2000).

15. D. Ulrich and N. Smallwood, *Leadership Brand: Developing Customer-Focused Leaders to Drive Performance and Build Lasting Value* (Boston: Harvard Business School Press, 2007).

16. B. Groysberg and S. Snook. "Leadership Development at Goldman Sachs," Harvard Business School Teaching Note 407–080, 2006:7.

Chapter Ten

1. W. Bennis and J. O'Toole, "How Business Schools Lost Their Way," *Harvard Business Review 83,* no. 5 (2005): 96.

2. S. L. Rynes, A. E. Colbert, and K. C. Brown, "HR Professionals' Beliefs About Effective Human Resource Practices: Correspondence Between Research and Practice," *Human Resource Management 41* (2002): 149–174.

3. E. E. Lawler and C. Worley, *Built to Change: How to Achieve Sustained Organizational Effectiveness* (San Francisco: Jossey-Bass, 2006).

4. T. C. Cummings and C. G. Worley, *Organization Development and Change* (Cincinnati, Ohio: South-Western College Publishing, 2004).
5. M. L. Tushman and C. A. O'Reilly, *Winning Through Innovation: A Practical Guide to Leading Organizational Change and Renewal* (Boston: Harvard Business School Press, 1997).
6. E. E. Lawler, *From the Ground Up: Six Principles for Building the New Logic Corporation* (San Francisco: Jossey-Bass, 1996).
7. P. S. Adler, B. Goldoftas, and D. Levine, "Ergonomics, Employee Involvement, and the Toyota Production System: A Case Study of NUMMI'S 1993 Model Introduction,"*Industrial and Labor Relations Review 50,* no. 3 (1997): 416–437.
8. Lawler, *From the Ground Up.*
9. L. V. Gerstner, *Who Says Elephants Can't Dance? Leading a Great Enterprise Through Dramatic Change* (New York: HarperCollins, 2002).
10. Lawler and Worley, *Built to Change.*

Epilogue
1. J. O'Toole and E. Lawler, *The New American Workplace* (New York: Palgrave Macmillan, 2006).
2. O'Toole and Lawler, *The New American Workplace.*

REFERENCES

Adler, P. S., Goldoftas, B., and Levine, D. "Ergonomics, Employee Involvement, and the Toyota Production System: A Case Study of NUMMI'S 1993 Model Introduction."*Industrial and Labor Relations Review,* 1997, *50*(3), 416–437.

Bains, G., and others. *Meaning Inc.: The Blueprint for Business Success in the 21st Century.* London: Profile Books, 2007.

Bartlett, C. A., and Ghoshal, S. "Building Competitive Advantage Through People."*MIT Sloan Management Review.* 2002, *43*(2), 36.

Becker, B. E., Huselid, M. A., and Ulrich, D. *The HR Scorecard: Linking People, Strategy, and Performance.* Boston: Harvard Business School Press, 2001.

Benko, C., and Weisberg, A. *Mass Career Customization.* Boston: Harvard Business School Press, 2007.

Bennis, W. *On Becoming a Leader.* Reading, Mass.: Addison-Wesley, 1989.

Bennis, W., and Nanus, B. *Leaders: The Strategies for Taking Charge.* New York: HarperCollins, 1985.

Bennis, W., and O'Toole, J. "How Business Schools Lost Their Way."*Harvard Business Review,* 2005, *83*(5), 96.

Benson, G., Finegold, D., and Mohrman, S. A. "You Paid for the Skills, Now Keep Them: Tuition-Reimbursement and Voluntary Turnover."*Academy of Management Journal,* 2004, *47*(3), 315.

Blasi, J., Kruse, D., and Freeman, R. B. "Shared Capitalism at Work: Impacts and Policy Options." In E. Lawler and J. O'Toole (eds.), *America at Work: Choices and Challenges.* New York: Palgrave Macmillan, 2006.

Boudreau, J. W., and Ramstad, P. M. *Beyond HR: The New Science of Human Capital.* Boston: Harvard Business School Press, 2007.

Cascio, W. *Costing Human Resources: The Financial Impact of Behavior in Organizations.* Cincinnati, Ohio: South-Western College Publishing, 2000.

Cascio, W. "Decency Means More Than 'Always Low Prices': A Comparison of Costco to Wal-Mart's Sam's Club."*Academy of Management Perspectives,* 2006, *20*(3), 26–37.

Cascio, W. "The Economic Impact of Employee Behaviors on Organizational Performance." *California Management Review,* 2006, *48*(4), 41–59.

Cascio, W. "The Economic Impact of Employee Behaviors on Organizational Performance." In E. E. Lawler and J. O'Toole (eds.), *America at Work: Choices and Challenges.* New York: Palgrave Macmillan, 2006.

Cascio, W. "The High Cost of Low Wages." *Harvard Business Review,* 2006, *84*(12), 23.

Center for Effective Organizations. *The Value of the PwC Professional Experience: What Employees Gain by Staying Longer at the Firm, and Why They Leave.* Los Angeles: University of Southern California, August 2004.

CFO Services and Mercer Human Resource Consulting. *Human Capital Management: The CFO's Perspective.* Boston: CFO Publishing, 2003.

Charan, R. *Boards That Deliver: Advancing Corporate Governance from Compliance to Competitive Advantage.* San Francisco: Jossey-Bass, 2005.

Conger, J. A. *Learning to Lead: The Art of Transforming Managers into Leaders.* San Francisco: Jossey-Bass, 1992.

Conger, J. A., and Benjamin, B. *Building Leaders: How Successful Companies Develop the Next Generation.* San Francisco: Jossey-Bass, 1999.

Conger, J. A., Finegold, D. and Lawler, E. E. "Appraising Boardroom Performance." *Harvard Business Review,* 1998, *76*(1), 136–148.

Conger, J. A., and Kanungo, R. N. *Charismatic Leadership in Organizations.* Thousand Oaks, Calif.: Sage, 1998.

Conger, J. A., Lawler, E. E., and Finegold, D. L. *Corporate Boards: New Strategies for Adding Value at the Top.* San Francisco: Jossey-Bass, 2001.

Cummings, T. C., and Worley, C. G. *Organization Development and Change.* Cincinnati, Ohio: South-Western College Publishing, 2004.

Davenport, T. H., and Hearris, J. G. *Competing on Analytics: The New Science of Winning.* Boston: Harvard Business School Press, 2007.

Deloitte Touche Tomatsu and the *Economist* Intelligence Unit. *Aligned at the Top.* 2007.

Finegold, D. "Is Education the Answer? Trends in the Supply and Demand for Skills in the U.S. Workforce." In E. E. Lawler and J. O'Toole (eds.), *America at Work: Choices and Challenges.* New York: Palgrave Macmillan, 2006.

Flamholtz, E. G. *Human Resource Accounting: Advances in Concepts, Methods and Applications.* Boston: Kluwer Academic, 1999.

Friedman, T. *The World Is Flat.* New York: Farrar, Straus, and Giroux, 2006.

Fulmer, R. M., and Conger, J. A. *Growing Your Company's Leaders: How Great Organizations Use Succession Management to Sustain Competitive Advantage.* New York: AMACOM, 2004.

Galbraith, J. R. *Designing Organizations: An Executive Briefing on Strategy, Structure, and Process.* San Francisco: Jossey-Bass, 1995.

Galbraith, J. R. *Designing the Customer-Centric Organization: A Guide to Strategy, Structure, and Process.* San Francisco: Jossey-Bass, 2005.

Gennaro, V. *Diamond Dollars: The Economics of Winning in Baseball.* Hingham, Mass.: Maple Street Press, 2007.

Gerstner, L. V. *Who Says Elephants Can't Dance? Leading a Great Enterprise Through Dramatic Change.* New York: HarperCollins, 2002.

Greiner, G., Cummings, T., and Bhambri, A. "When New CEOs Succeed and Fail: 4-D Theory at Strategic Transformation." *Organizational Dynamics,* 2002, *32*(3), 1–17.

Guzzo, R., and Nalbantian, H. "The Sound of Silence in Corporate Reporting." *Directors and Boards,* 2006, *30*(2), 16.

Hackman, J. R., and Lawler, E. "Employee Reactions to Job Characteristics." *Journal of Applied Psychology,* 1971, *55,* 259–286.

Hackman, J. R., and Oldham, G. *Work Redesign.* Boston: Addison-Wesley, 1980.

Hamel, G. *The Future of Management.* Boston: Harvard Business School Press, 2007.

Hatch, M. J., and Schultz, M. "The Dynamics of Organizational Identity." *Human Relations,* 2002, *55*(8), 989–1018.

Huselid, M. A., Becker, B. E., and Beatty, R. W. *The Workforce Scorecard: Managing Human Capital to Execute Strategy.* Boston: Harvard Business School Press, 2005.

Kaplan, R. S., and Norton, D. P. *The Balanced Scorecard: Translating Strategy into Action.* Boston: Harvard Business School Press, 1996.

Kaplan, R. S., and Norton, D. P. *Strategy Maps.* Boston: Harvard Business School Press, 2004.

Khurana, R. *Searching for a Corporate Savior: The Irrational Quest for Charismatic CEOs.* Princeton, N.J.: Princeton University Press, 2002.

Latham, G. P. *Work Motivation: History, Theory, Research and Practice.* Thousand Oaks, Calif.: Sage, 2006.

Lawler, E. E. *High-Involvement Management.* San Francisco: Jossey-Bass, 1986.

Lawler, E. E. *From the Ground Up: Six Principles for Building the New Logic Corporation.* San Francisco: Jossey-Bass, 1996.

Lawler, E. E. *Rewarding Excellence: Pay Strategies for the New Economy.* San Francisco: Jossey-Bass, 2000.

Lawler, E. E. *Treat People Right!* San Francisco: Jossey-Bass, 2003.

Lawler, E. E. "Reward Practices and Performance Management System Effectiveness." *Organizational Dynamics,* 2003, *32*(4), 396–404.

Lawler, E. E., Boudreau, J. W., and Mohrman, S. A. *Achieving Strategic Excellence: An Assessment of Human Resource Organizations.* Stanford, Calif.: Stanford University Press, 2006.

Lawler, E. E., and Finegold, D. "Individualizing the Organization: Past, Present, and Future." *Organizational Dynamics,* 2000, *29*(1), 1–15.

Lawler, E. E., and Finegold, D. "The Changing Face of Corporate Boards." *MIT Sloan Management Review,* 2005, *46*(2), 67–70.

Lawler, E. E., and Finegold, D. "Who's in the Boardroom and Does It Matter: The Impact of Having Non-Director Executives Attend Board Meetings." *Organizational Dynamics,* 2006, *35*(1), 106.

Lawler, E. E., Finegold, D., Benson, G., and Conger, J. "Corporate Boards: Keys to Effectiveness." *Organizational Dynamics,* 2002, *30*(4), 310–324.

Lawler, E. E. and Mirvis, P. H. "How Graphic Controls Assesses the Human Side of the Corporation." *Management Review,* 1981, *70*(10), 54–63.

Lawler, E. E., Mohrman, S. A., and Benson, G. *Organizing for High Performance: Employee Involvement, TQM, Reengineering, and Knowledge Management in the Fortune 1000.* San Francisco: Jossey-Bass, 2001.

Lawler, E. E., and O'Toole, J. (eds.). *America at Work: Choices and Challenges.* New York: Palgrave Macmillan, 2006.

Lawler, E. E., Ulrich, D., Fitz-enz, J., Madden, J., and Maruca, R. *Human Resources Business Process Outsourcing.* San Francisco: Jossey-Bass, 2004.

Lawler, E. E., and Worley, C. *Built to Change: How to Achieve Sustained Organizational Effectiveness.* San Francisco: Jossey-Bass, 2006.

Lev, B. *Intangibles: Management, Measurement, and Reporting.* Washington, D.C.: Brookings Institution Press, 2001.

Lewis, M. *Moneyball: The Art of Winning an Unfair Game.* New York: Norton, 2003.

Locke, E. A., and Latham, G. P. *A Theory of Goal-Setting and Performance.* Englewood Cliffs, N.J.: Prentice Hall, 1990.

McCall, M. W. *High Flyers: Developing the Next Generation of Leaders.* Boston: Harvard Business School Press, 1998.

McCall, M. W., and Hollenbeck, G. P. *Developing Global Executives: The Lessons of International Experience.* Boston: Harvard Business School Press, 2002.

Michaels, E., Handfield-Jones, H., and Axelrod, B. *The War for Talent.* Boston: Harvard Business School Press, 2001.

Mirvis, P. H., and Lawler, E. E. (1983). "Systems Are Not Solutions: Issues in Creating Information Systems That Account for the Human Organization."*Accounting, Organizations and Society,* 1983, *8,* 175–190.

Murray, A. *Revolt in the Boardroom: The New Rules of Power in Corporate America.* New York: HarperCollins, 2007.

Nadler, D. A., Behan, B. A., and Nadler, M. B. *Building Better Boards: A Blueprint for Effective Governance.* San Francisco: Jossey-Bass, 2006.

Nalbantian, H. R., Guzzo, R. A., Kieffer, D., and Doherty, J. *Play to Your Strengths: Managing Your Internal Labor Markets for Lasting Competitive Advantage.* New York: McGraw-Hill, 2004.

National Association of Corporate Directors, in collaboration with Oliver Wyman—Delta Organization & Leadership. *2007 NACD Public Company Governance Survey,* 2007.

O'Toole, J., and Lawler, E. *The New American Workplace.* New York: Palgrave Macmillan, 2006.

Pfeffer, J., and Sutton, R. I. *The Knowing-Doing Gap: How Smart Companies Turn Knowledge into Action.* Boston: Harvard Business School Press, 2000.

Pfeffer, J., and Sutton, R. I. *Hard Facts, Dangerous Half-Truths and Total Nonsense: Profiting from Evidence-Based Management.* Boston: Harvard Business School Press, 2006.

Porter, M. *Competitive Strategy.* New York: Free Press, 1980.

Prahalad, C. K., and Hamel, G. "The Core Competence of the Corporation."*Harvard Business Review,* 1990, *68*(3), 79–91.

PricewaterhouseCoopers. "9th Annual Global CEO Survey: Globalisation and Complexity; Inevitable Forces in a Changing Economy." PricewaterhouseCoopers, 2006, p. 2.

Roethlisberger, F., and Dickson, W. *Management and the Worker.* Cambridge, Mass.: Harvard University Press, 1939.

Rousseau, D. M. *I-DEALS: Idiosyncratic Deals Employees Bargain for Themselves.* Armonk, N.Y.: Sharpe, 2005.

Rynes, S. L., Colbert, A. E., and Brown, K. C. "HR Professionals' Beliefs About Effective Human Resource Practices: Correspondence Between Research and Practice."*Human Resource Management,* 2002, *41,* 149–174.

Rynes, S. L., Gerhart, B., and Parks, L. "Personnel Psychology: Performance Evaluation and Pay-for-Performance."*Annual Review of Psychology,* 2005, *56,* 571–600.

Schmidt, F. L., and Hunter, J. E. "Select on Intelligence." In E. A. Locke (ed.), *The Blackwell Handbook of Principles of Organizational Behavior.* Oxford, England: Blackwell, 2000, 3–14.

Schmidt, F. L., and Hunter, J. E. "The Validity and Utility of Selection Methods in Personnel Psychology: Practical and Theoretical Implications of 85 Years of Research Findings." *Psychological Bulletin*, 1998, *124*, 262–274.

Simons, R., and Davila, A. "Siebel Systems: Organizing for the Customer." Harvard Business School Case 9–103–014, 2002. Adapted by Christopher Worley.

Tam, P. W. "Boss Talk: Hitting the Ground Running; New CEO of HP Immerses Himself in Studying Company; 'Management Is a Team Sport.'" *Wall Street Journal*, Apr. 4, 2005, p. B1.

Teerlink, R., and Ozley, L. *More Than a Motorcycle: The Leadership Journey at Harley-Davidson*. Boston: Harvard Business School Press, 2000.

Tichy, N. M. *The Cycle of Leadership: How Great Leaders Teach Their Companies to Win*. New York: HarperCollins, 2004.

Tichy, N. M., and Bennis, W. G. *Judgment*. New York: Portfolio, 2007.

Tushman, M. L., and O'Reilly, C. A. *Winning Through Innovation: A Practical Guide to Leading Organizational Change and Renewal*. Boston: Harvard Business School Press, 1997.

Ulrich, D., and Brockbank, W. *The HR Value Proposition*. Boston: Harvard Business School Press, 2005.

Ulrich, D., and Smallwood, N. "Capitalizing on Capabilities." *Harvard Business Review*, 2004, *82*(6), 119.

Ulrich, D., and Smallwood, N. *Leadership Brand: Developing Customer-Focused Leaders to Drive Performance and Build Lasting Value*. Boston: Harvard Business School Press, 2007.

USC/Center for Effective Organizations and Heidrick & Struggles. *10th Annual Corporate Board Effectiveness Study, 2006–2007*.

Wanous, J. P. *Organizational Entry*. Reading, Mass.: Addison-Wesley, 1980.

Welch, J. *Jack: Straight from the Gut*. New York: Warner Business Books, 2001.

Welch, J. *Winning*. New York: HarperCollins, 2006.

White, E. "Opportunity Knocks, and It Pays a Lot Better." *Wall Street Journal*, Nov. 13, 2006, p. B3.

THE AUTHOR

Edward E. Lawler III is distinguished professor of business and director of the Center for Effective Organizations in the Marshall School of Business at the University of Southern California. He has been honored as a top contributor to the fields of organizational development, human resources management, organizational behavior, and compensation. He is the author of more than 350 articles and 43 books. His most recent books include *Achieving Strategic Excellence: An Assessment of Human Resource Organizations* (2006), *Built to Change* (2006), *The New American Workplace* (2006), and *America at Work* (2006). For more information, visit www.edwardlawler.com and http://ceo-marshall.usc.edu.

INDEX